T0305772

Modern Evolutionary Economics

Evolutionary economics sees the economy as always in motion
with change being driven largely by continuing innovation. This
approach to economics, heavily influenced by the work of Joseph
Schumpeter, saw a revival as an alternative way of thinking about
economic advancement as a result of Richard Nelson and Sidney
Winter's seminal book, *An Evolutionary Theory of Economic
Change*, first published in 1982. In this long-awaited follow-up,
Nelson is joined by leading figures in the field of evolutionary
economics, reviewing in detail how this perspective has been
manifest in various areas of economic inquiry where evolutionary
economists have been active. Providing the perfect overview for
interested economists and social scientists, readers will learn how
in each of the diverse fields featured, evolutionary economics has
enabled an improved understanding of how and why economic
progress occurs.

RICHARD R. NELSON is Professor Emeritus at Columbia University.
He served as a research economist and analyst at the Rand
Corporation and the US President's Council of Economic Advisors.
His most cited publications include his book with Sidney Winter,
An Evolutionary Theory of Economic Change (1982), *The Moon and
the Ghetto* (1977), and *National Innovation Systems* (1993). He has
received the Honda Prize, the Tinbergen Award, the Leontief Award,
and the Veblen-Commons Award for his research, and has been
awarded an honorary degree by several universities.

Modern Evolutionary Economics
An Overview

RICHARD R. NELSON
Columbia University, New York

GIOVANNI DOSI
Scuola Superiore Sant'Anna in Pisa

CONSTANCE E. HELFAT
Dartmouth College, New Hampshire

ANDREAS PYKA
University of Hohenheim

SIDNEY G. WINTER
Wharton School, University of Pennsylvania

PIER PAOLO SAVIOTTI
Utrecht University

KEUN LEE
Seoul National University

FRANCO MALERBA
Bocconi University

KURT DOPFER
University of St. Gallen

CAMBRIDGE
UNIVERSITY PRESS

CAMBRIDGE
UNIVERSITY PRESS

University Printing House, Cambridge CB2 8BS, United Kingdom

One Liberty Plaza, 20th Floor, New York, NY 10006, USA

477 Williamstown Road, Port Melbourne, VIC 3207, Australia

314-321, 3rd Floor, Plot 3, Splendor Forum, Jasola District Centre, New Delhi - 110025, India

79 Anson Road, #06-04/06, Singapore 079906

Cambridge University Press is part of the University of Cambridge.

It furthers the University's mission by disseminating knowledge in the pursuit of education, learning and research at the highest international levels of excellence.

www.cambridge.org
Information on this title: www.cambridge.org/9781108427432
DOI: 10.1017/9781108661928

First published 2018

A catalogue record for this publication is available from the British Library

Library of Congress Cataloging in Publication data
Names: Nelson, Richard R., author.
Title: Modern evolutionary economics : an overview /
Richard R. Nelson [and eight others].
Description: Cambridge, United Kingdom; New York, NY: Cambridge
University Press, 2018. | Includes bibliographical references and index.
Identifiers: LCCN 2018000013 | ISBN 9781108427432 (hardback) |
ISBN 9781108446198 (paperback)
Subjects: LCSH: Evolutionary economics.
Classification: LCC HB97.3.N45 2018 | DDC 330.1–dc23
LC record available at https://lccn.loc.gov/2018000013

ISBN 978-1-108-42743-2 Hardback
ISBN 978-1-108-44619-8 Paperback

Contents

Figures

Notes on Contributors

Kurt Dopfer is a Professor at the Department of Economics, University of St. Gallen, Switzerland, where he is also Chair of International Economics and Development Theory, Co-director of the Institute of Economics, a member of the University Senate, Emeritus, and a researcher for the Swiss National Science Foundation. He has published several books and numerous articles in twelve languages and has been a member of the editorial board of several journals, including the *Journal of Evolutionary Economics*.

Giovanni Dosi is Professor of Economics and Director of the Institute of Economics at The Sant'Anna School of Advanced Studies, Pisa, and serves as Director of the Industrial Policy and Intellectual Property Rights task forces at the Initiative for Policy Dialogue at Columbia University. Professor Dosi is a continental Europe editor of the journal *Industrial and Corporate Change*. A selection of his works has been published as *Innovation, Organization and Economic Dynamics* (2000) and *Economic Organization, Industrial Dynamics and Development* (2012).

Constance E. Helfat is the J. Brian Quinn Professor in Technology and Strategy at the Tuck School of Business at Dartmouth College, New Hampshire. She has published widely in academic journals and books, and co-authored *Dynamic Capabilities: Understanding Strategic Change in Organizations* (2007). She is a Fellow of the Strategic Management Society, and has received the Distinguished Scholar Award from the Technology and Innovation Management Division of the Academy of Management, the Viipuri Prize, and an honorary degree. She currently serves as co-editor of *Strategic Management Journal*.

Keun Lee is a Professor of Economics at the Seoul National University. He was awarded the 2014 Schumpeter Prize for his monograph on *Schumpeterian Analysis of Economic Catch-up: Knowledge, Path-creation and the Middle Income Trap* (Cambridge University Press, 2013). He is now the President of the International Schumpeter Society, a member of the Committee for Development Policy of the UN, an editor of *Research Policy*, a council member of the World Economic Forum, and a member of the governing board of Globelics.

Franco Malerba is Full Professor of Applied Economics and President of the research center ICRIOS, Bocconi University, Milan. He has published fifteen books internationally, including *Sectoral Systems of Innovation* (Cambridge University Press, 2005) and *Innovation and the Evolution of Industries* (Cambridge University Press, 2016). He is an editor of *Industrial and Corporate Change*, an advisory editor of *Research Policy*, and an associate editor of *Journal of Evolutionary Economics*.

Andreas Pyka is a Professor at the University of Hohenheim, Stuttgart, where he has held the chair for innovation economics since April 2009. His fields of research are neo-Schumpeterian economics and evolutionary economics with a special emphasis on numerical techniques of analyzing dynamic processes of qualitative change and structural development. He has published numerous articles and chapters on these subjects.

Pier Paolo Saviotti is a Visiting Research Fellow in Innovation Studies at the Copernicus Institute, Faculty of Geosciences, Utrecht University. He is the author of several publications about the economics of innovation, including *Technological Evolution, Variety and the Economy* (1996), which was awarded the 1997 Gunnar Myrdal Prize of the European Association of Evolutionary Political Economics (EAEPE). He is a member of EAEPE, of the Lisbon Civic Forum, and is Vice President of the International Schumpeter Society.

Sidney G. Winter is the Deloitte and Touche Professor of Management, Emeritus, at The Wharton School of the University of Pennsylvania. He is the author of *An Evolutionary Theory of Economic Change* (1982, with Richard Nelson), and of many articles in scholarly journals and symposia. His honors include the 2015 Global Award for Entrepreneurship Research.

I Economics from an Evolutionary Perspective

Richard R. Nelson

I.I WHAT IS THIS BOOK ABOUT?

This book is about modern evolutionary economics. It is designed for economists and other social scientists who want to become more familiar with this body of research and writing, and provides an overview of the field, its theoretical orientation, and the empirical findings it has achieved.[1] It brings together several different strands of work in evolutionary economics that have been developing relatively independently and displays the broad perspective on how modern economies work and evolve that together they bring into view.[2] And as evolutionary economics is a work in progress, it considers where the field seems to be going.

The term "evolutionary economics" has been used to denote a wide range of economic research and writing.[3] This book focuses on work aimed to illuminate empirical economic phenomena oriented theoretically by the proposition that the phenomena being studied have evolved, in a sense that will be laid out in what follows. While

---

[1] A strong background in economics is not required. However, a basic familiarity with the field would be very helpful to the reader, if not indispensable. A large share of the topics treated and concepts employed by evolutionary economists are traditional in economics, and readers will be assumed to have at least a rough understanding of these. And the significant differences between evolutionary and neoclassical economics will stand out more clearly for readers with a familiarity with the latter.

[2] We note that much of the work in evolutionary economics has been done by economists who have their home outside of standard economics departments, particularly in business schools and in programs focused on science and technology policy. Much of it has been published in journals outside of the economics mainline, we note in particular the *Journal of Evolutionary Economics, Industrial and Corporate Change*, and *Research Policy*.

[3] Here are a limited set of references to a vast literature: Veblen, 1898; Nelson and Winter, 1982; Hodgson, 1993; Metcalfe, 1998; Dopfer, 2005; Dosi, 2014; Winter, 2014; Malerba et al., 2016.

I

formal evolutionary modeling has played a significant role in developing and sharpening that perspective, the focus here is not on formal models but rather on the broad perspective on economic activity that they have helped to shape.[4] And, to keep reasonable constraint on the subject matter we will explore, while evolutionary economists clearly have a kinship with the broader body of evolutionary social science research and writing, we do not consider that extensive literature in any detail.[5]

This book is tightly focused this way because we, the authors, believe that the value of a broad theoretical perspective, such as that of evolutionary economics, should be judged in terms of the strength and quality of the understanding of empirical phenomena and the illumination of policy questions provided by research oriented by that perspective. We believe that the research done over the last thirty years oriented by evolutionary economic theory has amply demonstrated the value of that theory, and we want to increase the number of scholars who appreciate that.

This introductory chapter lays out the broad orientation taken by evolutionary economists and the questions they regard as central. The following chapters will describe in more depth the evolutionary perspective on fields of empirical study where evolutionary economists have been particularly active, and show the kind of picture of how economies work and change that they provide when they are put together. The concluding chapter considers the evolution of evolutionary economics.

I.2   CAPITALISM AS A DYNAMIC EVOLVING SYSTEM

At the root of the difference between evolutionary economics and economics of the sort presented in today's standard textbooks is the conviction of evolutionary economists that continuing change,

---

[4] The formal modeling of evolutionary economists is scattered and varied in style; for a sampling see Nelson and Winter, 1982; Metcalfe, 1998; Dosi, 2014; Malerba et al., 2016. For a survey of evolutionary game theory, see Weibull (1995).
[5] For a broad recent review, see Alex Mesoudi's *Cultural Evolution* (2011).

largely driven by innovation, is a central characteristic of modern capitalist economies, and that this fact ought to be built into the core of basic economic theory. Economies are always changing, new elements are always being introduced and old ones disappearing. Of course economic activities and economic sectors differ in the pace and character of change. In many parts of the economy innovation is rapid and continuing, and the context for economic action taking is almost always shifting and providing new opportunities and challenges. And while in some activities and sectors the rate of innovation is more limited, attempts at doing something new are going on almost everywhere in the economy, and so too change that can make obsolete old ways of doing things. Neoclassical theory, which is a significant influence on how most professionally trained economists think,[6] represses this.

With our central interest in innovation and the economic conditions continuing innovation generates, evolutionary economists are Schumpeterian, and as Schumpeter does we highlight the amazing, if uneven, economic progress that capitalism has engendered. Economies at the economic frontier today support a standard of living that would have been almost unthinkable two centuries ago, when capitalist economies were just emerging. For evolutionary economists perhaps the most challenging and important economic questions that need to be addressed are: How did the economic progress we have achieved come about? What can be done to enable those societies that to date have not shared in economic progress to do better? And what kind of progress can we expect in the future, and how can we influence the paths taken?[7]

[6] We recognize that many empirically oriented economists do their research and write it up under very little explicit influence of neoclassical theory. But we would argue that even in these cases the implicit influence can be significant. More on this shortly.
[7] Evolutionary economists also are much concerned with the "creative destruction" associated with innovation-driven economic development, and the fact that often the benefits or economic growth are not widely shared.

In having these questions at the center of their attention, modern evolutionary economists are returning to the perspective on the workings of market economies laid out long ago by Adam Smith,[8] and later Karl Marx, and more recently of course by Joseph Schumpeter. Long run economic development certainly is treated in today's standard economic textbooks, and technological innovation is recognized as the key driving source. However, this subject matter is presented as a special topic, rather than at the heart of economic description and analysis.

Evolutionary economists would argue that analysis of what goes on in the economy at any time cannot be separated from, but must involve in an integral way, explicit recognition of the dynamic processes involved in ongoing innovation-driven economic change. The core assumptions of neoclassical theory make it very difficult to do this.[9]

There is, first of all, the need to recognize the importance and nature of innovation. Innovation is an activity involving a vision of something that has not existed before and beliefs about its potential value. Inventors and innovators may draw as best they can from what is known empirically about what is and is not likely to succeed. But the imagination and sophistication guiding the effort, and luck, are at least as important in determining what paths are explored and the innovations that actually emerge. These aspects of what innovators see and believe, and don't see, do not fit in very well with a theoretical presumption that economic actors somehow know the best course of action for them.

And in a world of innovation-driven change, not just the innovators, but also many economic actors who would prefer to keep

---

[8] Recall that Smith begins his great book by describing innovation and productivity growth in pin making. His central interest clearly is in economic development.

[9] As we noted, many empirically oriented economists get around this problem basically by ignoring the canons of neoclassical theory in their empirical work and writing. Thus discussion of what is involved in industrial competition may well stress Schumpeter. But when the analysis is linked to formal theorizing, the emphasis is on how competition affects industry output and prices in equilibrium.

on doing what they have been doing often can't because the context they are in has changed, and therefore must take the actions they employ on the basis of limited relevant experience. Again, a theory that presumes that actors have a strong understanding of the context they are in and of appropriate actions to take would seem not to recognize important aspects of what is going on in many contexts.

Similarly, evolutionary economists see an inclination to presume that economic activity tends to be in or close to an equilibrium configuration as a hindrance for analyzing contexts in which innovation is going on, with a variety of new ways of doing things actively competing with each other and with prevailing practice. Some will be winners, and some losers, but the race must be understood as ongoing rather than already finished.

On the other hand, the nature of the economic dynamics we have been describing is readily interpretable as an evolutionary process. This certainly is not a new idea. Over a century ago Thorstein Veblen (1898) asked "Why Is Economics Not an Evolutionary Science?" While Alfred Marshall[10] generally is associated with the rise of neoclassical economics, in a famous statement he proposed that "The Mecca of the economist lies in economic biology ..." And Schumpeter (1950) argued that "in dealing with capitalism we are dealing with an evolutionary process." Thus many economists long have believed that the process through which economic change occurs has important aspects similar to those involved in biological evolution; this is why we and our forebears have used the term "evolutionary" to denote our theoretical orientation.

Later in this chapter we will discuss the aspects of economic evolution, and the similarities and differences from evolution in biology, in more detail. However, here we want to highlight the following essential features.

First, when we call the process of economic change evolutionary we do not mean to deny, or play down, the purpose, thought,

---

[10] The quote is from the eighth edition of Marshall's *Principles*, published in 1920.

and often the considerable sophistication that lies behind much of economic action taking. Rather, we use the term to highlight the incomplete character of human understanding even in contexts that are illuminated by a strong science, and the consequent uncertainties that surround important parts of economic activity, and which are always present when new things are being created and tried out. The outcomes of trying new things almost always differ, in some cases radically, from what the inventor or innovator had in mind. How things actually work only can be learned in actual practice, and even then reliable learning about the efficacy of new ways of doing things can be slow.

This characterization clearly fits efforts at significant innovation. But it also fits efforts by economic actors to respond to changes in the economic environment in which they operate, even if the appropriate new behaviors do not require any sophisticated action once they are found. Thus the responses of retail stores to changes in population density or location almost always involve considerable trial and error learning, and failures.

As a consequence, in any field of economic activity where innovation is under way, and we argued earlier that in modern economies no field is completely static, there is bound to be a variety of different ways of doing things employed by different actors. At the same time some of these practices, generally but not always ones that are relatively superior in some sense, are expanding in their relative importance, and others, generally relatively ineffective ones, are declining. And as this goes on new modes of operation may enter the picture. This is very much the way traits evolve in biology.

In many cases an important aspect of the selection processes going on in economic evolution is expansion of actors doing relatively well and the decline and possible disappearance of those doing poorly.[11] However, while there are exceptions, most empirical

---

[11] This statement is relevant to practices employed by firms in competition with each other. It has much less relevance to household practices.

studies of change in an arena of economic activity find that the principal mechanism through which a new and better practice takes over a large share of the action is adoption by increasing numbers of economic actors. As highlighted above, a principal difference between economic evolution and biological evolution is that economic actors generally are able to choose what they are doing and how they are doing it, and have the capability to learn not only from their own experience but from available information about alternatives. But this is a long way from proposing that economic actors "optimize."

This perspective on the process of economic change molds not only how evolutionary economists see economic dynamics, but also how they understand what is going on in the economy at any time: the prevailing allocation of resources across activities firms and industries, the technologies and business practices in use, the present quantities of production and consumption of different goods and services, their prices and the prices of the different factors of production, the current structure of industry, etc. We evolutionary economists see these features of economic activity not as an equilibrium configuration with all participants doing the best they can, but as more or less transient phenomena being generated by a path dependent evolutionary process.

Thus the considerable variation at any time in the productivity and profitability of firms within the same industry that is widely observed in market economies is something that evolutionary economists expect, while neoclassical economists have a difficult time explaining it. More generally, evolutionary economists would predict that at any time a number of firms (and households) are making decisions, doing things, that are poorly conceived and for that or other reasons will not turn out well for them. At the same time learning from experience and, for firms, competitive selection will have led to much of prevailing economic behavior being reasonably competent, given the range of practices that are available at that time, and in some cases remarkably effective.

Evolutionary economists of course are interested in what is relatively constant in an economy, as well as the processes of change. However, given their presumption of continuing change, we look for constancies in variables and relationships that tend to hold up in a dynamic economy, and which reflect the nature of the processes driving change. Thus evolutionary economists see the forces of dynamic competition in an economy as generally preventing average rates of profit in an industry from having a strong persistent drift in one direction or another. And while they would expect the prices of different goods and services to be continuingly changing, in many contexts they would expect the ratios of prices to costs to remain relatively constant over relatively long periods of time. On the other hand, evolutionary economists also see drastic breaks from paths that had been relatively stable as an important feature of the creative destruction involved in economic progress.

In short, evolutionary economics puts forth a very different view of what is going on in an economy than that laid out in today's more standard economics. That view highlights continuing change, much of that connected with processes that in the long run generate economic progress, and at the same time requires many economic actors to cope with new conditions. It sees the configuration of economic activity at any time as the current result of an evolutionary process whose workings over time have generated a variety of different behaviors which vary in effectiveness, which have been winnowed but not completely (among other reasons because of the continuing innovation going on). Evolutionary economists believe that this orientation provides a much better basis for understanding how modern capitalist economies work.

I.3 NARROWING THE DISTANCE BETWEEN ECONOMIC THEORIZING AND WHAT ECONOMISTS ACTUALLY BELIEVE

There is good reason to believe that a significant number of empirically oriented economists, who may present a neoclassical theory of economic activity when they are teaching theory or writing a theoretical article, in fact harbor an implicit evolutionary perspective regarding much of what is going on in the economic world. This is reflected in their writings and other presentations for general audiences regarding such matters as the nature and economic significance of competition in high tech industries, their identification of creative innovation as the key driving source of economic growth, arguments about the need for capital markets to finance the birth and growth of new entrepreneurial firms, and about the importance of flexible labor markets for coping with an economic context where the location and nature of jobs and the needed skills are constantly changing. And the top economic journals often are open to empirical research reports framed implicitly by a dynamic evolutionary point of view.

Evolutionary economists obviously see these developments in a very positive light. However, rather than regarding them as indicating that there is little need to push further, we believe they increase the importance of getting an explicit evolutionary perspective on economic activity better known and entertained more widely.

It is important to recognize that theorizing in economics is of several different kinds and involves different levels of abstraction and generality. Some of it is very general and abstract, providing a broad conception of what shapes what goes on in market economies and how they work. When economists employ the term "neoclassical theory" they tend to mean such a broad perspective on economics, and when we use the term "evolutionary economics" here we are denoting a similarly general and abstract theory of economic activity. At the present time neoclassical theory holds a near monopoly on conceptualizations at a general level of what economic activity and structure are about that professional economists know and teach. Evolutionary economists aim to break that monopoly.

Of course much of economic theorizing is focused not on an abstract view of economic activity in general but on particular sets of phenomena or economic questions. It is concerned with such matters as how labor markets work, how particular prices are determined, the determinants of the overall rate of inflation, the patterns of international trade, etc. A good portion of theorizing at this level is quite formal, often laid out mathematically. Economists often refer to formal theories at this more limited level of generalization as "models." While formal models have their own particular orientations, those that today are widely known by economists tend to have a general perspective that, not surprisingly, is broadly consistent with the broader conceptions of neoclassical theory. On the other hand, while their work may not be familiar to most economists, evolutionary economists also have been active in formal modeling.

However, what we want to highlight here is that much of the effort by economists to understand what is going on in the economy is abstract to a much more limited degree than the general theoretical orientations and the formal models we have referred to above. Rather, it is quite close to the empirical subject matter it is concerned with, and is the result of economists knowledgeable about that subject matter trying to identify the gist of the forces at work. It is to a considerable extent inductive in nature, and is less logically fleshed out than general theories and formal models. Nelson and Winter (1982) have called this kind of theorizing "appreciative" as contrasted with "formal" theorizing.

Virtually all appreciative theory is expressed verbally, and takes advantage of the richness of natural language, and its ability to describe qualitative as well as quantitative detail. But the cost of this is that it is much more difficult to check on the logical coherency of a complex verbally expressed theory than one that is sharper and articulated more formally, and the ability to explore and deduce implications is much more limited. On the other hand, the ability of formal theory to incorporate details that the analyst believes are important, particularly if these cannot be characterized quantitatively, is much more constrained.

Nelson and Winter (1982) argue that, if they are oriented the same way, appreciative and formal theorizing should be understood as complements. We propose that most of what economists know about how the economy actually works is contained in our appreciative theories. In contrast, formal theory ought to be understood as presenting allegories about what would happen under certain idealized conditions that are a significant distance from the actual context and course of economic action, but whose analysis can provide insights into the behavior of a more complex reality. In particular, if the broad theoretical orientations are mutually consistent, the stronger logical structure of formal theorizing can help to sharpen the focus and provide a way of thinking about the coherence and scope of the analytic arguments of appreciative theory.

Appreciative theorizing by evolutionary economists has been shaped and supported by formal evolutionary modeling in several of the areas of research we will consider in the following chapters of this book. Economists who are not knowledgeable about evolutionary economics tend not to be aware of these models, and the relationships they highlight and illuminate.

But even more important, we would argue, is the broad orientation to economic activity that is associated with an evolutionary perspective. We suggested above that, today, a good portion of the appreciative theorizing regarding what is going on in economics is being done by economists who have doubts about whether neoclassical theory provides much useful illumination of the empirical phenomena they are trying to understand and explain. But there is too much going on in any arena of economic activity for an empirical observer to see it all, even if the researcher has an open mind. Inevitably what is seen and not seen is going to be influenced to some extent at least by the general conceptions of what economic activity is all about, and the forces molding it, that one has in one's head.

Thus absent an explicit conception of the economy as an evolving system, economists doing empirical research and developing an appreciative theory about what is going – even who are drawn to an implicit evolutionary point of view – are unlikely to highlight the generally significant differences in the behavior and performance of competing economic actors, or recognize adequately the trial and error learning and selection going on, and at the same time the variety of innovations that are being tried out, most of which will not amount to anything but some of which could profoundly shape the path of future change. It takes the perspective provided by explicit evolutionary economic theory to bring phenomena like these into clear view.

This is why we think it so important that the broad evolutionary perspective that we lay out in this book be more widely known. Our argument is that this orientation to how an economy works can bring theory and empirical understanding more in line with each other.[12]

1.4   THE BEHAVIOR AND CAPABILITIES OF ECONOMIC ACTORS

These issues come out strongly when one considers how evolutionary economics understands the behavior and capabilities of economic actors. Since the days of Adam Smith a hallmark of economic theorizing has been the presumption that for the most part economic actors do *what* they do with purposes in mind and, in situations that are familiar to them, at least a rough understanding of the consequences of following various courses of action. It can be argued that, if treated with care, and recognizing human fallibility, the theory that economic actors usually behave rationally, in the sense above, has shown considerable explanatory and predictive power. Most evolutionary economists buy this argument.

However, modern neoclassical theory has abstracted the presumption that economic actors mostly act with purposes in mind and some knowledge about how to achieve them into the theoretical assumption that their behavior is optimal, in the sense that what they do is the best possible action for them to take, given their objectives and the constraints they face.[13] For the reasons laid out above, this

---

[12] And more in line with economic analysis of an earlier time.
[13] Of course this proposition often is put forth in terms of expectations.

abstraction of goal oriented behavior does not provide an adequate general basis for understanding the diverse actions being taken in an economy marked by continuing innovation and flux.

We note that the concerns of evolutionary economists about the theory of behavior that over the last half century has come to dominate mainline economics clearly overlap those that motivate modern behavioral economics.[14] However, the arenas of economic activity, and the particular aspects of behavior, on which these two bodies of economic analysis focus are different. Behavioral economics has focused almost exclusively on human behavior that is logically inconsistent, or more generally does not seem to further any considered objective the actor might have.[15] The context within which such ineffective or even harmful action is being taken is not highlighted as being new to the actor, but rather can be interpreted as not radically different from situations the actor faces relatively regularly. We evolutionary economists are not surprised by instances of the kind of behavior that behavioral economists highlight, even in contexts that are familiar to the actor. But our broad theoretical presumption is that in contexts that remain relatively constant and thus are familiar to the economic actors, while one certainly would expect to find instances of incompetent or even bizarre behavior, by and large learned actions result in satisfactory, if not optimal outcomes.[16]

We evolutionary economists make a distinction between action taking in familiar contexts, and action taking in contexts that are new to the actor and past experience is of little value. To date at least this is not a distinction that has drawn attention from the behavioral economics camp.

Given these interests, many evolutionary economists have been drawn to the conception developed by Herbert Simon and his

---

[14] For a fine broad review of behavioral economics see Diamond and Vartainen (2007) and Akerlof and Shiller (2015).

[15] For a recent discussion of these matters see Akerlof and Shiller (2015).

[16] We stress here that "satisfactory" does not connote "close to optimal." What the actors are achieving must of course meet survival needs, and what they will settle for. But this may be far from the best they could do if they knew better.

colleagues of "bounded rationality," which provides a basis for a general theory that recognizes both the factors behind the broad effectiveness of much of economic behavior in many contexts, and also the many exceptions to that tendency, and in particular supports a distinction between contexts that are familiar to the economic actor and those that are not.[17] The basic premise of the bounded rationality conception of behavior is that the contexts within which individuals and organizations make choices very often are much too complicated for them to understand all the factors bearing on how best to achieve their objectives. On the other hand, they may be able to observe and understand important aspects of the context they are in, and may have the reasoning power to draw out some implications of what they know or think they know. In particular, in contexts that are reasonably stable they may be able to learn from experience and reflection what, given their purposes and wants, seems to work and what seems not to work.[18]

In such contexts, and where the actions that need to be taken are recurring, evolutionary economists tend to join Simon and colleagues in proposing that learned "routines" tend to come into existence which, after they are established, are employed without much explicit thinking about the matter on occasions when action of a particular type is called for. This proposition holds for both individual and organizational actors.[19] If the context for action taking remains relatively constant, evolutionary economists would propose that forces of learning and selection are likely to result in the employment of routines that yield satisfactory or at least viable

[17] Simon would be considered by some contemporary behavioral economists as within their camp. However, his point of view is not central to most of the statements of what behavioral economics is about.

[18] The key references here are Simon, 1955; March and Simon, 1958; and Cyert and March, 1963.

[19] In Nelson and Winter (1982) we reserved the term "routine" to refer to organizational actions, and much of the subsequent literature follows that tradition. However, in this book the term "routine" will be used to refer to the standardized behavior of individuals as well as organizations.

consequences, if not optimal ones. An important part of evolutionary economics is study of how these learning and selection processes operate, and the nature of the routines they generate.

Effective routines need to be responsive to variations in the context for action that occur relatively commonly. Thus in a relatively stable environment one would expect consumers to learn to respond to increases and decreases in prices that fall within the range of normal variation by doing some switching among substitutes, and see suppliers responding to increases or decreases in demand by offering more or less. To learn to respond adaptively and relatively routinely in this way does not require the ability to optimize, and adaptive behavior can be far from optimal. But it is the kind of behavior that boundedly rational economic actors can be expected to have learned to adopt in relatively constant environments.

However, any particular routine, or way of doing things more generally, even one that has considerable built-in adaptability, and has served adequately for a long time, inevitably will be made obsolete or irrelevant by changes that have occurred. And for a variety of reasons economic actors may choose to, or be forced to, operate in contexts that are new to them and do things that they never have done before and where past experience provides little guidance to appropriate action. Search and problem solving activity aimed to identify or create a satisfactory course of action when suitable routines do not exist, or need to be modified, is another important component of the behavioral theory in evolutionary economics.[20]

Of course in the eyes of evolutionary economists, the kind of behavior associated with innovation is the principal driver of economic progress, and a central subject for research. There is no clear conceptual line where search and problem solving behavior begins to

---

[20] It might be noted that this distinction in Simon's behavioral theory between two different modes of arriving at an action – following a routine without much conscious thought, and more conscious thought and problem solving – is closely analogous to the two "systems of behavior" recently put forth by Daniel Kahneman.

involve efforts at innovation. However, innovation clearly involves the imagining of courses of action that lie beyond the actor's experience and understanding of what others are doing. Efforts at innovation require search and problem solving that must be effectively creative to work out well, and success also often requires a certain amount of good luck.[21] This certainly characterizes R&D done by firms and other organizations. It also characterizes the efforts of firm management to map out new courses of action.

The central importance evolutionary economists place on search, problem solving, and innovation, in the processes that generate what economic actors do leads them to put particular emphasis on how the ways of doing things that are available to an economic actor come to be evident or are discovered or imagined or constructed. This is a very different orientation than that of conventional decision theory in which the "choice set" generally is taken as a given, and the focus is on the objectives of the economic actors and how these influence choice among a given set of alternatives, rather than on why the alternatives that are considered are what they are. This of course leads evolutionary economists to a central interest in how available options are perceived and the processes through which new ways of doing things get conceived and developed.

These observations pertain to both individual economic actors and to formal organizations. Evolutionary economists recognize that much of economic activity goes on in formal organizations, and that in many contexts organizations are the key economic actors. In modern economies it is firms (and other organizations like hospitals and schools) that produce or provide most of the goods and services created in economic activity. In many arenas of economic activity most of the innovating is done by firms. A significant fraction of the

---

[21] We note that the treatment of bounded rationality by Simon and his colleagues deals with innovation hardly at all.

research and writing by evolutionary economists has been concerned with firm behavior, capabilities, and innovativeness.

How does the traditional presumption of economists – that what economic actors do in any context is molded by the objectives they have there and their beliefs about what actions are likely to be effective in pursuing these, and that the analyst can predict or explain changes in behavior that occur when the context changes on the basis of these presumptions – hold up under the relatively complex theory of behavior we have been describing? We would argue that it holds up pretty well as a rough first approximation, but that there are exceptions, and in any case to get beyond a rough first cut prediction or explanation of what economic actors are doing requires an understanding of the details, like the kinds of routines that are operative, and the way efforts at problem solving and innovation proceed.

When drawn into discussion of what really is going on in the economy, and the factors behind the behaviors of the economic actors involved, we believe that many economists who teach neoclassical economic theory would be in broad agreement with the above. And we would argue that the orientation of evolutionary economic theory provides a much more promising basis for getting at relatively detailed understanding of what economic actors are doing than the assumption that they "optimize."

1.5 THE NATURE AND ROLE OF MARKETS AND COMPETITION

Today's evolutionary economics stands squarely in the mainline tradition of economic analysis in seeing market organization of economic activity, with for-profit business as the principal suppliers of goods and services, and competition as the major regulatory mechanism, as the key institutions of capitalist economic systems. However, the view of how markets and market competition work is more Schumpeterian than today's standard theory. And the case put forth by evolutionary economics for the kinds of benefits society can gain from market organization of economic activity is different than the neoclassical case.[22]

In modern capitalist economies a staggering range of goods and services are potentially available to customers. These goods and services are largely provided by business firms, who in turn require a wide range of different kinds of inputs. Taken together the range of variables involved and the number of connections among them are enormous. "Solving" the system analytically for an allocation of resources and a production of goods and services that serves the vast variety of human needs reasonably well is a problem that defied Soviet style central planning. Even with the most elaborate economic models run on the most powerful modern computers, solving the allocation problem analytically still cannot be done today in a way that calculates the relevant details.

Yet market organization somehow is able to deal with this problem in a way that often is messy but which by and large "works." Evolutionary economists would take issue with the theory that the workings of markets generates an optimal, or even an efficient, or even an equilibrium, configuration of economic activity. The workings of markets, even widely supplemented as they are with a variety of government programs and regulatory regimes, clearly leave a number of needs, highly valued by many people, met to a meager degree, and allows and even encourages activities that many regard as positively harmful to society. But while evolutionary economists tend to be less positive about the way markets allocate resources than our more orthodox colleagues, we agree that what markets have achieved is quite remarkable. And they do so not in the simple static context assumed in neoclassical general equilibrium theory, but in one where technologies, available resources, and wants, are changing in unpredictable ways.

---

[22] Our orientation of course is Schumpeterian. For a modern statement see Metcalfe (2014).

Evolutionary economists, as our more orthodox colleagues, see prices as key variables that influence the behaviors of both demanders of a good or service and suppliers, and as usually adjusting to diminish conditions of excess demand or supply particularly when these become large. We tend to see significant changes in quantities or prices or both as usually reflecting shifts in demand or supply. That is, many evolutionary economists are quite Marshallian.[23] We are quite comfortable with a good portion of the causal arguments presented in today's standard price theory texts, if not with the theoretical assumptions used to rationalize those arguments. Thus while we assume that the behavior of economic actors is adaptive in the sense we discussed earlier, we do not assume that what they do is "optimal" for them. And while we, like our neoclassical colleagues, see prices as playing a key role in balancing supply and demand, and as enabling adjustment to changes, we do not assume that markets always are at or near to an "equilibrium" in the standard sense of those terms.

Moreover, evolutionary economists would highlight that markets and competition do a lot more than simply influencing prices and the allocation of resources among different lines of economic activity, given current know-how, which is the focus of neoclassical theory. At the same time markets provide an opportunity and an inducement for economic actors to try out new products and processes, and explore modes of doing and using things more generally that they have not engaged in before. And competition among firms in a market does a lot more than simply providing pressure to keep costs low and for prices not to diverge too much from costs. Competition raises the pressure for firms to innovate and to respond to a competitor's innovation, and increases the rewards from doing so successfully.

More generally, markets in capitalist economies are perhaps the most important among the varied institutions that shape the

---

[23] For an extended discussion see Nelson (2013).

processes of economic evolution. The advantages of market organization of economic activity are not only that this is a reasonably effective (if not an optimal) way of meeting present perceived wants, given present capabilities and knowledge. Evolutionary economists see it as even more important in the long run that market organization of economic activity and competition provide a spur and a context for the generation of new and potentially better ways of doing things and for sorting out the wheat from the chaff. The allocation of resources and the prices they generate at any time should be understood in this light.[24]

For market organization of economic activity to serve as an engine of progress obviously requires that innovators anticipate that they will be able to reap returns from their innovations when these in fact improve economic performance, and as our innovation systems work this generally involves their ability to garner at least temporary monopoly control over the use of their innovation. But on the other hand, if progress is to be broad and sustained, that monopoly must be limited and competition must not be eroded widely and durably. We have been highlighting the variation in patterns of behavior, including the technologies and other routines used, that one observes among firms in the same line of business, along with significant differences in productivity and profitability. This variation clearly is at least partially associated with the innovation going on by firms in an industry, which not only has advantaged some firms relative to others, but often has led them along different paths. But at the same time in most arenas of economic activity one can observe a basic broad similarity in what firms are doing. In many industries most firms employ the same basic technologies, if with different details and with different effectiveness. The broad design of the products or services they provide is similar. So too a wide variety of management practices.

[24] The perspective articulated here regarding what is driving positive change in market oriented economies is very close to that developed in Rosenberg and Birdzell (1986).

The basic reason is that, given the way that most markets work, while a successful innovator is able to hold control over its new ways of doing things and reap the returns from the advantage they give it over its competitors for a certain period of time, almost always aspects of new productive ways of doing things sooner or later become widely known, and the ability of the innovator to hold off its competitors from using that know-how generally is limited. As a result, the whole industry moves ahead over time. Market competition turns out to be an effective vehicle for collective evolutionary learning.[25]

This is a very different view of what markets do and how they work than articulated in today's standard economic texts. And yet, here too it would appear that many contemporary economists have a view of the advantages of market organization of economic activity, and competition, that is very much in line with the perspective presented above. It is the theory they espouse when presenting formal economics that ignores this. As we have argued, a major advantage of evolutionary economic theory is that it puts forth an abstract view of economic activity, and the role of markets and competition, that squares with what much of the profession actually believes.

We have highlighted that there is no argument here that market mechanisms allocate resources and efforts optimally. Winston Churchill's famous characterization of the virtues of democracy – democracy is the worst form of government except for all the others that have been tried – perhaps is equally apt for market organization of economic activity. But then, modern economies do not operate with market mechanisms and institutions alone. To this we now turn.

I.6   THE INSTITUTIONAL RICHNESS OF
MODERN CAPITALISM

Economists use the term "institutions" in a variety of different ways. Probably the most widely employed conception of institutions today

---

[25] Lundvall (1992) has stressed collective cumulative learning.

is as "the rules of the game" (North, 1990), or the somewhat broader concept of "governing regimes" associated with the structures, constraints, requirements, incentives, and norms operating in particular contexts, and molding the way things are done. As we noted above, economists traditionally have argued that the employment of privately owned for-profit firms and of markets to structure and govern much of economic activity are the hallmark institutions of capitalism. The economic behavior that one observes in capitalist economies certainly is strongly and widely molded by these institutions. For-profit firms operating on markets is the standard way of organizing and managing the production of goods and services in a wide variety of economic sectors. In most of these sectors and others markets provide the vehicle through which those who want something are able to obtain it, and those that have something they want to sell can find customers. Evolutionary economists are in full accord on the powerful role of firms and markets in enabling and molding coordinated behavior in modern capitalist economies.[26]

However, many evolutionary economists have a different view than is standard among economists these days on the other significant institutions of modern economies. The current standard position sees these either as supporting or subsidiary institutions needed to make firms and markets work well, or as responses to "market failures." Contemporary evolutionary economists, very much in the spirit of an older tradition of institutional economics, tend to be more inclined to consider the nature and operation of non-market institutions in their own right.[27]

We have noted the considerable research done by evolutionary economists on technological innovation in different economic sectors. In virtually all of the areas studied firms and markets have

---

[26] Thus in many cases the "routines" employed by economic actors in certain contexts are "institutionalized."

[27] For excellent general discussions of the new and the old institutional economics see Rutherford (1996) and Hodgson (2016). In his work Greif (2006), while oriented to the questions of today's institutional economics, develops the rich description and analysis associated with the older tradition.

played key roles in the innovation process. But in many areas universities have played key roles. In a number of technologies government procurement or other modes of public finance has been important, and government agencies have actively and effectively steered efforts to advance the field.

While unfortunately their empirical study has been limited, it is clear that scientific, technical, and professional societies play a significant role in the operation of modern capitalist economies, particularly in enabling that new advances in a field become available, if sometimes with a lag, to all those working in the field who have the relevant background understandings. It is these kinds of institutions that support the communal evolutionary advance of know-how.[28]

For evolutionary economists the proposition that these non-market institutions should be understood as there simply to support market processes and fill in for market failures just does not ring right. Thus the early work on computers was largely initiated and funded by government agencies, and for-profit firms and market arrangements (contracts) were used by the government as part of the apparatus it put in place to develop an effective computer. Similarly, in the efforts to find a prevention or a cure for AIDS government agencies and non-profit foundations have been very much in the lead.[29]

More generally, there is a lot more to the institutional structure of modern economies than for-profit firms and markets. Firms and markets do play a role in almost all arenas of economic activity, but in most they share the stage with other institutions. In many sectors firms and markets clearly are the dominant institutions, although almost all such industries are regulated to some degree, and in many publicly provided goods or services are essential to their operation. Think of airlines and airports and traffic control systems. In many sectors non-market institutions play the central guiding roles with

---

[28] Murmann (2003) provides a fascinating discussion of how this system worked in the evolution of the German dyestuffs industry.

[29] Mazzucato (2013) also has stressed the range of technological fields where government programs have been in the lead.

market mechanisms subsidiary. National security, education, criminal justice, and policing are good examples. Some sectors, like medical care, are extremely "mixed," and one cannot understand the activity going on in them, or the ways in which their structure, ways of doing things, and performance have evolved, if one pays attention only to firms and markets.

Also, evolutionary economists are coming to recognize that the evolution of the institutions constraining and molding economic activity is a central aspect of the process of long run economic change. The nature of firms evolves. New kinds of industries and new kinds of markets come into existence. Changing government programs and policies, and changing laws, both are responses to and forces pushing changes in economic activity. While most of the research by evolutionary economists, and scholars more broadly, on innovation has been oriented to technological innovations, increasingly organizational and institutional innovation is on the agenda.

As these recognitions sink in, many evolutionary economists have come to treat modern economies as intrinsically mixed, with political, social, and cultural aspects intertwined with market ones, and to see the theory of the economy as basically a clean simple market system, which has played such a role in influencing the thinking of the profession since Walras, not just as highly abstract and simplified (which is appropriate in a theory at this level of conceptualization) but badly distorting. As we have noted, the "innovation systems" concept has taken strong root among evolutionary economists.[30] There is increasing recognition that the economic growth process involves the evolution of governmental policies and programs, and institutions more generally, as well as technologies and industries. In a number of ways these developments can be seen as a returning to a pre-Walrasian view of political economy, which is well suited to analysis from an evolutionary perspective.

---

[30] The key references here are Lundvall (1992) and Nelson (1993).

However, it is fair to say that this recognition of the institutional complexity of modern capitalist economies is not yet as ingrained in evolutionary economics as the other perspectives discussed earlier. The broader building of institutional richness into the basic analytic conceptions of evolutionary economists is a work in progress.

1.7 EVOLUTIONARY ECONOMICS AND EVOLUTIONARY BIOLOGY

The term "evolutionary economics" obviously carries the connotation that this orientation to economic analysis has something in common with the perspective of Darwinian evolutionary biology. In this section we flesh out our earlier brief discussion of the similarities and differences.

One basic similarity is that both theories play down the role of deliberate long run planning in determining the prevailing state of affairs. Darwin's theory provides an explanation for the remarkably good design that existing animals and plants possess for living in their environments, that does not involve the mind and hand of God. Evolutionary economics provides an explanation for the often striking effectiveness of the ways economic actors presently go about doing things that does not assume an ability to reason, foresee, and control the path of future events that vastly exceeds what we know about human capabilities.

And in both evolutionary biology and evolutionary economics the state of affairs at any time needs to be understood as a frame in a motion picture. While not always directly relevant to understanding of what is going on at present, understanding of why the current phenomena are as they are hinges on analysis of how they came to be.

Further, at a broad level the dynamic mechanisms argued by the two theories to have brought us to where we are, and which will take us to where we will go from here, have similar elements. The dynamic processes in both theories feed off of variety. Both involve selection mechanisms that winnow that variety, increasing the relative importance of some variants and decreasing that of others. In both systems continuing change requires the continuing introduction of new variety, mutations in the case of biology and innovations in economics.

But as we have stressed, there also are important differences. The most fundamental one is the central role played by human purpose, understanding or belief, and deliberate decision making in the economic (cultural) evolutionary processes going on.

It is likely that one reason why many economists have tended to shy away from considering evolutionary economics as a serious approach to analysis of economic behavior and phenomena is their conviction that human beings are not like fruit flies. Evolutionary economists do emphasize the bounded nature of human rationality, that often what economic actors do is a matter of routine, and that their conscious deliberations inevitably are limited in scope and depth. But evolutionary economics does not treat human actors, individuals or organizations, as like fruit flies, locked into particular patterns of behavior by their genes. They can and do change what they are doing, and try out new practices, based on their notions about what they need to do to prosper or at least survive.

One important consequence is that the distribution of practices going on in an economy tends to change much more rapidly than the population of economic actors changes. We do not want to play down the role of "creative destruction" in the processes whereby a superior new way of doing something replaces an established less effective way; in many cases the process involves the disappearance of many of the older firms. But on the other hand, in many cases the shift over of an industry from one technology to another superior one is accomplished largely by extant firms adopting the new, with the death of established firms and the birth of new ones playing only a modest role. This is very different than in biological evolution where a change in the distribution of phenotypes and genotypes is strongly linked together. And it means that the distribution of practices and understandings being employed in an economy can change very fast.

Also, humans can hold possibilities in their heads, often with the aid of supporting mechanisms like books and the web, and analyze them "offline" before deciding whether or not to employ them in actual practice. Thus many designs are considered by engineers before they decide what they actually want to try out in practice. A wide range of business plans may be conceived, discussed, and analyzed, before a firm decides whether or not to go into a new market. As a consequence, the range of alternatives in play at any time may greatly exceed the number in actual use. And conscious decision making, oriented to meeting objectives more fully, and guided by beliefs about what will do that, plays a central role in economic evolution.

But as we have stressed actions taken on the basis of conscious choice often yield consequences very different from what was intended, and in any case virtually always can be improved by subsequent action undertaken on the basis of learning by doing and using. Actual experience in practice, and what economic actors make of that experience, remain essential aspects of the cumulative change process even in areas where there is strong scientific knowledge. This fact makes it especially important that there generally are a number of economic actors doing and experiencing the consequences of doing different things. Where one observes powerful sophisticated ways of doing things, these virtually always are the result of a cumulative learning process, where generally a number of different actors have been involved. These factors and others have led us to call the dynamic processes involved evolutionary.

A related difference is that the advance of know-how in economic evolution is, to a considerable extent, a collective phenomenon. The successful innovations of one or a few economic actors relatively quickly become part of the knowledge that the collectivity of economic actors can access.

Today's standard economics takes the remarkable productivity of modern economies for granted. In most of economics this is taken as a given, with the analysis focused on other aspects of what is going on. But what is going on in contemporary economies at any time cannot be understood without recognizing the amazing range of capabilities that today's economic actors have and can work with.

Both evolutionary economics and evolutionary biology highlight that one needs to understand what exists at the present as being the result of the workings of long run path dependent dynamic processes. The present is part of history. It cannot be understood otherwise.

Thus as should be obvious evolutionary economics is very much connected with scholarship on economic history. And a large portion of the writings of economic historians take an evolutionary perspective, explicitly or implicitly.[31]

It is interesting to note that theories that human culture and institutions evolve, in the sense of evolution in evolutionary economics, long preceded Darwin. Hume and Mandeville were cultural evolutionary theorists, and so of course was Smith. And, as we have highlighted, in the years since Darwin a number of economists – Veblen, Marshall, and Schumpeter prominent among them – have proposed that economics as a field of analysis is much closer to biology than to physics. In a very real sense today's evolutionary economists are arguing a point of view that has been around for a long time.

I.8   A ROADMAP

The following five chapters describe what has been learned from research over the last three decades on the principal subjects on which work oriented by evolutionary economics has been concentrated. These areas are: technological advance, firm capabilities and behavior, Schumpeterian competition and industrial dynamics, long run economic development in economies at or close to the frontier, and catching up by economies that are lagging. Research in these

---

[31] Mokyr (2009, 2017) is prominent among economic historians taking an explicit evolutionary point of view. The dynamics described by North (1990) and Rosenberg (for example, 1994, and with Birdzell, 1986) also clearly are evolutionary.

different areas often has proceeded with only limited communication across them. The authors of this volume believe that, in fact, the different pieces largely complement each other, and together provide a broad and coherent picture of the economic workings and dynamics of modern market economies.

Given their central interest in illuminating the sources of the remarkable increases in living standards that much of the world has achieved over the past two centuries it is not surprising that one of the principal clusters of research by evolutionary economists has been on technological advance. Chapter 2 will describe the orientation of this research and what has been learned.

Economists have been interested in technological advance at least since the days of Adam Smith; recall his famous analysis of the sources of productivity growth in pin making. But empirical research on technological advance received a major stimulus from the development during the 1950s and 1960s of neoclassical analyses of long run economic growth that gave much of the credit to technological advance. Somewhat ironically, the new empirical knowledge about how technological advance actually occurred led a number of the economists doing that research to propose that those processes were inconsistent with neoclassical theory and, rather, called for an evolutionary perspective. However, because an evolutionary theory of technological advance runs counter to the general body of theory held by most of the economics profession, it is not surprising that much of the research described in Chapter 2 has been done not in economics departments but by economists and other scholars at schools or departments concerned with science and technology policy or innovation management.

Earlier we highlighted how evolutionary economists have come to recognize the importance both of the significant differences at any time among firms operating in a field in the details of their technological knowledge and operations, and at the same time the substantial body of relevant knowledge that is held by virtually all actors operating in a field. While successful innovators may try hard to keep what they have achieved proprietary, sooner or later the gist of new technology almost inevitably becomes part of the public domain. The term "technological paradigm" has been used to characterize this body of broadly shared knowledge. Chapter 2 considers both the mechanisms that often make new technology private for a while, and those that sooner or later open up access to know-how, and the important consequences of this kind of an evolutionary process.

In most technologies firms play a central role in technological innovation. And there has been considerable interaction between scholars in business schools studying the dynamic capabilities of firms and scholars studying technological advance more generally. However, usually firms (and private inventors and entrepreneurs) are not the only actors involved. In a number of fields university researchers play an important role. Today most fields of technology are supported by university based research in particular fields of science and engineering. In a number there is significant government funding and in some government agencies play a significant role in orienting inventive effort. Considerable research has been directed toward trying to illuminate the division of labor that exists in different fields, and how the "innovation system" fits together. Chapter 2 will discuss research on industry differences as well as features that seem common to technological progress in general.

Chapter 3 surveys the considerable research that has been done on firm capabilities and behavior, viewed from an evolutionary perspective. A good understanding of business firms obviously is an essential part of any broad understanding of how capitalist economies work, since firms are the principal suppliers of goods and services in most (not all) economic sectors, and firms have played central roles in the advance of technologies, and the advance of economic capabilities more broadly. At the same time, understanding the determinants of firm capabilities and behavior is of central interest to management, and to the teaching mission of business schools. And much of the research described in Chapter 3 has been done by scholars at business schools.

Like the evolutionary perspective on technological advance, the emergence of an explicitly evolutionary theory of firm behavior was induced by the perception of some economists that neoclassical theory bearing on the subject had serious problems. For these economists the proposition that the behavior of firms should be understood as the successful result of their efforts to find and implement actions that would maximize their profits seemed to assume cognitive and calculational capabilities that firms did not have, and also to be refuted by the detailed empirical studies that had been done of how firms actually went about making decisions. And the argument that competition assured that only firms that did in fact implement profit maximizing policies would survive seemed quite inconsistent with the variety of firm behaviors that empirical studies had shown to exist. Evolutionary analysis of firm behavior aimed to provide an alternative perspective.

The theory of the firm that has emerged is based on the proposition that much of firm behavior is built into the routines that a firm has developed over the years. Some routines involve the technologies used by a firm and the division of labor and modes of coordination that are operative in production. Others involve the standard ways a firm goes about such matters as ordering new inventory, mounting a new marketing campaign, or setting the prices it charges for its products. The role of management is seen as monitoring what is going on in the firm, and holding it to a standard, and assessing when firm routines need to be changed and if so in what direction. A considerable body of research has been concerned with the "dynamic" capabilities of firms, which includes prominently capabilities for effective innovation. Firm innovation itself involves considerable use of established routine, along with conscious analysis and deliberation, and explicit managerial decision making. Chapter 3 will discuss these matters in detail, and also present other findings of evolutionary research on firm capabilities and behavior.

The body of research surveyed in Chapter 4, concerned with Schumpeterian competition and industrial dynamics, overlaps somewhat the more general literature on technological advance as an evolutionary process surveyed in Chapter 2, and also is linked with some of the work surveyed in Chapter 3 on firm capabilities and behavior. In recent years data sets have become available that enable one to see the diversity of firms underneath the industry averages, and identify the characteristics of firms that are growing and declining. We thus have a much better picture now than we used to of the dynamics of firms and industry structures in industries where technological advance is rapid.

The chapter also surveys the now substantial body of research concerned with what happens in an industry as the new technology that launches it emerges, develops, and matures. While all industries are different, many of them conform to a particular pattern in which industry structure concentrates as an underlying technology matures. In recent years there also has been substantial research on how industry specific institutions emerge as the industry develops.

This analysis of dynamics at a sectoral level nicely sets up the review, in Chapter 5, of research on long run economic development viewed in the framework of evolutionary economics. Research on this topic has followed several broadly different paths, each of which will be discussed separately, and then integrated.

Research on one of these paths has focused on the driving force of innovation, and the creative destruction that innovation sets in train. In contrast with the neoclassical growth models that for the past half century have dominated most of mainline economic analysis of economic growth, evolutionary analysis recognizes the diversity of firm practice that co-exists in the economy at any time, and sees the economic development process as involving, on the one hand, an increase in the use of more productive practices and the decline and ultimate disappearance of less productive ones, and on the other hand continuing innovation that renews variety. Recent models of this genre have recognized the many sectors that comprise an economy at any time, with the growth process involving centrally the birth of new sectors and the decline and disappearance of older ones. Chapter 5 will pay particular attention to this body of writing and the view of long run economic development that it highlights.

Another strand of research on economic development by evolutionary economists has been concerned with the roles played by institutions in fostering the development of new technologies and industries, and in turn with how changing economic structures call for institutional innovation and reform.

Most of the research and analysis we describe in Chapter 5 has been addressed, explicitly or implicitly, to economic development in countries at or near the technological and economic frontiers. In recent years a significant body of evolutionary writing has emerged concerned with countries significantly behind the economic frontiers and striving to catch up. We discuss the evolution of evolutionary analysis of the economic catch-up process in Chapter 6.

Earlier analyses of the challenges countries behind the economic frontier faced in trying to catch up with the leaders presumed, explicitly or implicitly, that while intellectual property rights might be an obstacle to adopting some of the technologies used in higher income countries, the basic challenge for countries aiming to catch up was to increase significantly their investments in human and physical capital, and adopt economic policies that reward effective economic operation in a market context. This still is pretty much the view of much of the analysis of catching up presented by economists of relatively orthodox orientation. In contrast, studies by evolutionary economists have highlighted the considerable learning by doing and using, and capability building, that is involved in successful efforts of catch-up. Much of this needed capability building is in firms. But the emergence and development of capable firms is greatly facilitated by, and may be impossible without, the emergence of a strong group of engineers and applied scientists who are capable of understanding the technologies being adopted, and the development of the kind of institutions needed to support efficient operation of the industries and technologies being taken aboard.

A few countries that used to be significantly behind the economic and technological frontiers in recent years have achieved the capabilities to compete internationally in industries where technology is very sophisticated and, further, is continuing to change rapidly. A portion of the research reported in Chapter 6 is concerned with how countries like Korea and Taiwan were able to do this.

We believe the bodies of research, reviewed in Chapters 2–6, all guided by the perspective of evolutionary economics, when fitted together, provide a coherent and illuminating characterization of how modern market economies work, and the nature of the economic dynamics going on. As stated earlier, our principal orientation in these chapters is to empirical phenomena, and the light on them that an evolutionary perspective gives. But there also has been considerable amount of research by evolutionary economists of a more abstract nature. While not the focus of this book, some of this more abstract and formal theorizing by evolutionary economists is described in appendices to several of these chapters.

While Chapters 2–6 cover most of the empirically oriented research done to date by evolutionary economists, the domain is broadening. We, the authors of this volume, believe that much of the traditional subject matter of economics can be understood better if viewed from an evolutionary perspective than from a neoclassical one. In Chapter 7 we reflect on the future evolution of evolutionary economics.

2 Technological Advance as an Evolutionary Process

Giovanni Dosi and Richard R. Nelson

2.1 INTRODUCTION

We have highlighted that evolutionary economics sees the economy as always in motion, always changing, and in many respects (if certainly not all) generally progressing, in the sense of improving its ability to provide goods and services that meet human needs and wants. Evolutionary economists would insist that a fundamental part of the understanding we need of how modern economies work must involve centrally understanding of how the remarkable capabilities that we now have, compared with those of an earlier era, got developed, and the ways in which the basic dynamic processes at work continue to drive economic progress today.

More than a century ago Thorstein Veblen (1898), in his famous article calling for economics to be an evolutionary science, pointed to the research path evolutionary economics needed to follow: "For the purposes of economic science the process of cumulative change that is to be accounted for is the sequence of change in methods of doing things."

The "methods of doing things" in use in a modern economy at any time are extremely numerous and varied. Many can be called "technologies." But there also are methods of doing things that generally would not be called technologies, like ways of dividing up a complex task and organizing and coordinating work, and methods of making various kinds of decisions, and trying to assure that these are carried out. Evolutionary economics recognizes all of these, and some have been the subject of considerable research. But the principal focus of evolutionary economists, and of economists more generally trying to understand long run economic growth, has been on technologies and on the processes involved in technological advance. Economists long have considered technological advance to be the key driving force behind economic growth. It is less easy than some think to cleanly distinguish methods of doing things that might reasonably be called technologies from other methods of doing things. But the focus here is on the design of the artifacts produced and services rendered, and the physical processes involved in their production and implementation.

It is not surprising that developing a good understanding of how the advance of technology, in the above sense, comes about has been one of the principal motivators for the development of modern evolutionary economics, and this is the focus of this chapter. The evolution of other "methods of doing things," or rather their co-evolution with technology, will be explored in other chapters.

Like the development of an evolutionary theory of firm behavior and capabilities, which we will consider in the following chapter, the development of an evolutionary theory of technological change was motivated by the perception of a number of economists that the way the mainline discipline was treating the subject seemed at best inadequate and in some respects inconsistent with what was going on. Neoclassical growth theory and the associated empirical growth accounting studies had highlighted the importance of technological advance in the economic growth process, and induced a body of empirical research on the microeconomic details of how new technology got conceived and developed. The findings of this research could not be squared with the assumptions of the theory that motivated it. In particular, the empirical studies exploring the details of how technological advance in a field came about almost always showed divergent views among various inventors regarding the most promising approaches to take, with many different efforts going on but only a small percentage of these succeeding, with the outcomes – both the winners and the losers – of one round of efforts setting the stage for the next round. None of this was built into the prevailing theory, and indeed it seemed to some scholars that these empirical facts were fundamentally inconsistent with what that theory assumed (for an early discussion along these lines see Nelson, Peck, and Kalachek, 1967).

To some of these scholars, the process seemed to warrant the term "evolutionary," in the sense that at any time there were a variety of efforts going on to advance the technology which to some extent were in competition with each other as well as with prevailing practices, with the winners and losers being determined largely through how they worked in practice. And like evolution in biology, the current state of technology generally was the cumulative result of a myriad of advances made over many years.

This was far from a wholly new idea. It was implicit if not explicit in the writings of a number of earlier scholars who had studied technological advance (Mandeville, 1714; Smith, 1776). In recent years the proposition has been put forth independently by several scholars outside of economics. However, bibliometric studies show clearly the major influence that the development of evolutionary economics has had on this field of research (Fagerberg and Verspagen, 2009; Fagerberg, Fosaas, and Sapprasert, 2012). Today the proposition that technological advance is an evolutionary process is widely held by scholars in a number of disciplines. The list includes Landes, 1969; Nelson, 1981; Dosi, 1982, 1988; Freeman, 1982, 1991; David, 1985, 1989; Pavitt, 1987; Mokyr, 1990, 2002; Vincenti, 1990; Metcalfe, 1994, 1998; Ziman, 2000; Foray, 2006.[1]

The emergence and development of an empirically oriented research community dedicated to studying technological advance viewed as an evolutionary process owes greatly to the perspective and energy that developed at SPRU (The Science Policy Research Unit) at the University of Sussex, under the leadership of Christopher Freeman, SPRU's director for many years. A significant fraction of the articles and books cited in this chapter are by SPRU members,

---

[1] Much of the formal theoretical structure was first presented in Nelson and Winter (1977, 1982). This chapter draws extensively on Dosi and Nelson (2010).

or scholars who got their training at SPRU, or more recently, their students. More generally, SPRU played the central role in establishing the core intellectual perspective of the broad community of scholars of technological evolution whose work we review here.

The proposition that technology evolves in the sense described above in no way denies or plays down the role of human purpose in the process, or the sometimes extremely powerful body of understanding and technique used by those working to advance a technology. Efforts at invention and innovation are by no means totally blind, or strictly random, as often is assumed regarding biological mutation.[2] Particularly where technological and scientific knowledge is broad and strong, an important part of the variation and selection of possible paths for advancing the technology is pursued in the human mind, in thinking and analysis, in discussion and argument, in exploration and testing of models, as contrasted with in actual practice. That is, much of the effort to advance a technology proceeds "offline" as it were. Research and development is the term customarily given to such offline activities, particularly when they involve groups of scientists and engineers working within a formal organization who have such work as their principal activity. Technologies and industries vary in the investments that are made in R&D and in the effectiveness of such work.

However, even in fields where the underlying science is strong, highly trained and experienced professionals almost always will be far from of one mind regarding the kinds of technological advances most worth trying for, or the best way to try to achieve any of these. There are several reasons. Prevailing technological practice, the artifacts and processes being produced and used, rarely are completely understood scientifically. Professionals are sure to differ at least somewhat in how they understand the reasons why certain things work well and others do not, and in their beliefs about how to fix the latter. Second

---

[2] We note that much of current writing on biological evolution no longer treats mutation as strictly random.

and related, efforts at inventing and solving problems inevitably will reach beyond the areas that are well illuminated by existing knowledge, and involve the hunches of professionals based on their own particular experiences and thoughts. And more generally, while technological professionals in a field may share a good part of the knowledge they possess, particularly the part of knowledge that is taught and written about, their personal experiences with the technology in question and on other matters each regards as relevant inevitably are different.

As a consequence, in most fields of technology one sees a variety of different inventive efforts going on. Many will vary in the aspects of prevailing best practice they seek to advance. But in many cases they will be in direct competition with each other, representing different approaches to the same problem or objective. Some will be winners and others losers.

If scientific knowledge were strong enough so that sophisticated technologists could judge reliably ex-ante which new departures would be worthwhile and which would not be, much of this variety of inventive efforts, and the fact that there are many losers as well as winners, would be evidence of wastefulness. But in no arena of technological advance that has been studied in any detail empirically has ex-ante knowledge been this strong. What kinds of advances are worth the cost, and what works effectively and what works better than what, can only be judged reliably in actual practice. In all the fields that have been studied, learning by doing and using not only is an essential part of the process which determines which new departures get into widespread use and which ones are abandoned or returned to the drawing board, but also plays a significant role in stimulating further R&D to correct or take advantage of the characteristics about a new artifact or procedure that were learned when it was actually put to practice.

We already have sketched broadly an important part of what researchers guided by an evolutionary perspective have learned in recent years about how technological advance comes about and the factors influencing its rate and direction. We have highlighted the role of the variety that exists at any time, the selection mechanisms that winnow on that variety and the continuing innovation which refreshes it, and the cumulative collective learning that is the result of these processes. In the rest of this chapter we flesh out this description as follows:

In Sections 2.2 and 2.3 we discuss what is now known about how factors on the supply side and on the demand side affect the rate and direction of investments in efforts to advance technology, and the nature of the technological advance that is achieved. The question of how individuals and organizations who invest in invention and innovation get returns from their investment is considered in Section 2.4, where particular attention is paid to the role of intellectual property rights.

One important fruit of an evolutionary conception of technological advance has been the development of the concept of a "technological paradigm" which involves all of these factors influencing how a technology evolves. We discuss technological paradigms in Section 2.5.

In Section 2.6 we discuss two other important bodies of understanding that have come out of the research we describe here: first, a sharper recognition of significant differences across economic sectors in the pace and character of technological advance and the actors and factors driving and molding it, and second, recognition of the wide range of institutions involved in technological advance in different sectors. While until recently these topics have tended to be treated as separate, in fact they are closely related, and we treat both in Section 2.6.

In the concluding section we step back from the detail and discuss the dynamics of the evolution of technologies more broadly.

The focus of this chapter is on technological advance at the frontiers. Chapter 6 is concerned with research by evolutionary economists on the catching up process of countries behind the economic and technological frontier.

2.2 TECHNOLOGICAL CAPABILITIES

It is an old adage that "necessity is the mother of invention." Indeed. But there also is the proposition that in this age of powerful science, new technology flows from new science. Certainly, as Mowery and Rosenberg (1979) argued, there are many things that society wants that technological advance has not been able to deliver, and many of the advances that society has welcomed came about only after technological understanding had reached a level where these became feasible. Economists studying technological advance have paid a great deal of attention to the role of demand side and supply side factors in influencing the allocation of efforts to advance technology, and what those efforts achieve. They have come to understand that while both influences are important, they operate in different ways. In this section we consider technological capabilities, the factors affecting the ability to make different kinds of technological advances. In Section 2.3 we turn to influences on the demand side.

Clearly at any time society has a range of pressing wants that in principle could be satisfied by better technologies. However, for many of these, while the rewards to successful invention and development would be great, technologists simply lack the capability to make the needed advances. What scholars of technological advance have come to call "technological opportunities" vary greatly from field to field, and change over time. In this section we review what has been learned about technological opportunities as a result of empirical research on that subject over the past thirty years.

Scholars working in this field of study have come to recognize three broad variables. One is the strength of relevant scientific knowledge. This factor has become increasingly important over the years. A second is what has been learned from experience with the technology and its uses. In most fields of technology learning by doing and using continue to be important factors contributing to the ability to make advances. And third, the materials, components, processing equipment, and other artifacts that technologists can work with, and employ, in their R&D work and in the designs they develop.

While these variables are conceptually different, in practice they interact strongly.

Both case studies and survey research suggest strongly that the "sciences" that are most drawn on in R&D tend to be the engineering disciplines and other applied sciences like electrical engineering, materials science, pathology, agronomy (Klevorick et al., 1995; Nelson and Wolff, 1997). These fields of scientific research are consciously aimed to advance understanding relevant to solving particular kinds of problems and improving particular technologies. They aim to achieve a deeper understanding than can be gained simply through learning by doing and using, but in a sense can be regarded as furthering that kind of learning through systematic science. While today these fields find their homes in universities and formal research institutions, the origins of many of them clearly go back to the experimental approaches and scientific perspectives of many of the sophisticated inventors working during the industrial revolution (see Mokyr, 2002, 2010).

Modern science is widely thought to be oriented to seeking knowledge of what and how and why, but not as strongly oriented to developing practical know-how. However, for the engineering and other applications oriented sciences, seeking illumination that will lead to the advance of practice is the central objective. And funding and efforts go into those sciences in pursuit of that objective. In a sense, therefore, much of modern science, like much of the effort to advance technology directly, is pulled by demand.

It is clear that knowledge of what is likely to work, and of how to do things, can be quite strong even if there is no deep understanding of why and how things work as they do. Steam engine design improved dramatically over the first half of the nineteenth century even though the designers lacked understanding of the physics involved. Thermodynamics emerged later as a field of science dedicated to developing that deeper understanding. The scientists at

Bell Labs who created the first transistor did not understand how it worked; that understanding had to be developed through advances in solid state physics. A good portion of today's knowledge of how to treat various diseases is knowledge of what seems to work, but with limited understanding of just how that treatment works.

On the other hand, deeper scientific knowledge underpinning know-how can greatly facilitate technological progress. The achievement of stronger knowledge of the physics involved helped engineers design better engines. While the efficacy of inoculation to prevent some diseases was discovered before there was any knowledge of how vaccines worked, the development of understanding of immune reactions and the development of immunology as a field of science helped greatly to focus efforts to develop new vaccines. And of course the emergence of some fields of technology was only made possible by advances in basic scientific understanding. Electrical and nuclear technologies are obvious examples.

Put compactly, while the sciences that are drawn upon directly by those seeking to advance product or process technology tend to be the engineering disciplines and the application oriented sciences, the strength of these fields generally depends in good part on the power and illumination provided by more basic knowledge, which is mostly the result of research in the more fundamental sciences.

The presence of strong scientific understanding of how a technology works greatly enhances the ability to learn how to improve it by calculation and analytic modeling, and experimenting with simplified physical models of the system, that is learning through offline R&D. Of course inventors have always tried to learn what might work by sketching and calculating the characteristics of the designs they thought might work, and by experimenting with pilot versions of their creation, but the importance of offline R&D in technological advance clearly has increased enormously over the last century and a half.

On the other hand, it is a mistake to think that R&D is the only way that technological learning occurs these days. Earlier, we stressed the continuing importance of learning by doing and using even in technologies where scientific knowledge is strong. Nelson (2008b) discusses in detail the roles of and interactions between learning through R&D and learning by doing and using in the advance of medical technologies.

We have noted that the scientific knowledge drawn on by inventors in a field generally is open and available to all those skilled in the art. (On the importance of open science to technological advance in a field see David, 2001a, 2001b, 2004, and Nelson, 2004.) In contrast, much of what is learned through practice tends to be inventor or firm specific, at least when the learning is new.

Individual technologies do not stand alone. The ability to make technological advances of a particular sort very often is dependent on the artifacts that other technologies can make available.

Thus the ability to discover and design new pharmaceuticals is dependent on the scientific instruments that can be used in R&D. These days the design of new aircraft involves the use of computer power both for simulation and for calculation. The design, as well as the production of new semiconductors, is strongly dependent on computer capabilities.

And what can be used in a design to meet a particular want is constrained by the materials and components that can be used to make it up, and the production processes that can be used to make it. Advances in the materials and components that can be used can have a strong liberating effect on the ability to advance "downstream" technologies. Thus the development of efficient steam engines in the late eighteenth and early nineteenth centuries, and later the development of economical methods for making steel, led to the development of steam powered railroads and ships, which revolutionized transport technology. We note that, in turn, the design and production of efficient steam engines would not have been possible had there not been earlier advances in the technology for boring gun barrels which, shifted to use in another area of design, enabled the construction of precision chambers and other steam engine components.

The development of efficient compact electric motors had a similar wide ranging revolutionary effect on technologies in the early twentieth century. Semiconductors have been playing a similar role in the twenty-first. Technologies that have this kind of broad (generally downstream) effect have been called "general purpose technologies" by scholars working in this field.

2.3   THE ROLE OF DEMAND

It has been proposed that in fields where the underlying science is strong, efforts to advance technology tend to be triggered by new scientific knowledge, and are directed to taking advantage of that new knowledge. But while there certainly are a number of examples of the latter mechanism at work, the evidence is that this is not the usual case, with the inducement of particular inventive efforts generally being the result of demand side variables. (For an excellent survey study asking about the sources of stimulus for new projects, see Cohen, Nelson, and Walsh, 2002.) Perception that there is need and demand for a particular kind of technological advance may be induced by feedback from customers of a product, or (for process R&D) from knowledge of weaknesses or desirable improvements on the production line, or from visionary assessments of the likelihood of positive response of users to various advances in technology.

The kind of inventions that potential users will welcome often is not obvious. It is all too common for a new product or production process that works well technologically to be rejected by potential users as not suited to their needs and constraints. One widely cited empirical study (Project Sappho, see Freeman, 1982) identified careful and accurate assessment of what users wanted to be a major factor determining whether an inventive effort was successful or not. As noted above, the desirability of a new product or process only can be determined in actual use. However, it clearly enhances the chances of success of an inventive effort when user needs are well analyzed.

User markets differ greatly in the nature of the user needs and preferences they reflect, how potential inventors are able to assess these, and in the sophistication of the users and the roles they play in how new technology is developed.

Thus to be successful in the market for the next generation of TV sets, a company that designs and produces them may need to do good consumer research to assess what users value and what they might be willing to pay. But other than that users do not play a role in influencing the R&D that is done in this area.

In contrast, to sell their wares to the airlines, the producers of large passenger aircraft know their designs have to meet a long list of quite precise requirements, and that the airlines have the sophistication both to specify many of these, and to evaluate plane designs offered to them in their light. To develop a new design that has a good chance of being successful, companies that design and produce aircraft need to engage in dialogue on complex technical issues with potential customers both before and often during the R&D process.

What will be successful on the market may depend not only on what potential users want, but also on a sometimes complex web of other requirements and constraints. Thus for a company to be able to sell its new aircraft design, the plane must meet a number of regulatory requirements, as well as appealing to the airlines. A new pharmaceutical must meet a number of regulatory requirements and pass a series of tests before it is allowed to enter the market. In some industries the knowledge possessed by a company of regulatory requirements and how to meet them may be as important to its success as knowledge of what customers want.

If they have the competence, users themselves often do some of the experimenting, inventing, and evaluating that are needed to improve the technologies they are using, or to explore the potential of radically new ones. This is particularly true of specialized production technologies used by technologically sophisticated firms. But von Hippel (1988) has identified many other examples, particularly in cases where the users were highly trained professionals.

In general – there certainly are exceptions – where potential users are business firms or other formal organizations, one finds much more explicit interaction between users and those doing R&D that influences the orientation of the R&D effort than one finds where the potential users are households or individuals. This is partly a matter of differences in user expertise. It also is partly a matter of whether the aim of the R&D effort is a product with a mass market, or a more specialized and concentrated set of users.

In the latter cases, particularly where there is a single intended potential user or a very small group of them, one often sees some user support of R&D and a commitment to buy and try out at least a few early versions of the artifact being designed. Thus in many cases there is shared support by both equipment suppliers and users for R&D on new specialized production equipment for firms who do not do their own process R&D. And where the government is the sole or prime user, and particularly for artifacts desired by the Department of Defense, government R&D support is the rule not the exception. On the other hand, where the aim of R&D is to achieve a product that will serve a mass market, there generally is no direct user involvement in the R&D process.

But we want to highlight that almost always when a new product or service is introduced to the market that differs significantly from those with which users have had experience, it takes a bit of time before they are able to sort out what they like and don't like about it, and even the uses for which it is fit. In Chapter 4 we discuss in more detail what is now known about how new technologies take hold in a market. But generally the process involves a considerable amount of user learning which in turn feeds back to influence the direction of efforts aimed to make the product or service more attractive.

There is strong evidence that inventive effort tends to be attracted by large markets. And as certain markets grow and others shrink the allocation of inventive effort tends to shift toward the former. Thus as shown in Schmookler's pioneering studies (Schmookler, 1966), the rise in sales of automobiles and of motorized tractors and the decline in the use of horses for transportation and for farm work clearly was associated with the rise of patenting relating to the former two products, and a decline in patenting relating to horse shoes. Schmookler showed that this relationship was quite general; patenting tends to grow in growing industries, and to shrink in declining ones. And many subsequent studies have supported the argument that inventing tends to follow the market.

There are many forces influencing the way markets change over time, and pull inventive efforts in the direction of change. One important factor, of course, is growth of per capita incomes, and the changes in the pattern of demand that are associated with increasing affluence. Wars, and defense buildups, have played an important role. Much of contemporary electronics technology was originally pulled into existence by military demands. The sharp increases in oil prices that occurred during the 1970s induced a significant increase in the amount of inventing concerned with saving energy costs.

Another matter that has attracted considerable attention by economists is how conditions of factor supply – for example the cost and availability of skilled labor, or various kinds of raw materials, or the cost of designing and building specialized machinery – affect the kinds of production processes that are developed in an economy. Thus in a famous work, John Habakkuk (1962) argued convincingly that the high price and limited availability of skilled labor in the United States during the early nineteenth century, relative to the situation in England, was an important factor inducing the development of machinery in the US and the use of higher capital labor ratios in manufacturing than in England. Gavin Wright (1997) has argued that the availability of low cost raw materials in the US was an important factor leading to the development of production processes that used raw materials intensively, even wastefully, and also to the development in the US of a variety of technologies for raw materials extraction. As suggested above, recent studies have shown that effort dedicated to the development of technologies that save on the use of energy is quite responsive to the price of energy. All these are examples of what economists have called "induced innovation theory" at work, where market conditions influence the kinds of production process innovations producers would welcome and support. (For a general review of induced innovation theory, and cases relating to agriculture, see Binswanger and Ruttan, 1978.)

As Karl Marx (1847) argued a long time ago, and Rosenberg (1976) has argued more recently, the kinds of innovations affecting how production is organized and done that managers welcome is not determined by factor prices and perceptions of factor quality and availability alone. One of the reasons why, in the nineteenth century English firm managers welcomed mechanization, is that this put them less vulnerable to strikes and other forms of pressure from skilled labor. Coriat and Dosi (1998) have argued that control continues to be an important influence on management desires regarding production processes, and thus continues to be an objective sought through technological innovation.

The stochastic way that technology advances itself often is associated at any time with imbalances in the capabilities of different components or aspects, or other obvious needs for further advances of a particular sort, that attract inventive efforts. Hughes (1983), in his study of the development of electric power systems, has called these "reverse salients," a term he meant to indicate aspects of a system left conspicuously behind the advance of other parts.

Rosenberg's (1963) study of the development of machine tools in the United States during the nineteenth century provides a fascinating example. Users of machine tools always wanted them to cut faster, and inventors and designers responded. However, as higher cutting speeds were achieved, this put stress on the metals used in the blades. New blade materials were invented. And higher cutting speeds also increased the temperatures at which the blades operated. Cooling methods were invented and developed.

We note that these advances of machine tool technology led to increased capabilities of machinery producers to design and produce specialized production equipment for the wide range of American industries seeking to mechanize production to cut down on labor costs that we described earlier. This is another example of the intertwining of demand and supply side factors in influencing that allocation of inventive effort and the kinds of technological advances that are achieved in an economy.

2.4   PUBLIC AND PROPRIETARY ASPECTS OF TECHNOLOGICAL KNOWLEDGE

Economists long have recognized that technological knowledge has some attributes generally associated with the term "public goods." In particular, once a body of technological knowledge has been developed that knowledge can be used widely, say to produce many goods of a particular kind, without developing that knowledge again. And that knowledge can be used for different purposes; the use for one does not preclude using that technology for another purpose at the same time, although some modification of the basic design or procedure may be needed to achieve multiple uses.

While this may involve significant efforts at learning, economic actors other than the creator of the technology can use it without diminishing the ability of the inventor to use it. Indeed an important vehicle through which effective new technology increases the effectiveness of economic activity is through its spread among users as well as uses. Most new technology sooner or later enters the public domain, becoming part of the broad body of knowledge known and used by most professionals in a field. Indeed this is the principal reason why the technological advances that have been achieved over the past couple of centuries have lifted productivity and incomes so broadly.

At the same time, there is a tension here. While going public rapidly can enhance significantly the gains in economic performance that a new technology can engender, the spread of users may erode significantly the returns reaped by the inventor. In turn, this can diminish the incentives for efforts at invention in the first place.

In most economic sectors business firms and independent inventors are the principal sources of efforts aimed directly at creating or improving product and process technologies. They do so for a variety of reasons. Particularly when a technology is new both independent inventors and firms often engage with it because of enthusiasm for its promise and a desire to be part of an exciting effort. But clearly the most important reason that firms and private inventors put in the resources and time to advance a technology is that they hope and expect to profit from their efforts. Their ability to gain returns from their work then depends to a considerable degree on their ability to control the use of their inventions.

The tension here is real. For effective economic development there needs to be some balance between the forces that make new technology public, and those that provide incentive for efforts to advance it further.

There now are a considerable number of empirical studies of how the creators of new technology gain returns. This work recently has been reviewed by Hall et al. (2014). The conventional wisdom long was that the establishment of intellectual property rights, particularly through patenting, was the principal vehicle. But from the earliest of these studies (Scherer et al., 1959), economists studying the question have come to understand that this presumption is highly misleading.

Much of the more fine grained evidence we have now has been obtained through studies that used questionnaires responded to by firm officials responsible for R&D. The studies by Levin, Cohen, and Mowery (1985) and Cohen et al. (2002) set the mold for this kind of research, and as reported in Hall et al. the findings of these earlier studies have been repeated in more recent ones.[3]

There are some industries where the survey respondents said that patent protection is effective and is the principal means firms have for profiting from their innovations. Pharmaceuticals, chemical products, and some portions of the scientific instrument industry, are

---

[3] Most of these studies have focused on the US, but a number have been concerned with Europe. See for example Arundel, van de Paal, and Soete (1995).

prominent among these. But most industries reported that patents were not the principal means through which their firms were able to profit from their innovations. The simple gaining of a head start over their competitors, the building up of marketing and servicing capabilities, and continued improvements associated with moving down learning curves ahead of their followers, were (with differing emphasis) reported as more important than patents. David Teece (1986, 2011) and followers have written extensively on how firms are able to profit from innovating through mechanisms such as these, particularly when patent protection is not effective.[4]

In many industries keeping as much of the technology secret was also stated as important, particularly for innovations firms made that improve their production processes. For obvious reasons, keeping product design technology secret is more difficult than keeping process technology under wraps.

In a number of these industries, respondents reported that patents were not effective. In others they reported that patents were valuable to them, but were useful primarily as a support and complement to the potential advantages of a head start. In some industries patents were viewed more as a vehicle for holding off patent suits from other firms, and for bargaining with them regarding access to technologies they both need, than as a vehicle for protecting their own innovations.

Large firms tended to use patents more than did small firms, and small firms were less likely to say that patent protection was effective. This finding is highly relevant since much of the political argument in favor of strong patent protection is that this is needed by small firms. While to our knowledge there has been no similar survey of independent inventors, numerous case examples indicate strongly that like small firms independent inventors have trouble with the expense and expertise required to enforce a patent.

---

[4] For a review of this literature see the special issue of *Research Policy*, 2006.

The question of how strong and wide control over the use of their inventions inventors ought to have is a complicated and controversial issue. To the extent society depends on the expectation of profit to induce the inventive activity it wants, it is in society's interest that invention and innovation be attractive ventures for profit seeking organizations and individuals. There also is the argument that inventors should have the right to decide just how their inventions are used, and by whom.

However, the overall economic gains that a new technology can enable depend on the range of uses and users that can employ it effectively, and economists and other analysts of technological advance long have recognized that monopolization of an invention generally means restriction of its use, through high prices and other limits on access imposed by whomever controls the technology, which denies society the ability to benefit from it as fully as would be possible if its use were open. The conflict and tradeoff here has led to controversy on several different policy fronts. One is the question of what should be patentable and what should be the terms of a patent. A second is regarding whether the results of publically supported R&D should be patentable, or whether the results should be placed in the public domain. Third, the issues here raise questions regarding appropriate anti-trust policy.

Traditionally the social costs that economists have most focused on of having new technology be proprietary concerned new products where the establishment of strong intellectual property enabled the inventor to monopolize and price accordingly. Where the new product meets an important need that cannot be met in any other way, the cost to those who are foreclosed from using it because they cannot afford it can be substantial. As a frequently highlighted case in point, consider a new pharmaceutical that enables much more effective treatment of a devastating disease than was possible earlier. As noted, in pharmaceuticals patents are strong and pharmaceutical companies generally price new pharmaceuticals as high as they think they can without drastically curtailing sales. And this certainly cuts out some potential users, as well as causing high financial costs to those that do buy.[5]

As this example illustrates, the seriousness of the problem depends on the importance of meeting the need the new product does meet, and the availability of satisfactory substitutes. Much of the earlier analysis by economists was concerned with optimal patent duration, under the assumption that, while longer patent life meant greater incentive for invention and more inventing, this came at the cost of longer monopoly pricing. Much of the more recent discussion of patents on pharmaceuticals has been concerned with how long the developer of a new drug ought to have before other producers are permitted to produce and sell "generic" versions.

But more recently, clearly supported by the increasing understanding of technological advance as an evolutionary process, there has been growing recognition that patent scope often can be the more important variable. Particularly in fields where technology is advancing rapidly, the limits on the monopoly power of a patent holder are coming to be seen as largely determined by how rapidly competitors come up with competing products and processes, that are not blocked by patents. If the patent or patents granted to a particular inventor are very broad, other inventors may be stymied, or made to operate under significant legal threat. Early in the twentieth century, the Selden patent on a broadly defined automobile design, and the Wright brothers patent on a broadly defined steering and stabilizing system for an aircraft, clearly held back the development of automobiles and aircraft for many years, as other inventors in the field worked under a cloud of actual or threatened law suits (see Merges and Nelson, 1994). More recently, researchers seeking to advance biotechnology sometimes have worked under a similar cloud.

In addition to contexts in which particular firms or inventors hold a broad patent that blocks efforts at competition across a wide

---

[5] Of course this cost tends to be picked up by insurance companies or the government these days.

front, scholars of technological advance have come to recognize that the technology behind many important product designs and production processes involves complex systems with many parts or aspects. These would include automobiles and aircraft, and telecommunication systems and computers and a range of other electronic devices. Here technological advance may be made difficult if there are a number of different patents on different components or aspects of the system, so that designers of new artifacts need to negotiate a number of patent licenses to go forward, or are forced to design themselves components for which satisfactory designs already exist. Merges and Nelson (1994) discuss this problem in detail. Heller and Eisenberg (1998) call it the problem of the "anti-commons." In many industries in which technologies are "systems" one finds widespread cross licensing by firms in the industry which may largely solve the problem for incumbents, but also may make entry of new firms very difficult.[6]

More generally, economists studying technological progress increasingly have become concerned about the conditions under which intellectual property regimes make invention and innovation more difficult and costly than would be the case if technology were open.

This point of view obviously cuts across the grain of conventional beliefs, and the arguments of interested parties, that in order for an economy to generate significant invention and innovation it needs to grant strong intellectual property rights on inventions. However, some years ago Edwin Mansfield (1986) asked company officers connected with R&D how many of the inventions they had introduced to the economy would not have been brought into practice had no intellectual property been available. Even in pharmaceuticals and chemical products, the answer was that less than a third would not have been developed. For most industries the answer was 10 percent or less.

---

[6] Allen (1983) on blast furnaces and Nuvolari (2004) on pumping in mines provide interesting nineteenth century examples of historical cases of this sort.

This is not an argument for junking the patent system or significantly weakening patents across the board. But it certainly should warn against proposals that increasing patent strength is a good way to increase the inventing we get. (For reviews of the empirical work on this matter see Mazzoleni and Nelson, 1998; Granstrand, 1999; and Dosi, Marengo, and Pasquali, 2006.)

In recent years the argument about how the issuance of broad patents affects technological progress has been particularly sharp in fields where technological advance is closely connected with the advance of a science. In these fields a patent controlling the use of the relevant science may block anyone who does control the patent or have a license to use the phenomena or processes the patent controls from effectively inventing in the field. This issue here has become prominent as a result of the increasing proclivity of university researchers and administrators to take out patents on research results, a development, spurred in the US by the "Bayh–Dole" act passed by Congress in 1980, which was induced by the broad belief that when university research results are patented this makes it more likely that they will get into practice. A number of other countries have passed similar legislation, on the basis of the same argument. However, empirical research indicates strongly that the role of patenting in facilitating technology transfer from universities to firms has been greatly exaggerated (see Mowery et al., 2004; David and Hall, 2006; Nelson 2006; and Dosi et al., 2006). These studies discuss the problems for those seeking to advance a technology caused by the impingement of intellectual property rights into the realm of basic scientific understanding relevant to that technology. The current discussion in the US regarding what kind of scientific research results should be patentable and what aspects kept open and in the public domain increasingly is recognizing these issues.

These kinds of issues also have influenced thinking about antitrust policy. In particular, growing recognition that new firms often are the source of radical innovations in fields where established firms have concentrated on improving aspects of prevailing technologies has led to concern that where industries are marked by dominant firms this not only tends to lead to high prices, but also to constraints on the kinds of innovations that are likely to occur. This has revitalized the orientation of anti-trust policies of trying to restrain policies of dominant firms that increase the difficulty of new entry into the industry. Some of the policies that have been attacked for this reason involve the use of intellectual property rights to block entry. Others involve mechanisms for locking in customers. The latter have been particularly prominent among firms working through the internet.

2.5 TECHNOLOGICAL PARADIGMS AND TECHNOLOGICAL TRAJECTORIES

A characterization of the state of technology at any time needs to recognize at least the following three aspects: 1) the body of technological artifacts and processes in use, and the way they are used; 2) the body of understanding, both scientific and experiential, supporting the technology and illuminating the key factors determining how it works; 3) assessments of the strengths and weaknesses of prevailing best practice, and perceptions of promising and unpromising approaches to further improvement. Dosi (1982, 1988) has proposed that, when they are basically held in common by those knowledgeable about the technology, these bodies of practice, knowledge, and approaches to advancing the state of the art together define what might be called a "technological paradigm," somewhat analogous to what Thomas Kuhn (1962) has called a scientific paradigm. The conception of a "technological regime" put forward by Nelson and Winter (1977) is similar.

As we argued earlier, most studies of technological advance clearly show that well informed individuals working in a field of technology do share a common body of knowledge and technique. The paradigm concept is meant to characterize the sweep and structure of what is largely shared. In addition, of course, individual professionals and firms have their own private experience and understandings, but these should be understood as supplementing the shared paradigm.

Prominent within the shared paradigm are basic design concepts. The fact that members of the technological community tend to work with the same basic design concepts is an important part of the reason why at any time there often is strong similarity among the range of artifacts produced by different firms, and why often the production processes used in the industry are very similar. Commercial airliners produced by different companies tend to be tailored to the particular tasks and routes they are intended to serve, but otherwise are much alike. Similarly automobiles and television sets. The mass production arrangements at one car company usually have much in common with those at another. Similarly plant and procedures used in the oxygen process for making steel.

In many industries and technologies the presence of a strong technological paradigm results in the presence of what has come to be called a "dominant design" (Abernathy and Utterback, 1978; Rosenbloom and Cusumano, 1987; Henderson and Clark, 1990). One finds dominant designs in all of the fields mentioned above.

The proposition that a dominant design exists in a field is not meant to argue that there is little variety, but rather that variety is relatively tightly constrained. It is clear that for many years there has been a dominant design of automobile sedans. While Chevrolets, Toyotas, and BMWs surely are not all the same, someone who did not know much about automobiles and was not familiar with the different models might say they all seemed much the same to them. And it is likely that a car company who designed and produced a sedan that was very different than the norm would have trouble getting many sales.

On the other hand, potentially many customers of new cars clearly see these different makes as very different, and consumer reports tell us that their performance and quality vary considerably. Car manufacturers differ significantly in terms of the productivity they are able to achieve on their production lines. And the fact that Tesla is in fact selling pretty well shows that some deviation from the standard can be very profitable, for at least some individual producers.

If user groups differ strongly in their needs and preferences, a strong technological paradigm can be consistent with a very diverse range of products, tailored to the different demands. A case in point is pharmaceuticals, where companies and scientists clearly share basic scientific and technological knowledge, and understandings about how new pharmaceuticals can be developed, but there are a variety of different pharmaceuticals on the market tailored to different human ailments. In fields like this, analysts would agree that there is no dominant design. Murmann and Frenken (2006) provide a good general review of what is known about the conditions under which dominant designs do and don't emerge from a technological paradigm.

In addition to specifying broad design concepts, technological paradigms generally involve a shared appreciation of what is strong and what is weak about prevailing practice, and plausible approaches for advancing the technology in different ways. The former of course is associated with perceptions of what users want, a topic discussed in Section 2.3. The latter involves understandings about how the technology works, a topic discussed in Section 2.2, along with heuristics for problem solving that generally have a strong experiential as well as a scientific basis. Constant (1980) has provided us with a beautiful study of these at work in the progressive development of turbo jet engines.

Particularly where a technological paradigm is associated with a dominant design, it also often is associated with what has been called a "technological trajectory," a strong tendency for the artifacts and processes that are the working part of the technology to progress over time in particular directions in the space defined by their relevant technical characteristics. The particular directions of advance of course determine the kinds of needs and wants of the technology's users that are being met better over time. It is a good bet that the wants being met better are ones where innovators can gain profit from the advances they make, a topic considered in Section 2.4.

We note that the trajectories followed by particular technologies tend to be sensitive to some user needs and some social costs but not others, particularly if these do not impinge strongly on the incentives for inventors and innovators. The paths followed by coal and oil electricity generating plants during the last half of the twentieth century are good cases in point. As changes in the orientation of energy generating technologies in recent years suggest, regulation often is necessary to put and keep technological advance on socially desirable tracks.

The proposition that technological advance in a field largely follows a particular technological trajectory is not meant to play down the fact that at any time there generally is considerable variation in the advances occurring. Rather, the argument that technological advance is proceeding along a trajectory is meant to highlight that a large share of the individual advances being made have a family resemblance. But that family can be quite varied. And, within a broad paradigm and the associated broad trajectory of technological advance, the particular general orientation of innovation can change somewhat over time as conditions – in particular the nature of dominant user demands, the availability and costs of different inputs, and regulatory structures – change. But conceived of as pathways, technological trajectories tend to remain oriented in particular directions for long periods of time.

There are empirical studies of the technological trajectories that have been prominent in a wide range of product and process fields. Of course many of the particular directions taken by technological advance are particular to the technology, its characteristics, and how it is used. However, there would appear to be several technological trajectories that one finds quite widely.

Thus a common feature of technological trajectories in process technologies and the artifacts that are used in them is a powerful trend toward mechanization, and growing capital intensity. We note that Adam Smith wrote about this in his famous discussion of what was happening to pin making in the mid and late eighteenth century. Karl Marx argued that this was a general feature of manufacturing industry in capitalist economies. The recent study by Klevorick et al. (1995) suggests that trends in the late twentieth century are similar to those of the nineteenth. The reason for the trend is that, on the one hand, with high and (until recently) rising costs of labor, manufacturers are willing to pay significantly for machinery that enables them to cut back on the labor they need to hire, and on the other hand that from the times of Adam Smith inventors have been able to visualize ways to mechanize operations that are being done by hand.

While to our knowledge there is no recent study that has looked at this phenomenon in detail, it is quite clear that over the past quarter century a widespread tendency in the evolution of process technologies has been the development of computer linked hardware and software to automate operations that had been being done by persons. The reasons are similar to the above.

But of course the characteristics of the trajectories followed by different technologies to a large extent need to be described in terms of the specific characteristics of those technologies. Perhaps the technological trajectory most familiar to many readers is that followed by transistors, integrated circuits, microprocessors, and more generally the heart components of microelectronics, which was described many years ago by Gordon Moore, and which continues to hold to the present. The elements of these electronic devices have progressively become smaller, and more tightly packed, with the result that the capacity of devices of a given size has increased dramatically, as have operation speeds, while unit operation costs have declined amazingly.

The trajectory followed now for half a century in semiconductor electronic devices reflects the key forces influencing how efforts at advancing technology are focused that we discussed earlier. Users of semiconductors, generally as components in the electronic and other product systems (like aircraft engines) that they design produce and sell, are willing to pay for faster more compact devices. And improvements in understanding and the creation of devices that enable the design and construction of more tightly packed chips with smaller components, have progressively opened opportunities for designers of chips to improve their products in these dimensions. (See Dosi, 1984 for a perspective on these developments.)

We note that, in turn, the evolution of semiconductor technology in these directions has led to trajectories of improvement in a wide range of devices that use semiconductors as key components that take advantage of their progressive miniaturization, and greater capacities and faster speeds. These trajectories show up in products as diverse as computers, television sets, and hearing aids. (For a discussion see Nordhaus, 2007.)

The trajectories followed by aircraft engines and aircraft bodies is another area that has been studied relatively intensively (Sahal, 1985; Saviotti, 1996; Frenken, Saviotti, and Trommetter, 1999; and Bonaccorsi, Giuri, and Pierotti, 2005). The efficiency of aircraft engines is increased if they are able to operate at higher temperatures and pressures. Both the development of new materials that could be used in engines, and better control mechanisms, has enabled engine technology to progress in these dimensions. In turn, aircraft body design has evolved to accommodate the streamlining challenges associated with the increased speed that more powerful engines make possible. And the range of aircraft designed for transcontinental flight also has increased. The advances in electronic devices described above also have helped to enable movement along these trajectories.

Empirical research has shown that the evolution of many other technologies display these kinds of trajectories. For general reviews see Sahal (1981, 1985) and Dosi (1982, 1984).

A somewhat separate body of research and writing – focused on "learning curves" – has developed over the years concerned with what happens to unit costs, or sometimes output per worker, or measures of product performance, as a new product gets into production and matures. The independent variable is cumulative output, which clearly grows over time, and is interpreted as a measure of experience with the product. The mechanisms at work discussed in this literature include some also treated in the trajectory literature. For example in many of the cases studied the decline with experience in unit costs or labor per unit of output is ascribed in part to learning to mechanize various operations. But the causal elements discussed in the learning curve literature also include such general developments as identification of particular production problems and bottlenecks, and restructuring of the production process, and in some cases the design of the artifact, to deal with these.

A striking characteristic of the learning curve literature is that almost always it shows that the rate of cost reduction or quality improvement per unit of time diminishes as output and experience increase over time. In addition to the learning curve literature, there is a wide range of evidence that technological advance within a given technological paradigm often proceeds with increasing returns but at diminishing rates. As this happens, a renewal of rapid progress may require a paradigm shift. Relatedly, a large shift in the nature of demands, costs, or regulations, together with changes in the scientific and technical knowledge, may induce inventors and innovators to abandon prevailing paradigms and trajectories and attempt to establish others. These are matters we discuss in Chapter 4.

2.6 GROWING UNDERSTANDING OF SECTORAL
DIFFERENCES AND THE COMPLEXITY OF
INNOVATION SYSTEMS

When the research by economists on technological advance that we are surveying in this chapter began to surge in the 1960s, it is fair to say that their background understanding of the subject was rather limited. In this section we focus on two related areas where the initial narrow conception has broadened out considerably.

First, the early work tended to proceed as if the way technological progress occurred was pretty much the same in all economic sectors, and therefore the quest was to understand a quite general process. Increasingly it has come to be recognized that there are major differences across economic sectors in the way progress proceeds and the major influences on its rate and direction. Second, the early work tended to see the activities involved in technological innovation as largely done by firms or independent inventors and conducted in a competitive market context, with other kinds of actors and institutions very much in the background. Since that time it has come to be recognized much more clearly that a variety of institutions are involved in the activities that generate technological advance, and that non-market mechanisms and actors as well as market ones play key roles.

These two aspects are closely related. The important differences across economic sectors are to a large part associated with differences in their innovation systems: the kind of organizations most active in innovation, and their modes of interaction. Therefore, in this chapter we treat the subjects together.

From the beginnings of this stream of research, economists were aware that Schumpeter had, at different times, made two quite different propositions about how innovation occurred in capitalist economies, and in particular about the kind of firms involved and how they operated. In his early *Theory of Economic Development* he argued that innovation largely occurred through the establishment of new firms by entrepreneurs, who used bank finance to enable them to develop inventions and introduce them to the market; this structure came to be known in the literature as Schumpeter Mark I. In his later *Capitalism, Socialism and Democracy*, Schumpeter argued that in the modern world of science based innovation, technological innovation had become the province of large firms with internal R&D facilities, who did their inventing in-house, and were able to finance this work internally; Schumpeter Mark II.

In these early days of the research tradition being reviewed here, a considerable amount of research was done trying to determine which of these models better fit the facts about innovation in the years after World War II. Initially most of the argument was posed generally. A major question explored empirically was how firm size and industry concentration was related to various measures of technological progress in an industry. As general research in the field progressed, the roles of technological opportunity and the ability of innovators to reap returns that we discussed earlier became increasingly recognized, and various indicators of these and other variables were introduced to the regressions.

In a fine general review of this research, Cohen and Levin (1989) report that, particularly when these other variables are considered, there seems to be little general relationship between technological progress in an industry, and firm size or market power. In some industries where firms are large and have considerable market power significant innovation is going on; telecommunications systems is a good example. In other industries also marked by large firms, technological advance is relatively slow, for example in recent years in steel production. Similarly, there is rapid innovation in some industries where firms are small, but in many such industries innovation is slow.

More generally, it gradually came to be recognized that sectors where considerable innovation was going on differed considerably in the kind of firms who were making the principal innovations. In some industries the important innovators tended to be small, often new firms, as in Schumpeter Mark I, in others large established firms, as in Schumpeter Mark II. (See, e.g., Dosi et al., 1995; Malerba and Orsenigo, 1997; Breschi, Malerba, and Orsenigo, 2000; Marsili, 2001.) During this same period of time recognition sharpened that in some industries suppliers played a major role as a source of innovation. (Recognition of the often important role of users came somewhat later, largely through the work of von Hippel.) And technological innovation in some industries clearly depended heavily on research undertaken at universities and public laboratories.

The taxonomy developed by Keith Pavitt in 1984 of the locus in different industries of the principal innovative activity going on, and the nature of most of the innovation, was a first cut at characterizing this diversity. Pavitt proposed it was useful to distinguish among the following classes of industry.

One class he called "scale intensive." The industries he included in this class all were marked by large firms engaged in mass production for markets for broadly standardized products. Some of the industries produced materials like steel and glass. Others produced complex artifacts like automobiles and television sets. While firms in the former kind of industry did little product R&D, firms in the latter often did considerable product R&D. And in both of these kinds of industry most of the firms in these industries engaged in R&D to make their production processes more efficient and reliable. In some specialized equipment suppliers also were a source of process improvement. In the industries producing and marketing complex artifacts there often was significant R&D work that goes into design, and occasionally significant product innovation. As the television set example illustrates, product innovation in these industries also often benefited from component innovations resulting from the R&D of suppliers.

Certain other industries Pavitt proposed were largely "supplier dependent" regarding the sources of the technological progress they were experiencing. Here the firms were smaller than in the industries he called scale intensive, and did little R&D on their own. Some of these industries produced commodities, like yarn and fabric, or provided general services, like airline and bus transportation. Others provided products or services tailored to particular users, like building construction and dental and medical care. Technological advance in these industries depends largely on the effective implementation of new materials, machinery, and other artifacts being offered by their upstream suppliers.

As his discussion of both of these industry classes indicates, Pavitt was especially interested in highlighting the role of suppliers of specialized machinery, components, and instruments, in the technological progress being made in a wide range of industries. However, his identification of a class he called "supplier dependent" shows his sharp recognition that the importance of suppliers varied across industries.

As we argued earlier, in many industries there is strong interaction between suppliers and users in the design of new production equipment. And in many fields of technology users play an important role in advancing technology more generally. When Pavitt was writing the recognition among scholars in the field of an active user roles in innovation was limited, but nonetheless it is interesting that Pavitt did not see a category of industries in which users played a major role. Clearly, as the importance of suppliers, the importance of users in the innovation process varies greatly across industries.

A recent study by Arora, Cohen, and Walsh (2016) begins to help us sort out these differences. They note the importance of sophisticated user-customers of the products of high tech industries like semiconductors. Undoubtedly the downstream innovation going on here is in sophisticated user firms like computers and telecommunications. As von Hippel has suggested, user innovation is to be expected where the users are highly sophisticated technologically. But users also play a role in the development of things like sporting equipment.

Earlier we noted that, as a result of the growing range of the applied sciences, a large number of technologies are becoming more closely linked with a field of science. However, Pavitt was surely correct in identifying technological advance in a few industries as particularly "science based." He singled out electronics, and some of the chemical industries including pharmaceuticals. Today we certainly also would include some of the industries whose products and processes are based on biotechnology. The Arora et al. study, concerned with the role of outside sources of innovations introduced by an industry, identified pharmaceuticals, medical equipment, semiconductors, and (perhaps surprisingly) automobiles as industries where research at universities was an important source.

A great deal more is known now than earlier regarding the roles that scientific research plays in technological innovation, and in how universities and public laboratories are involved in the processes involved. As was discussed earlier in this chapter, an important part of what has been learned is the pivotal role of the applied sciences and engineering disciplines. These are the fields most generally cited as most relevant to technological advance in their field by respondents in business forms. It is a good bet, therefore, that engineering and medical schools are the principal loci within the university of the university inventions that the firms in the Arora et al. study reported as the sources of their principal innovations.

This is not to play down the importance of advances in understanding won in the basic sciences to the technological progress that has been made over the last century and a half. However, the pathway from an advance in basic scientific understanding to use of that understanding to advance an area of technology generally runs through the applied sciences and engineering disciplines.[7] The effectiveness of these pathways depends both on the power of the new knowledge on which the applied sciences can draw, and the resources dedicated to research in those applications oriented fields.

While there is a tendency among economists, as among lay persons, to talk or write about the rate of technological advance in general, in fact the rate of technological progress has differed greatly across industries and sectors, and in terms of progress in meeting different kinds of human wants. In recent years various studies have explored the factors that seem to lie behind these differences (see for example Nelson and Wolff, 1997, and Nelson, 2008b). Both comparative case studies and statistical analysis suggest strongly that a key factor is the strength of the scientific knowledge supporting efforts to advance technology in a field. In fields where that knowledge is

---

[7] We do not want to draw too sharp a distinction between the basic and applied sciences. As the late Donald Stokes (1997) argued, many sciences are in "Pasteur's Quadrant" with the objective both of advancing useful knowledge and the gaining of fundamental understanding to enable this.

strong, this has induced both relatively high levels of R&D aimed to advance the technology and significant productivity of that R&D. In contrast, in fields of technology where the underlying body of scientific understanding is weak, efforts to push for more rapid advance through increasing R&D funding have born little fruit, and have not been sustainable. Education is a good example (see Nelson, 2008b).

Government policies clearly matter. Economic sectors and the technologies used by them differ greatly in the strength and nature of the public programs directed to supporting them. In the United States and several other countries the electronics and aerospace industries have received very high levels of government support, not simply in the funding of R&D but through procurement. Government programs oriented by perceived national security interests have provided direction as well as support for the development of important new technologies, like the internet, that later found widespread civilian use. Most of the examples used by Mariana Mazzucato (2013) to support her argument that the government can and has been extremely effective in developing new technologies relate to defense programs.[8]

US public programs have also played a major role in stimulating, and guiding, the emergence and development of a wide variety of medical technologies, from new drugs to new medical devices to research techniques and instruments. And as in defense (but along different lines) public support of the purchase and use of medical technologies has played a major role in their emergence and evolution. A third area where public support of R&D, plus major influences on the product market, has played a large role (although less so in recent years) is in technologies relevant to agriculture.

In all of these fields technological progress has been relatively rapid. It is noteworthy that in all of them public support has been substantial for the underlying sciences as well as for applied R&D, and those underlying sciences have become strong. Public support of

---

[8] See also Ruttan (2006).

R&D, and efforts to strengthen the underlying sciences, have been less successful in education and housing.

Taking these diverse strands together, the view we now have of the activities and actors involved in technological advance is much richer than the picture we had at the start of the research tradition reviewed here, which was focused almost exclusively on for-profit firms and private inventors competing on markets, with university research in the background. The concept of an "innovation system" has taken hold, concerned with the wide range of actors and institutions involved, the division of labor among them, and their modes of interaction.

Much of the early work oriented by the "innovation system" concept was motivated by an interest in identifying and analyzing what appeared to be significant differences across nations in the way industrial innovation was supported and organized, and in particular in the roles of government in different countries. To a considerable extent this interest was induced by the emergence during the 1970s and 1980s of Japanese firms as industrial leaders in steel, automobiles, and electronics, and a belief that a major reason was the support by the Japanese government of cooperative research by firms in those industries. Attention also was paid to the long run perspectives believed to be held by Japanese firms, and bank finance that supported this. Freeman's 1987 book, *Technology Policy and Economic Performance: Lessons from Japan*, was perhaps the most influential of these studies of the Japanese innovation system, and how it differed from that of the US and those of the UK and northern Europe.

Several other studies were oriented more broadly at differences across nations. Lundvall (1992) and Nelson (1993) compare a wide range of national systems. The goals of these studies, as the earlier one by Freeman, were to highlight differences across nations in the ways industrial innovation was supported and organized, and to induce nations to adopt those structures and policies that seemed to be most effective.

But increasingly it came to be recognized that a major part of the reason why "national" innovation systems differed was that countries differed significantly in the sectoral focus of innovative activity, and sectoral innovation systems differed greatly, in all of the variables we have discussed above. And gradually the focus of innovation systems research has shifted to the sectoral level (see Malerba, 2004).

The concept of a national innovation system is a useful one, if its limitations are recognized. To the extent that the national innovations systems concept has broadened the scope of analysis and perceptions about policies beyond the quite narrow conception of these that was common years ago, this has been an important plus. And the comparative orientation of the national innovation systems concept certainly has resulted in country policy makers becoming more aware of what policies are in other countries, and trying to take aboard those that appear to be effective if they fit the national context.

However, as we have highlighted, one of the most important things that has been learned in the research we have been discussing is that there are major sectoral differences. A one size shoe does not fit all feet. Policies that are effective for one sector or to foster the development of one class of technologies may be ineffective when used in other domains. As a result of this growing understanding, increasingly the innovation systems concept has been oriented to particular economic sectors, with the research aimed both to identify aspects of what goes on in an economic sector that significantly influence the structure of the innovation system of that sector in all countries, and to identify country differences that matter. The research of Malerba (2002) has been particularly prominent here.

2.7 TECHNOLOGICAL PROGRESS AS AN EVOLUTIONARY PROCESS

The description and analysis of technological progress we have been giving is not simple or easily stated in a compact fashion. A number of different kinds of actors and activities are involved, and both market and non-market institutions.

To further complicate matters, technological progress in one sector or broad field of technology is likely to be different in important ways from what goes on in other fields. There are national differences broadly, and in terms of what goes on in particular sectors. And obviously the nature of technological advance today is different in a number of ways from what was the case a century ago, or even half a century. Indeed, one of the most important things that empirical scholars of technological advance have learned from their research over the past half century is that it is a mistake to repress these differences.

Nonetheless, we propose that technological advance generally should be understood as an evolutionary process. This recognition highlights the uncertainties involved in almost any attempt to develop a new way of doing things that differs in non-trivial ways from prevailing practice. And as a result of the fact that almost always there are multiple actors oriented to advancing a technology, at any time there are a variety of approaches being tried out in competition with each other and with existing technology. Without denying the often great sophistication that is involved in these efforts, to a considerable extent the winners and losers are determined on the basis of evaluation of actual operating experience. And as a result of today's round of efforts and selection, the conceptual basis for the next round is enhanced.

Perhaps most important, understanding technological advance as an evolutionary process is recognition that the amazingly powerful technologies we have today in many areas of economic activity almost never are largely the result of the genius of one particular individual or organization, but virtually always the cumulative result of many different advances made over a considerable period of time by many different contributors. Three hundred years ago Bernard de Mandeville, commenting on what he regarded as one of the most complex and sophisticated artifacts of his era – the (then) modern kind of warship called the Man of War – observed as follows:

> What a Noble as well as Beautiful, what a Glorious Machine is a First Rate Man of War ... We often ascribe to the Excellency of Man's Genius, and Depth of his Penetration, what is in reality owing to the length of Time, and the Experience of Many Generations, all of them very little different from one another in natural Parts of Sagacity. (Mandeville, 1714, vol. II: 141–142)

Technology, as that term generally is understood, clearly is a very important part of the "methods of doing things" used in an economy that Veblen argued evolutionary economics needed to illuminate. However, as we suggested at the start of this chapter, if one adheres to the common use of the term "technology," the body of practice employed in modern economies includes much more than technologies. While one of us (Nelson) has proposed a broad concept of the "technologies" in use that includes a much wider range of practice than usually covered by the term, there certainly are important distinctions to be made. In particular, it is important to recognize explicitly that a good part of the methods used in an economy are basically concerned with the organization and management of work in activities where effectiveness requires the coordination of a number of different individuals or groups.

In contemporary economies the modern business firm is perhaps the most important structure housing these kinds of activities and the practices governing them. We now turn to survey evolutionary research and understanding concerned with the behavior and capabilities of business firms.

Appendix to Chapter 2: Formal Modeling of Problem Solving and Knowledge Accumulation

Giovanni Dosi

The theorizing about technological advance described in the text of Chapter 2 has been largely inductive. As noted in Chapter 1, this book is principally concerned with showing how the broad perspective that the economy should be understood as an evolving system orients empirical research and the kinds of understandings that orientation yields. However, as also noted, there also is a significant body of more abstract theorizing concerned with exploring logically some of the processes and relationships that an evolutionary economic theory brings to the fore. In this appendix to Chapter 2, we describe some theoretical models of problem solving and cumulative learning in firms and other organizations. The focus of the theorizing is on problem solving and learning systems in which there is division of labor, and structured patterns of communication among the actors. The earlier work of Alfred Chandler, James March, Richard Nelson, Herbert Simon, and Sidney Winter has argued that this context is an important one in the processes through which technological advance occurs. This appendix draws significantly upon Dosi et al. (2011) and Dosi et al. (2017a, 2017b).

Firms "do things" (whether material as a car or more "immaterial" as a software program or an airline reservation system), try to improve over time what they do, and quite often also try to innovate and find new things. "Problem solving" is a synthetic notion covering both the current operations of an organization and its search for novel ones. Here we shall survey those endeavors which try to account for organizational problem solving in terms of explicit sequences of activities and procedures nested into specific organizational arrangements prescribing "who send which signals to whom" and "who does what and in which sequence."

The problem solving activities of the firm can be conceived as combinations of physical and cognitive acts, within a procedure, leading to the achievement of a specific outcome. Its internal organization determines the distribution of the informational inputs across specific task units and, as such, the division of the cognitive labor. The general idea is that firms possess the specific problem solving competencies associated with their own operational procedures and routines, in turn embedded into the patterns of intra-organizational division of labor and assignments of decision entitlements.

A.2.1 KNOWLEDGE ACCUMULATION: SEARCH PROCEDURES, PROBLEM SOLVING, AND ORGANIZATIONAL LEARNING

There are different but complementary styles in the formalization of the processes of search and learning.

NK Models

A big family of evolutionary models of organizations have been inspired by the "NK model" (Kauffman, 1993), a formalization that biologist Stuart Kauffman introduced to study the relation between selection and self-organization in complex systems, starting from the idea that adaptive evolution is a hill climbing process that typically progresses through small changes involving a local search in the space of possibilities.

The model is named NK because its basic features are captured by two variables: N refers to the number of parts of a system, while K reflects how richly cross coupled the system is, measuring the richness of interdependences among the components of the system. A system is conceived as a string of N elements $(i = 1,...,N)$; for each element i, there are A possible states. In the simplest case, each part can occur in two states $(A=\{0,1\})$. The set of all possible configurations (strings) of the system elements is called the space of possibilities of the system, whose size is given by A^N in general, while in the binary case the total number of possibilities is 2^N.

For each configuration that the system can assume, a value $f \in [0,1]$ can be assigned to measure its relative performance in the environment (fitness). The fitness of an entire system depends on the contributions of all its parts, and often in complex systems the fitness contribution of each component also depends on the state of the other elements: the set of these interdependencies (or *epistatic interactions*) between elements in a system is captured by the parameter $K \leq N - 1$. In particular, it is assumed that each element undergoes the same number of influences as all the others; i.e., that K is the same for all elements.

The number of values that each component can take is A^{K+1}, (2^{K+1} in the binary case), since its contribution depends upon its own state and upon the state of K other elements, hence upon $K+1$ loci; to each of these combinations, a different fitness contribution f_i is assigned at random, and the overall fitness of a configuration is defined as the average of the contributions of all its elements:

$$F = \sum_i^N f_i / N \qquad (1)$$

The space of possibilities is characterized by a fitness landscape made of the distribution of fitness values to all possible configurations. Each configuration is a one mutant neighbor of all those accessible by mutating a single element from one state to another. Each configuration is a one mutant neighbor of other $N(A-1)$ ones when each of the N part can assume A states, or of other N ones in the binary case. The number of one mutant neighbors gives the number of directions in which each configuration can change to another by a minimal alteration.

The specification of K, the degree of epistatic interactions, determines the smoothness of the fitness landscape. When $K = 0$ (minimum complexity: no element is in relation with another), the landscape has a single global optimum that can be climbed by all other suboptimal configurations via fitter neighbors, and all one mutant neighbors have nearly the same fitness, i.e., the landscape is smooth (highly correlated). When $K=N-1$ (maximum complexity: each element is epistatically affected by all the others that compose the system), there is an extremely large number of local optima, any configuration can climb to only a small fraction of the local optima, and only a small fraction of the configurations can climb to any given optimum. Moreover, the fitness of one mutant neighbor configurations is entirely uncorrelated with the starting point (the landscape is maximally rugged).

One of the earliest applications of the NK approach to organizational analysis was presented by Levinthal (1997). Each element (a gene in the original model) of the organization can be thought as an attribute of an organization's form ("strategy, personal system, structure, etc."), that can take two alternative states. In his simulations, populations of randomly generated structures (organizations) evolve on a fitness landscape, whereby the evolution is driven by variation selection and retention processes.

One major and quite general result is that when $K>0$, the landscape shows an increasing number of local optima on which subsets of organizations will converge according to their initial configurations, displaying a path dependent pattern of adaptation; local adaptation will reduce the heterogeneity but will never make it disappear. As such, this result provides a simple and intuitive explanation of the persistence of heterogeneity among firms, a piece of evidence widely reported by the literature but at odds with standard theories, according to which deviations from the only best practice should be only a transient property inevitably due to fade away as market selective forces operate. Note also that as K increases not only does the number of local optima increase, but also the size of the basin of attraction of each of them tend to shrink. It could well be therefore that none of the organizations might be located in the basin of attraction of the global optimum and therefore no organization will ever find the globally optimal configuration.

Levinthal's analysis has been developed in quite a few works, addressing the relationship between organizational design, environmental complexity, and search outcomes: see Rivkin and Siggelkow (2003), Siggelkow and Levinthal (2003), and Siggelkow and Rivkin (2005). Moreover, the NK formalism has been fruitfully used to study the tradeoff between exploration and exploitation in firms' strategy (March, 1991): see Ethiraj and Levinthal (2004) and Fang, Lee, and Schilling (2010) among a few others.

Cognition and Learning

In general, the NK modeling folds together cognition, action, and rewards into "traits" which are either rewarded or penalized. However, the formal apparatus is plastic enough to be applied to different domains of learning and adoption. So, for example, Gavetti and Levinthal (2000) make use of it to address cognition and learning, even if applied somewhat metaphorically to organizations rather than individuals. More specifically, their analysis of search processes look at the relations between forward looking and backward looking search and their effects on performances. The roots of the distinction between the two search processes go back to Simon (1957b): the former involves cognition ridden, forward looking choices based on offline evaluation of alternatives, even very distant from current behavior; the latter entails experiential choice based on online evaluation of a limited set of alternatives which are close to current behaviors.

In Gavetti and Levinthal (2000)'s model, the organization chooses a policy on the basis of a simplified and incomplete "cognitive model" of its environment, entailing "templates" which cannot directly prescribe actions. In this context, existing practices function as defaults for elements not specified by the cognitive representation and allow the identification of a specific course of action. Thus, it may happen that actors with the same cognitive template may engage in different behaviors.

These hypotheses are translated into a NK based model in which the organization's limited cognition corresponds to a simplified representation of the fitness landscape which is assumed to be of lower dimensionality than the actual landscape ($N1<N$), even if grounded in it. This is captured by the assumption that for each point of the cognitive representation (of the perceived landscape) there are 2^{N-N1} points in the actual fitness landscape that are consistent with this point. The fitness value assigned to each point of the cognitive representation corresponds to the average fitness values of these 2^{N-N1} points.

Gavetti and Levinthal (2000) show that in a context of competitive ecologies in which low performance organizations are selected out, organizations which adopt a joint cognitive and experiential search dominated the population. This becomes particularly evident under rugged landscapes, in which organizations which use purely experiential search are trapped into local optima.

This is indeed a promising route of analysis, explored among others by Gavetti (2005) and Knudsen and Levinthal (2007). Still, the nature of the "problem" to be solved and the cognitive and practical strategies to do that are utterly simplified in such a framework.

A.2.2   DECOMPOSITION AND PROBLEM SOLVING

Following Simon (1981), Marengo and Dosi (2005) focus on strategies for the reduction of problem complexity through the division of problem solving labor, that results in the decomposition of large and complex problems into smaller subproblems which can be solved independently. In fact, the Smithian process of division of labor is a major and long neglected driving force in explaining the inner features and boundaries of economic organization. In particular, traditional organizational economics has concentrated upon the governance of transaction and contractual relations between given "technologically separable" units, but does not tackle the analysis of where such technologically separable units come from or, even more importantly, of whether organizational structures have some at all.

The issue bears a fundamental importance because, first, most processes of division of labor take place within organizations and, second, it empirically happens that most of the times technologies are born in a highly integrated fashion, and possibly undergo subsequent vertical disintegration both within and among firms. In other words, one could say that "in the origin there were organizations" and then markets develop along the lines defined by the processes of division of labor, rather than the other way round as postulated by transaction costs economics.

In Marengo and Dosi (2005) different organizational structures (with varying degrees of vertical integration) are compared in terms of their dynamic problem solving properties determined by their patterns of division of labor and problem decomposition. The basic assumption is that solving a given problem requires the coordination of N atomic "elements" or "actions" or "pieces of knowledge," which we can generically call components, each of which can assume some number of alternative states. The one bit mutation algorithm at the basis of the NK model can be conceived as a particular case in which the problem is fully decomposed and the search process is fully decentralized: each subproblem consist of a single component (bit). On the opposite extreme, there is the case of no decomposition at all, corresponding to a strategy in which all the components (bits) are simultaneously mutated.

Note that the effectiveness of the decomposition, in terms of system performances, is strongly affected by the existence of interdependences among the components of the problem: so, for example, separating interdependent components and then solving each subproblem independently will prevent the very possibility of overall optimization. Note also that, as pointed out by Simon, because of the opaqueness of the interrelations between components, an optimal decomposition – a division of labor that separates into subproblems only the components that are independent from each other – cannot be generally achieved by bounded rational agents, who normally are bound to aim at *near decompositions*, that is, decompositions that try to put together within the same subproblem only those components whose interdependences are "more important" for the performance of the system.

APPENDIX TO CHAPTER 2 81

More formally, one can characterize a problem by the following elements: the set of components: $C = c_1, c_2, ..., c_N$, where each component can take one out of a finite number of states. Normally, a binary set of components is assumed for simplicity: $c_i \in 0,1 \forall i$. A configuration, that is a possible solution to the problem: $x^i = c_1{}^i c_2{}^i \cdots c_N{}^i$. The set of configurations: $X = \{x^1, x^2, ..., x^{2^N}\}$.

An ordering over the possible configurations: $x^i \neq x^j (or\ x^i > x^j)$ holds whenever x^i is weakly (or strictly) preferred to x^j. A problem is fully defined by the pair $(X, \neq)$. As the size of the set of configurations is exponential in the number of components, whenever the latter is large, the state space of the problem becomes much too vast to be extensively searched by agents with bounded computational capabilities. One way of reducing its size is to decompose it into subspaces.

Coordination among blocks in a decomposition may either take place through market like mechanisms or via other organizational arrangements (e.g., hierarchies). Dynamically, when a new configuration appears, it is tested against the existing one according to its relative performance. The two configurations are compared in terms of their ranks and the superior one is selected, while the other one is discarded.

The analysis of the patterns of problem solving and recombination can be usefully undertaken at the level of elements of knowledge (i.e., subproblems), or artifact components. And both domains of analysis have still a long way to go. However, as promising as they are, they still fall short of any semantics on what agents and organizations actually do.

Cognition, Action, and Learning

A step nearer to such task are models explicitly accounting some relation between (i) true "states of the world," (ii) their imperfect or even faulty representations, (iii) actions, (iv) environmental rewards.

Classifier Systems are a good initial candidate.

Let us start by considering those (still few) models whereby information processing and problem solving activities are represented by ensembles of condition action (that is, "if...then...") rules.

Marengo (1992, 1996) and Dosi et al. (2017b) present a model which focuses upon the modification of such information processing capabilities of individuals or subunits within the organization, i.e., a process of "structural" learning. Agents are imperfect adaptive learners, as they adjust their information processing capabilities through local trial and error. This adaptive learning is (at least partly) driven by the information coming from the environment and/or from other members of the organization.

Let

$$S = \{s_1, s_2, ..., s_N\} \tag{2}$$

be the set of the N possible states of nature and

$$A = \{a_1, a_2, ..., a_k\} \tag{3}$$

the set of the k possible actions the decision maker can undertake. The payoff to the agent is given by a function:

$$\Pi: A \times S \to R \tag{4}$$

where the agent's payoff to action a_i when the state of the world s_h occurs will be indicated by π_{ih}. The action the agent chooses depends obviously on the level of its knowledge about the state of the world. The agent's state of knowledge (or information processing capabilities) can be represented by a collection of subsets $P(s_i) \subseteq S$ where $P(s_i)$ is the set of states of the world which the agent considers as possible (or cannot tell apart) when the real state is s_i.

The basic component of this learning system is, as mentioned, a condition action rule, where the execution of a certain action is conditional upon the agent's perception that the present state of the world falls in one of the categories it has defined in its mental model. The condition part is a category, that is a subset of the states of the world, and is activated when the last detected state of the world falls in such a subset.

Practically, the condition is a string of N symbols (as many as the states of the world) over the alphabet $\{0,1\}$ and it is satisfied whenever the last state of the world corresponds to a position where a 1 appears. All in all, the condition:

$$c_1c_2...c_N \quad with \quad c_i \in \{0,1\} \tag{5}$$

is satisfied when, if s_k is the last observed state of the world, we have $c_k=1$. Thus, a set of conditions defines a subset of the power set of S. It is important to notice that each condition defines one subjective state (or category) of the world, as perceived by the agent, and defines its relationship with the objective (true) states of the world. This relationship remains anyway unknown to the decision maker, who is aware only of its subjective states.

The action part is instead a string of length k (the number of the agent's possible actions) over the same alphabet and with the following straightforward interpretation:

$$a_1a_2...a_k \quad with \quad a_i \in \{0,1\} \tag{6}$$

has one and only one position which equals 1, $a_h=1$, meaning that the action "h" is chosen, and "0's" everywhere else. The decision maker can be therefore represented by a set of such condition action rules:

$$R=\{R_1, R_2, ..., R_q\} \tag{7}$$

where:

$$R_i:c_1,c_2...c_N \Rightarrow a_1,a_2...a_k \quad with \quad c_i, a_h \in \{0,1\} \tag{8}$$

Each rule is assigned a "strength" and a "specificity" measure. Strength basically measures the past usefulness of the rule, that is the rule's cumulated payoff. Specificity measures the strictness of the condition: the highest specificity (or lowest generality) value is given to a rule whose condition has only one symbol 1 and therefore is satisfied when and only when that particular state of the world occurs, whereas the lowest specificity (or the highest generality) is given to a rule whose condition is entirely formed by 1's and is therefore always satisfied by the occurrence of any state of the world.

Such a basic modeling structure can withhold the formal representation of both organizational routines and organizational memory. Both entail an "if...then..." structure. Signals from the environment, as well as from other parts of the organization, elicit particular cognitive responses, conditional upon the "collective mental models" that the organization holds, which are in turn conditional upon the structure of its cognitive memory. Cognitive memory maps signals from an otherwise unknown world into "cognitive states" ("...this year the conditions of the market are such that demand for X is high..."). Conversely, the operational memory elicits operating routines in response to cognitive states ("...produce X..."), internal states of the organization ("...prepare the machine M to start producing piece P..."), and also environmental feedbacks ("...after all X is not selling too well..."). In turn, the organizational memory embodies the specific features of what an organization "thinks" and does, and what it is "good at," that is, its distinct capabilities.

This is what one formalizes in Dosi et al. (2017b), trying precisely to map patterns of environmental dynamics, structures of organizational cognition, and environmental performance feedbacks.

A.2.3   CONCLUSIONS

At last, one has begun to couple the empirical investigation on what goes on within the Rosenbergian "black box" with modeling attempts which explore the properties of different search and learning processes. It is just a beginning but a promising one. There are multiple challenges ahead. Here are two. First, one needs to further develop the implication for the theory of the firm. Second, there is hardly any link between the genre of research discussed here and the much more "black boxed" technological learning familiar in the models of industrial evolution.

3 The Behavior and Capabilities of Firms

Constance E. Helfat

3.1 INTRODUCTION

The theory of firm behavior and capabilities and the associated empirical work surveyed in this chapter, along with the research on technological advance treated in the previous chapter, is one of the clusters of research and writing where evolutionary economic theory has had its greatest influence. Two somewhat different kinds of concerns and interests have led to work along these lines.

First, dissatisfaction arose with respect to the neoclassical theory of firm behavior that had become the standard in academic economics, along with a desire to build a theory that explained firm behavior and what goes on in firms more generally in a way more consistent with detailed observation. Among economists who studied how firms made decisions, a significant current arose that firm behavior could not be understood simply as profit maximization. The procedures that firms actually used to make decisions, such as deciding what prices they should charge for their products, did not appear to involve explicit maximization (Cyert and March, 1963). And the fact that many firms did very poorly in market competition, and indeed many failed, suggested strongly that their behavior was often far from optimal.

Milton Friedman (1953) famously responded to this line of criticism by arguing that the outcomes of firm behavior were consistent with profit maximization, so it was appropriate to proceed "as if" firms actually maximized profits. He argued that competition ensured that firms that survived in the market were the most profitable, no matter how that behavior came about. This argument, of course, did not address the fact that at any time most industries comprise a diversity of behaviors among firms, with some firms faring better than others.

At roughly the same time Armen Alchian (1950) wrote an article proposing that, in the contexts of uncertainty that characterize many important industries, the concept of an optimal set of firm actions is not well defined. On the other hand, it is possible to orient the theory of firm behavior around analysis of the behaviors that competition encourages, what competition allows, and what competition tends to eliminate.

There clearly is a suggestion here that the economic theory of firm behavior ought to be built on a theory of competitive evolutionary process. Tjalling Koopmans (1957) endorsed this argument. And in his early research, Sidney Winter (1964, 1965) began the work of doing that.

In the line of argument and writing just described, there is no particular emphasis on the kinds of issues raised by Schumpeter (1934, 1950). Schumpeter argued that continuing change was the hallmark of most economic sectors, with innovation by firms the principal driver of change. Both innovating firms and those not eager to innovate faced the need to adapt their policies and develop new capabilities to deal with contexts that were new to them and for which their established ways of doing things were unlikely to be viable – a central concern in the work of Nelson and Winter (1982).

These two different sources of interest in developing an evolutionary theory of firm behavior and capabilities have been brought together recently in research on the "dynamic capabilities" of firms that enable firms to innovate, adapt, and change. Technological innovation has played an important role in this literature, and the discussion in this chapter pays particular attention to this body of writing.

The following survey begins with an examination of the fundamental underpinnings of firm behavior in evolutionary economics, namely, organizational routines, and explains how these routines support organizational capabilities. The discussion then turns to the ways in which routines and capabilities emerge and develop, and the implications for firm performance. Building on this understanding of routines and capabilities, the discussion next examines profit seeking search for innovation. Particular attention is paid to dynamic capabilities directed toward change, particularly with respect to technological innovation, given the importance of technical advance in evolutionary economics.

3.2 ROUTINES AND CAPABILITIES

Consideration of how firms behave and make decisions forms an important point of departure for evolutionary economics. The assumption in mainstream economics that firms maximize profits presumes that firm decision makers can accurately size up the often complex and confusing context that they are in, and identify and implement the best possible actions they could take, given that context. But as Herbert Simon (1957a) observed, individual rationality is "bounded." Information and analytic requirements for making decisions and taking actions that are truly optimal are beyond human capabilities. Firms do as well as they can, and often are able to achieve what they realistically can hope for. In Simon's language, they "satisfice." This does not mean that firms ignore profits. Instead, firms are "profit seeking."

Profit seeking behavior encompasses ongoing firm operations and decision making, as well as search for new ways of doing things and new resources (tangible and intangible assets). Bounded rationality implies limited ability to consciously think through all possible options, so firms rely on routines for carrying out activities instead. Organizational routines play a critical role in an evolutionary economic analysis of profit seeking firm behavior. Indeed, we might say that routines are the building blocks of firm behavior, as next explained.

Routines

An organizational routine can be viewed as a pattern of behavior or as a set of rules, procedures, or techniques (Nelson and Winter, 1982; see also Becker et al., 2005). This discussion focuses on routines in the latter sense, consistent with research on firm capabilities discussed later. A routine, in the sense of a procedure, consists of a series of steps in a process for executing a task or activity. Thus, a routine can be viewed as a "technology" (Nelson, 2008c). This approach is consistent with the view of a routine as embodying a propensity or disposition to use a particular procedure when undertaking a task, as distinguished from the behavior itself (Hodgson, 2005).[1]

Routines can have tacit and implicit aspects, as well as codified and explicit ones. Codified information, however, rarely suffices to enable performance of a task. Instead, the use of such information "presumes the availability of intelligent interpreters" (Nelson and Winter, 1982: 82). That is, even routines that rely largely on codified information have an important, and usually critical, tacit element. Moreover, many routines are largely or even completely tacit. This tacitness is often accompanied by complexity. Examples of the complex nature of many routines abound, ranging from the studies of pricing by Cyert and March (1963) and more recently by Zbaracki and Bergen (2010) to Adler's (1993) study of the routines involved in the NUMMI plant joint venture between Toyota and General Motors.

Organizational routines involve teams of individuals that perform specific activities, including within functional areas (e.g., manufacturing) and across functional areas (e.g., design-for-manufacture). Because organizational routines involve multiple individuals that interact, routines entail a division of labor as well as coordination between individuals, and sometimes between teams or organizational units. Such coordination entails communication via "a stream of messages" that "in turn are interpreted as calling for particular performances by their recipients" (Nelson and Winter, 1982: 103). Becker et al. (2005: 778) bring these observations together

---

[1] Issues regarding the nature of routines have engendered much discussion in recent years. Some of this can be found in Feldman and Pentland, 2003; Felin and Foss, 2011; and Winter, 2013. A variety of perspectives on organizational routines can also be found in Becker (2005).

in noting that: "A routine, as a way of doing something in an organization, has two aspects. One is like a recipe or a program. The other is the way the work is divided up among individuals and organizational sub-units, and coordinated and managed."

Routines are persistent features of an organization that support "most of what is *regular and predictable* about business behavior ... especially if we understand that term to include the relatively constant dispositions and strategic heuristics that shape the approach of a firm to the nonroutine problems it faces" (Nelson and Winter, 1982: 15, original emphasis). Routines permeate virtually every facet of firm behavior, involving both routines for conducting activities and routines for making decisions (the latter are termed "decision rules"). They "range from well-specified technical routines for producing things, through procedures for hiring and firing, ordering new inventory, or stepping up production of items in high demand, to policies regarding investment, research and development (R&D), or advertising, and business strategies about product diversification and overseas investment" (Nelson and Winter, 1982: 14). In addition, routines that are most closely connected to production of goods and services are likely to depend heavily on, and be intertwined with, the associated technologies. Repetition plays an essential role in preserving routines, because "organizations 'remember' a routine largely by exercising it" (Nelson and Winter, 1982: 99). Thus, routines serve as organizational memory.

The preservation of routines through repetition makes routines analogous to the genes of an organization, undergirding constancy in behavior over time. At the same time as routines enable patterned behavior, routines are not rigid and can flexibly adapt to changing circumstances. For example, actors that confront new problems may respond by altering routines, such as the engineer called in to deal with a recalcitrant machine described by Nelson and Winter (1982).

Not only do routines themselves adapt over time, but routines can also facilitate organizational adaptation to external circumstances on a regular basis. Nelson (2015) has argued that routines frequently have a built-in adaptive responsiveness that can enable organizations to flexibly adjust to variations in conditions in which the routines are used. Adaptive responsiveness may include consideration of alternative choices and adjustments to behavior, but not extensive search and deliberation. Decision rules such as setting prices according to price-cost margins or setting R&D spending according to a percentage of sales are examples of adaptively responsive routines (Nelson and Winter, 1982). Another example is the well known Toyota routine that workers should stop the auto assembly line when they observe defects or problems. As these examples suggest, individual routines may contain different options that are suited to different circumstances.

Capabilities

Dosi, Nelson, and Winter (2000: 2) observe that: "To be capable of something is to have a generally reliable capacity to bring that thing about as a result of intended action." Winter (2000: 983) defines an organizational capability as "a high-level routine (or collection of routines) that, together with its implementing input flows, confers upon an organization's management a set of decision options for producing significant outputs of a particular type." To say that an organization possesses a capability means that the organization is able to operate a bundle of routines and coordinate them. Thus, an organizational capability, as a coordinated bundle of routines, provides the capacity to perform an activity for an intended purpose, in concert with the services of firm assets and other input flows.

A parallel stream of research in strategic management, particularly research on what is known as the Resource-based View of the firm, has taken a similar approach of linking organizational capabilities to the capacity to utilize firm resources (tangible and intangible assets). Amit and Schoemaker (1993: 35, original emphasis) define an organizational capability as: "a capacity to deploy *Resources*, usually in combination, using organizational processes, to effect a desired end. They are information-based, tangible or intangible processes that are firm-specific and are developed over time ... based on developing, carrying, and exchanging information through the firm's human capital." From the perspective of evolutionary economics, this emphasis on processes and exchange of information suggests that routines are involved, and subsequent scholarship on firm capabilities in strategic management has moved in this direction.

Given that organizational capabilities consist of routines, many of the characteristics of capabilities derive from the characteristics of routines. Within firms, routines and capabilities rest often on firm specific communication codes that enable the exchange of information and coordination. The underpinning of capabilities by routines also implies that capabilities involve patterned behavior, and that the function that a capability performs is repeatable and has a predictably reliable outcome (Helfat et al., 2007). In addition, like routines, capabilities are context dependent, and are specific to the organizational activities that they support.

Organizational capabilities, as collections of routines, relate to larger chunks of organizational activity than do individual routines (Dosi et al., 2000). Capabilities also refer to the capacity to perform activities that affect the ability of organizations to survive and prosper, as opposed to less critical undertakings (Winter, 2000). In addition, capabilities generally (but not always) entail greater intentionality than do routines. Thus, a capability has an intended purpose, even if not fully explicit.

3.3 EMERGENCE, DEVELOPMENT, AND ALTERATION OF ROUTINES AND CAPABILITIES

The characteristics of routines and capabilities just described derive in part from the ways in which they emerge and develop. Capabilities and their associated routines often emerge as profit seeking firms attempt to solve problems or find new ways of doing things. Some of these routines pertain to what is conventionally called research and development (R&D). In addition, search and problem solving activities take place elsewhere in the organization, such as in marketing departments that search for new customer segments and product ideas. Manufacturing units may also search for improved production processes so as to lower the cost or raise the quality of output, and must often find ways to solve problems that arise from internal or external sources, such as changes in the composition or quality of inputs received from suppliers.

As a general proposition, search tends to be "local," focused in the immediate area of a particular problem or in the neighborhood of existing routines, capabilities, and resources (Cyert and March, 1963). That is, firms tend to search in the neighborhood of what they know (Helfat, 1994a). Firms may also observe opportunities for profit not easily accessed through existing routines and capabilities. Organizational personnel may hear about alternative ways of doing things through membership in professional societies, read about them in professional publications, or observe them being implemented in other firms. Thus, organizations may seek to imitate methods or innovations of other firms, leading to the emergence of new routines. And as profit seeking entities facing competition, firms also pursue deliberate efforts at innovation aimed at beating their competitors and securing at least a temporary competitive advantage.

Routines develop over time in part through learning by doing through trial and error and repeated performance of activities. This form of learning has been observed at the team level, as in the study of Cohen and Bacdayan (1994) in which two person teams learned to configure playing cards in a specified manner by repeatedly playing a card game. Numerous studies of learning curves and productivity improvements in manufacturing have also provided evidence of learning by doing at the organizational level (Argote, 1999).

In addition to learning by doing, the development of routines and capabilities often takes place through deliberate learning processes. These processes include knowledge articulation, in which individuals discuss and compare their experiences, such as through debriefing sessions and performance evaluations (Zollo and Winter, 2002). When organizations subsequently codify their understanding of how routines and capabilities function, this provides guidelines for subsequent utilization of the capabilities in question (Zollo and Winter, 2002). In these ways, knowledge articulation improves the understanding of cause and effect relationships, which in turn improves the functioning of routines and capabilities. Knowledge codification helps to improve the reliability of capabilities.

At some point in the development of a routine, capability learning through intertwined processes of deliberate and trial and error learning may cease. This tends to occur when the performance of the task has reached what is considered a satisfactory level, determined in part by the aspirations of the organization or the relevant team (Winter, 2000). Because aspirations are likely to adapt to the context of capability learning, aspirations for further improvement tend to fall as outcomes improve. Capability development also entails costs – both direct costs as well as opportunity costs of other endeavors – that affect the willingness of organizations to continue capability learning. These costs affect the satisficing level of performance; higher costs are associated with a lower level of satisficing performance. Of note, these costs of investment in capability development are largely sunk, because they are embedded in a particular team and organization, and are therefore difficult to recoup.

This process of capability emergence and development often restarts as new problems in the functioning of routines and capabilities present themselves. For example, Hoopes and Postrel (1999) documented the way in which "glitches," or costly errors, caused a firm to improve its product development routines. Lazaric and Denis (2005) also documented the creation of new routines and the alteration of existing ones as a company implemented new ISO 9000 standards. The pursuit of innovation further suggests that new routines and capabilities may be required. Thus, the process just outlined tends to recur, leading to ongoing evolution of routines and capabilities within firms.

This continuing process of firm evolution leads to commonalities across firms operating within industries as well as heterogeneity among organizations in their capabilities and routines. Commonalities arise as firms seek to master commonly available know-how, often a legacy of a long history of advances in the industry, in an effort to survive competition. Firms also seek to imitate one another so as not to fall behind, such as by reverse engineering competitors' products and reading patent disclosures, leading to broad similarities in routines and capabilities. In addition, firms in an industry may have some of the same suppliers, customers, and complementary product producers ("complementors"), from whom firms glean information. And firms share information with one another through trade associations, standard setting organizations, and other business organizations (such as chambers of commerce in the United States). The well accepted concept of "industry recipes" for conducting business (Spender, 1989) suggests that firms within an industry often think in some of the same general ways about how to do business.

Notwithstanding these commonalities, capabilities and routines differ in economically significant ways among firms in the same industry. Organizations have different starting points, including times and places of entry as well as different initial sets of assets and individuals. As capabilities develop, this heterogeneity may persist because capability learning takes place within a particular firm context. A path dependent process of capability accumulation – which depends on the individuals involved, their skills and cognitions, the initial choices they made, and subsequent feedback and learning – results in capabilities and routines that are organization specific in many respects. As Nelson (1991) has observed, diversity of firms, their capabilities, and their behaviors is a natural consequence in evolutionary theory.

Although firms can and do imitate one another, there are many factors that limit the ability of firms to do so. For example, it is well documented that firms often use secrecy to keep innovations and knowledge proprietary rather than disclosing them through patenting (Levin et al., 1987; Cohen, Nelson, and Walsh, 2000). The tacit elements of routines and capabilities, along with the knowledge that underlies them, also impede the transfer knowledge across firms. Even within firms, knowledge transfer is difficult (Szulanski, 1996). As Rumelt (1984) has pointed out, "causal ambiguity" – in which firms have difficulty understanding cause and effect relationships involving resources, capabilities, and outcomes – makes it difficult for firms to transfer knowledge and capabilities internally and to fully imitate the behavior of their rivals.

With respect to technological innovation, a central concern for evolutionary economics, empirical research has provided evidence of intra-industry differences in firm behavior. For example, Helfat (1994a, 1994b) has shown that although the major US oil companies as a group tended to concentrate their R&D in several areas related to oil, gas, and alternative energy during the 1970s and 1980s, the firms differed persistently in the amounts and specific types of R&D pursued. Evidence from the pharmaceutical industry also indicates that firms differed in the amount of R&D spending in different therapeutic drug classes (Henderson and Cockburn, 1996). Winter (2005) observes that heterogeneity in firm behavior tends to hold especially strongly in industries characterized by high levels of complexity, in the sense of high levels of interactions among organizational choices, because this complexity makes imitation across firms more difficult. Given this, it is notable that recent survey data show that even relatively simple managerial and workplace practices differ among firms (Bloom and Van Reenen, 2010).

Heterogeneity in firm behavior due to heterogeneity in the underlying routines and capabilities may lead to heterogeneity in economic performance, particularly if firms do not operate in tight selection environments that efficiently weed out differences between firms in their routines, capabilities, and behaviors. Economists have now accumulated substantial evidence of heterogeneity in firm productivity (for a review, see Syverson, 2011). In addition, many studies in strategic management have documented heterogeneity of firm performance within industries linked to heterogeneity of firm resources and capabilities (see for example, Rumelt, 1991, and research discussed in Hoopes, Madsen, and Walker, 2003, and Jacobides and Winter, 2012).

3.4   SEARCH, INNOVATION, AND DYNAMIC CAPABILITIES

Evolutionary economics holds that not only do routines and capabilities underpin firm behavior, but also that firms are constantly evolving and innovating (Winter, 2006). As Schumpeter (1934) observed, in order to survive, firms in many fields must innovate or at least stay close to the frontier of the capabilities of competitors and the products that they offer. Thus, because firms are profit seeking and operate in a competitive environment, they regularly search for innovations in an effort to improve their profitability.

The concept of "dynamic capabilities" put forward by Teece, Pisano, and Shuen (1997) brings together the view in evolutionary economics of firm behavior as underpinned by routines and capabilities with the emphasis on firms as sources of innovation and growth. Dynamic capabilities refer to firm capabilities to "change the product, the production process, the scale, or the customers [markets] served" (Winter, 2003: 992) or that more generally enable "a firm to alter how it currently makes its living" (Helfat and Winter, 2011). This includes the capability to "create, modify, or extend" the resources and capabilities of an organization (Helfat et al., 2007: 4) and to alter elements of the firm's external environment (Teece et al., 1997; Teece, 2007).

Like organizational capabilities in general, dynamic capabilities are comprised of routines and have an intended purpose. As Nelson and Winter (1982: 17) stated early on: "we view firms as possessing routines which operate to modify over time various aspects of their operating characteristics." Winter (1986) later proposed that firms may have "superordinate adaptation routines" for organizational change, such as "high-level" routines for learning and search. These types of routines and their associated dynamic capabilities enable firms to promote change on a repeated basis, in contrast with "ad hoc problem solving" on a one-off basis (Winter, 2003). And like other capabilities, dynamic capabilities develop through experimentation and learning (Zollo and Winter, 2002), including deliberate learning mechanisms, and enable reliable, practiced, and patterned behavior (Winter, 2003; Helfat and Winter, 2011).

Dynamic capabilities differ from other organizational capabilities "in their purposes and intended outcomes" and are directed toward "economically significant change" (Helfat and Winter, 2011: 1245, 1249). In particular, dynamic capabilities contrast with "operational" or "ordinary" capabilities that enable a firm to maintain how it currently makes a living (Winter, 2003: 992). That is, operational capabilities enable firms to perform activities "on an ongoing basis using more or less the same techniques on the same scale to support existing products and services for the same customer population" (Helfat and Winter, 2011: 1244). Research often refers to hierarchies of capabilities: operational capabilities are often referred to as zero-order or lower-order capabilities, and dynamic capabilities, which can be used to alter operational capabilities, are referred to as first order or higher order capabilities (see Collis, 1994; Winter, 2003).

Helfat and Winter (2011) have observed that as a practical matter, it can sometimes be difficult to cleanly distinguish dynamic from operational capabilities, because this requires ascertaining what constitutes economically significant change, which in turn may depend on the point of view of an observer. Nevertheless, some chunks of firm activities and their underlying capabilities are clearly aimed at modifying organizational resources, operations, products, and markets in a significant manner and thus qualify as dynamic capabilities. Some capabilities may also have dual operational and dynamic purposes, such as marketing capabilities directed toward maintaining current customers as well as attracting new ones (Helfat and Winter, 2011; Kahl, 2014). Other capabilities such as those for collaboration may have dual variants, one directed toward change and the other directed toward maintaining the status quo (Helfat and Winter, 2011).

Dynamic capabilities are especially important in market environments characterized by technological change. The initial conception of dynamic capabilities by Teece et al. (1997) emphasized the importance of dynamic capabilities directed toward new process and product development, for example through formal R&D. Thus, early research by Tripsas (1997) documented the existence of a "dynamic technical capability" in the typesetter industry that enabled some firms to develop new generations of technology and overcome the threat posed by radical technological changes. This dynamic capability consisted of the capacity to absorb and integrate knowledge external to the firm (per Cohen and Levinthal, 1990), and the capacity to develop new technical capabilities through geographically distributed internal research sites. In another early study of dynamic capabilities and R&D under changing market conditions, Helfat (1997) examined the accumulation of knowledge and R&D capability in the US petroleum industry. The study found that firms with greater prior R&D in technologically related businesses devoted the most effort to developing knowledge and capability in alternative fuels technologies through R&D.

In a similar vein, Danneels (2012) has argued that dynamic capabilities enable firms to engage in Schumpeterian competition through innovation in new technologies, inputs and resources, products, and organization. Research has noted that dynamic capabilities also matter in environments characterized by moderate rates of change (Eisenhardt and Martin, 2000; Helfat and Winter, 2011). Moreover, the actions of firms themselves affect the pace of change in the market environment, such as through the introduction of new products or the replication of retail sales outlets in multiple locations (Winter and Szulanski, 2001). In this way, profit seeking firms propel industry growth and change.

Studies of technological change and innovation have also documented the ways in which dynamic capabilities develop and the associated impact on firm performance. In a study of the semiconductor industry, Macher and Mowery (2009) measured the deliberate learning mechanisms of knowledge articulation and codification proposed by Zollo and Winter (2002), which in turn underpin the development of dynamic capabilities for new process development and introduction, and assessed the impact of these mechanisms on performance outcomes. The study found that these learning mechanisms for dynamic capability development positively affected performance in terms of lower cycle time and greater yield, and that firms differed in both their learning mechanisms and their performance outcomes. In a related study, Verona and Ravasi (2003) examined the processes through which a major producer of hearing aids was able to continuously innovate and bring new generations of products to market. The study showed the importance of processes for knowledge creation and absorption, knowledge integration, and knowledge reconfiguration.

Additional studies have uncovered other ways in which dynamic capabilities for innovation develop. A study by Danneels (2008) of US manufacturing firms examined "R&D competence," measured as the ability to set up new types of manufacturing operations, learn about and assess the feasibility of new technologies, and recruit engineers for new technical areas. The study found that development of this dynamic capability was facilitated by a willingness to cannibalize old products, engagement in constructive conflict within the organization, scanning of the external environment, and organizational slack. In the pharmaceutical industry, Narayanan, Colwell, and Douglas (2009) found that antecedents to the development of dynamic capabilities for drug discovery and development included the cognitive orientations of senior managers and the orchestration by senior managers of new routines for developing the capabilities lower down in the organization. These findings point to the importance of managers in the development of dynamic capabilities (Adner and Helfat, 2003; Augier and Teece, 2009; Helfat and Martin, 2015).

Given that dynamic capabilities are directed toward economically significant change and given that there are many vehicles for such change, it is not surprising that the concept encompasses a large range of firm activities. As just noted, quintessential dynamic capabilities are those directed toward technological innovation. But in addition, dynamic capabilities extend to other activities directed toward change on a regular basis (Eisenhardt and Martin, 2000). Examples include capabilities for: replication of routines and business models in different geographic locations (Winter and Szulanski, 2001); acquisitions (Capron and Mitchell, 2009); alliances (Helfat et al., 2007); internal firm collaboration (Helfat and Campo-Rembado, 2016); and market entry (Franco et al., 2009).

When they originally introduced the idea of dynamic capabilities, Teece et al. (1997) suggested a framing of "positions-processes-paths." At any point in time, a firm has a "position" consisting of internal resources, capabilities, and other attributes, as well as an external positioning in the marketplace. A firm also has internal "processes" (including routines) through which dynamic capabilities operate, which in turn can alter the firm's existing positions and chart new "paths" to pursue. This original framing of dynamic capabilities is highly consistent with evolutionary economics in suggesting path dependent and capability based organizational change. That is, the firm is a dynamic entity, continually evolving and innovating.

Teece (2007) later elaborated on the core functions that dynamic capabilities perform, breaking these into "sensing" new opportunities and threats, "seizing" new opportunities through investment and construction of business models, and "transforming/reconfiguring" the organization in order to seize subsequent opportunities and deflect threats. A related function of "asset orchestration" to assemble, configure, align, and coordinate assets within the organization is part of both seizing and reconfiguring (Helfat et al., 2007). These core functions are part and parcel of the way in which firms "transform" regularly themselves and their industries through activities such as new product development, acquisitions, market entry, and the like.

Given that dynamic capabilities facilitate innovation and transformation both at the firm and industry level, we would expect that firms that possess more of these capabilities, or better variants of them, would tend to perform better (all else being equal). Consistent with this expectation, several studies have shown that a dynamic capability for innovation is positively related to innovative output. In a study of young biotechnology companies, Deeds, DeCarolis, and Coombs (1999) showed that the number of new products per firm was positively related to dynamic capabilities as measured by the quality of scientific personnel and the R&D management skills of CEOs and other top management team members. Using R&D expenditures as a proxy for a dynamic capability for R&D in the pharmaceutical industry, Rothaermel and Hess (2007) found a positive relationship between R&D capability and innovative output in the form of new patent applications in biotechnology. This finding echoes that of Henderson and Cockburn (1996) that higher R&D spending at the therapeutic class level was associated with more patents in pharmaceutical firms. Rothaermel and Hess (2007) also found that greater intellectual human capital in the form of research scientists was positively associated with innovative output, as in the study of Deeds et al. (1999). In a related study of the semiconductor industry, Dutta, Narasimhan, and Rajiv (2005) found that firms with high R&D capability had greater technological output as measured by patent counts and better financial performance as measured by Tobin's q. Yet additional evidence comes from a study by Stadler, Helfat, and Verona (2013) of the upstream petroleum industry, which found that firms with more advanced dynamic technological capabilities for seismic imaging and well drilling had greater success in finding and developing new oil reserves.

Dynamic capabilities also have implications for firm growth, and by implication for industry growth. Many dynamic capabilities can enable growth in firm size (Helfat et al., 2007), including capabilities for technological innovation, market entry, acquisitions, and the like. Evidence regarding persistence of firm growth is thus relevant; should studies show an absence of growth persistence, this would cast doubt on the claim that firms have dynamic capabilities to a meaningful extent. In assessing this claim, it is important to do so in settings in which dynamic capabilities and growth persistence might reasonably be expected to hold. Consistent with dynamic capabilities, research has found evidence of growth persistence in the high growth period of the 1950s in the US (Geroski, Machin, and Walters, 1997) and in the pharmaceutical industry in which firms have used R&D as part of an explicit strategy for growth and profitability (Bottazi et al., 2001). However, much more empirical research is needed on the linkage between individual firm dynamic capabilities for technological innovation and technological advance and innovation at the industry level.

3.5   CONCLUSION

The research surveyed in this chapter takes as a starting point that firms do not and cannot optimize. Instead, firms make decisions and undertake activities that are satisfactory given the contexts in which they operate. Firms are thus profit seeking rather than profit maximizing. Organizational routines, and the capabilities that they support, form the foundation of this profit seeking behavior. These routines and capabilities include those for making decisions as well as for conducting operations. In addition, profit seeking firms undertake search in order to address problems that arise in their current operations, and to find and exploit new opportunities for profit. Some of this search proceeds through the application of existing decision rules and other search proceeds through "dynamic capabilities" directed toward organizational and strategic change. Because search is often local, in the neighborhood of existing routines, capabilities, knowledge, and resources, the evolution of firms and the industries that they comprise unfolds through a history dependent process.

Profit seeking firms operate in competitive environments. The pursuit of new products and processes offers a potential means to beat the competition. Technological innovation can prove especially powerful in reframing the terms of competition to the advantage of the innovating firm. The Schumpeterian vision of "creative destruction" through innovation is therefore part and parcel of an evolutionary economic view of firm behavior. Not surprisingly, the literature on dynamic capabilities incorporates technological innovation as an important route to firm change. And from the perspective of the economy as a whole, the innovative efforts of firms are one of the most important engines of economic growth.

4 Schumpeterian Competition and Industrial Dynamics

Andreas Pyka and Richard R. Nelson

4.1 THE NATURE AND ROLE OF ECONOMIC COMPETITION

Schumpeter's argument that modern capitalist economies must be seen as dynamic systems inducing continuing innovation and creative destruction, and that economic performance must be seen in this light, has been basically ignored by the mainline economics profession, which has continued to frame its positive and normative analysis in terms of an economy operating under conditions of equilibrium. Nowhere is the conflict between these two points of view greater than in the way competition among firms is interpreted and evaluated. And the difference shows up most sharply in analyses concerned with economic activity and competition at the level of an industry or sector.

In this chapter we review the research by evolutionary economists on competition and industry dynamics in industries where innovation is important. This body of research and writing treats an industry as an evolving system. We want to highlight that, like the evolutionary perspective on firm behavior and capabilities described in the preceding chapter, viewing an industry as an evolving system is a radical departure from the way of looking at economic behavior and performance that has been standard in economics for the last fifty years.

Analysis of industry behavior in today's economic textbooks is largely focused on the determinants of industry outputs, how these are produced, and the prices of its products. The theoretical argument is that these are the outcomes of profit maximizing decisions of the firms in the industry and utility maximizing choices made by its customers, under conditions of an industry equilibrium with prices such that the total output offered by the firms just equals the quantities customers want to buy. The normative considerations brought into the discussion relate to how efficiently firms operate and how close price is to cost at industry equilibrium. The roles of competition are seen as forcing firms to operate efficiently in order to survive, and keeping down the gap between price and cost.

Particularly in the years after World War II, alongside analyses of the equilibrium conditions in competitive and less competitive industries along the lines sketched above, there also has been a tradition of quite detailed empirical economic research on what was going on influenced by the then new theoretical literature concerned with imperfect competition, and many of the studies were concerned with industries operating under conditions of monopoly or oligopoly. In many of these industries product differentiation was an important factor (for a broad overview see Schmalensee and Willig, 1989). An objective of many of these studies was to help identify the kinds of anti-trust or regulatory policies that were needed if competition otherwise was too weak to generate socially optimal industry behaviors. But for many economists interested in industry behavior and performance, empirically oriented studies of this sort became an important kind of economic research in its own right.

These studies almost always involved a careful treatment of the industry's history. And while only a few explicitly challenged textbook theory, the history of these industries was rich with phenomena not treated in the standard theoretical formulations. Particularly the early history of most of these industries was marked by considerable entry of new firms, and by the exit of firms that had given the market a try and had failed to succeed. Many industries, including relatively mature ones, experienced turnover of the industry leaders. Innovation clearly played a major role in the history of many of these industries, and as a result there often was considerable change over time in the nature of the products produced and the processes of production employed by firms in the industry. The empirical industry studies often provided a considerable amount of information regarding the sources of the innovations driving change. And a number of the economists doing these industry studies were proposing that the changes over time in the industry structure they observed had a lot to do with the rate and kind of technological change going on.

More generally, many of these empirical studies provided a view of what was going on in an industry that was much more consonant with a Schumpeterian theoretical perspective than with the post Marshallian neoclassical theory of industry behavior. For Schumpeter the driving force in industry behavior was innovation, and innovation was a far more important vehicle of competition than simply pricing low.

> In the capitalist reality as distinguished from its textbook picture it is not that kind of competition which counts but the competition from the new commodity, the new technology, the new source of supply, the new type of organization ... This kind of competition is much more effective than the other as a bombardment is in comparison to forcing a door, and so more important that it becomes a matter of comparative indifference whether competition in the ordinary sense functions more or less promptly. (Schumpeter, 1942: 84)

And industries where innovation is important are characterized by continuing disequilibrium, not equilibrium in the sense of the economics textbooks. At the same time progress in meeting human needs better may be rapid and continuing.

The dynamics of industry behavior obviously depends on the rate and nature of the innovation going on. The commonly held view of industries where innovation is rapid tends to see innovation as largely product innovation, with newly designed and introduced products viewed by customers (or at least some groups of them) as superior to older ones. In such a context the ability of a firm to make profits depends on its ability to be at the forefront of product

SCHUMPETERIAN COMPETITION AND INDUSTRIAL DYNAMICS 107

innovation, or close to it, and firms that are at the forefront may be able to charge very high prices for their products, until other firms are able to provide products that meet or exceed their qualities. But when that happens, price competition becomes quite relevant. Also, there are a number of industries where technological innovation is rapid but is largely in the form of improvements in production methods that reduce costs with little change in the products produced. Here the ability of the innovator to profit handsomely is very much dependent on how it prices its products. Thus while the quote from Schumpeter presented above might lead one to think otherwise, prices and price competition remain important economic influences even in industries where innovation is rapid.

Like price competition, active competition through the design and production of better products and the development of more efficient and less costly modes of production, imposes a discipline on the firms in the industry. Unless a firm can lead or stay close to a moving frontier of product and process quality, it can be in deep economic trouble, and forced to leave the business. And like price competition, competition of the sort Schumpeter described yields major benefits to consumers.

The standard view of industry behavior and the role of competition tends to stress the less than optimal behavior of industries where one or a few firms control most of the output, and have considerable market power. Under prevailing standard theory, in industries dominated by one or a few large firms, output is lower and prices higher than they would be if competition was greater. But in his *Capitalism, Socialism and Democracy* Schumpeter argued that by the mid twentieth century large firms with R&D facilities of their own had become the principal sources of innovation. Thus society ought to welcome their presence rather than seeking to break them up. A number of interpreters of Schumpeter argued that his proclivity to downplay the importance of price and price completion led him to downplay generally the role of competition. However, Schumpeter's position was not that at all, but rather that in an economy where innovation was important the actual market power of large firms was limited and fragile, as they always were under threat of having their market position undermined by innovative competitors. A successful innovator might indeed come to dominate an industry, but this monopoly power was only temporary and would erode quickly as its competitors innovated.

With the vision of hindsight it is clear that Schumpeter was quite right that most monopoly positions were temporary, and that the development of new technology by other firms was the principal reason for their erosion. However, there certainly are cases in which the strong market power of a firm that has come to dominate an industry in part at least because of its superior product or process technologies has lasted for a long time. IBM's long dominance of the mainframe computer market is a good example, as is Microsoft's market power over various kinds of software. One can be a strong believer in Schumpeter's view that innovation is the most effective form of competition, and still believe that a forceful anti-trust policy is necessary.

In any case, it now is clear that Schumpeter was only half right about the dominance in innovation of large firms. In many industries, particularly ones that are just emerging as a result of the development of radically new technologies, relatively small firms and often new ones are the principal source of innovation. One of the most interesting and important questions for evolutionary economists is the nature of the most innovative firms (e.g., Lazonick, 2005), and how this relates to various industry characteristics, like age.

These ideas have in recent years led to the development of a significant body of theoretical and empirical work by evolutionary economists on Schumpeterian competition and industrial dynamics. This body of research and writing has interacted strongly with the research by evolutionary economists on technological advance, and on firm capabilities and behavior, described in Chapters 2 and 3. But evolutionary industrial dynamics deserves to be considered a field in its own right. An important portion of this research has been oriented to study of particular industries. But much of the research and writing has been aiming to develop a broad view of the subject, concerned with industry more generally. This chapter will focus on the latter body of research. As we have highlighted, industries differ significantly. As a consequence research of this genre has been concerned both with illuminating the characteristics of Schumpeterian competition and industrial dynamics that seem quite general and hold across a wide range of industries, and the important industry differences that seem to exist.

4.2   SOME GENERAL ASPECTS OF INDUSTRIAL DYNAMICS

In recent years economists studying industry dynamics have had available to them a wealth of new data that enables analysis both of the cross section of firms that are listed as being in an industry at a given time and of how this cross section moves over time, and the movements over time of individual firms within these cross sections (Dosi, 2007; Dosi et al., 2012). These data sets have become available for a wide range of industries in a number of different countries.

Perhaps the first thing that struck economists looking at these newly available data sets was the great variation among the firms in the industry, in a number of different dimensions. Firms in an industry tend to vary greatly in their size, measured either by sales or employment. This was not so surprising for many economists who studied industry, but an important strand of economic thinking at that time presumed that there was an optimal firm size, and the data certainly did not support that notion. And firms also differed significantly in their productivity (measured in different ways) and their profitability (where plausible measures could be obtained). This was more surprising, and certainly cast doubt on the standard presumptions that industries generally operated close to an equilibrium and that firms that were not up to the average in productivity and profitability could not last for long and therefore would have only limited presence in the industry at any time. But the significant presence in most industries of firms with productivity levels less than one quarter that of the leaders tends to discredit those presumptions.

Part of the variation here almost surely reflects that standard industrial classifications encompass firms doing a variety of different things, and catering to somewhat different markets. However, as Griliches and Mairesse (1997) observed:

> We ... thought one could reduce heterogeneity by going down from general mixtures as "total manufacturing" to something more coherent like petroleum refining or the manufacture of cement. But something like Mandelbrot's fractal phenomenon seems to be at work here also: the observed variability-heterogeneity does not really decline as we cut our data finer and finer. There is a sense that different bakeries are just as much different from each other as the steel industry is from the machinery industry.

But the presence and particular position of firms within their industry distribution is far from static. In most industries there is considerable entry of new firms and the exit of others. As we will consider in more detail later, entry tends to be more extensive when an industry is young than when it is more mature, but is a non-trivial feature of many mature industries. But generally new entrants are small and fragile. While some come to be industry leaders, this generally takes considerable time. And much of the exiting from an industry is of firms that had entered a short time before and did not manage to catch up with, much less surpass, the crowd.

Existing firms in the industry grow at different rates. Firms that are highly productive and profitable tend to expand relative to firms that are less so. But perhaps surprisingly, this tendency is not very strong. And while over time there is some regression toward the mean regarding productivity and profitability, this tendency too is not strong. Firms that are leaders, and laggers, in these variables tend to remain so for a considerable period of time.

The early interpretations of Schumpeterian theory tended to assume that innovators were more profitable and grew faster than their non-innovating competitors (for an overview see Scherer, 1984). And some early empirical studies seemed to support this proposition. However, as discussed in Chapter 2, it came to be recognized that a very large share of innovations failed to make any profit, and some lost considerable money. As a consequence, even in industries where innovation is rapid, a firm might do better responding rapidly to the successful innovations of its competitors than innovating itself. Late movers often can learn by observing both the successes and failures of the firms that are in the lead. As a result of these new understandings, the question of how innovators in an industry fared relative to non-innovators became more open empirically. The studies we are reporting on here show no clean general results. In some industries and eras innovators are on average especially profitable and grow rapidly, and in others this is not the case, or there are more complex dynamics at work.

In virtually all of the industries where we have cross section time series data, the average productivity of the firms in the industry increased over time, almost certainly largely as a result of the innovation going on. An important question for Schumpeterian/ evolutionary economists is the relative importance in the productivity growth process of, on the one hand, expansion of the more productive firms relative to the less productive ones, and on the other hand, improvements in productivity at the firm level that includes a large share of the firms in the industry, those lagging somewhat behind the leaders as well as the leaders. In most of the industries where this question has been explored empirically, the expansion of highly productive firms relative to less productive ones seems to have played a relatively minor role in overall industry productivity growth. In industries marked by high average productivity growth, in most cases a large percentage of the firms have been increasing their productivity.

This is an extremely interesting finding. In fields where there are reasonable opportunities to improve product and process performance, competition definitely seems to discipline firms to innovate, or at least stay up with advancing technology, as best they can. In most industries apparently competition and selection forces are not strong enough to keep all firms close to the frontier, but it does force them to be adaptive. We note that various studies have shown that, in industries where firms tend to operate multiple plants, the development of new technology tends to lead to the firms cutting back or abandoning their use of older plants, as they build and come to operate new ones, even though the overall size of the firm may not change much. More generally, many studies have shown that the diffusion of productive new technology tends to be relatively rapid. Thus as Schumpeter argued, an innovative industry leader must innovate continuingly if it is to stay a leader in the industry. Schumpeterian "creative destruction" clearly is operative at the firm level, and as we shall see in the next chapter the development of new industries often leads to the decline and disappearance of older ones. However, the principal force of creative destruction seems to be at the level of practice – the nature of the products produced and the processes used by firms.

What we have been describing is patterns of industry dynamics that seem common to a wide range of industries. But as we have noted, industries differ significantly one from another. There has been little research that has attempted to highlight and explain differences across industries in the patterns we have described. One might expect, for example, that there might be a considerable difference in the variance of productivity among firms, and in the extent to which productivity growth occurred widely among firms in the industry as contrasted with being concentrated in a few dominant firms, between industries where the bulk of technological advance in the industry was coming from sources outside the industry, for example suppliers or universities, as contrasted with industries where technological advance was largely the result of innovation by firms in the industry. To our knowledge, this question has not been explored.

Another feature that almost surely makes a difference across industries is the age of the industry. We observed above that entry and exit tend to be greater in new industries than in more mature ones, but again there exists very little research on this issue using these data sets. However, there is now an extensive body of research and writing concerned with what happens in an industry over its life cycle. We now turn to that material.

4.3 INDUSTRY LIFE CYCLES

There now is a substantial body of theoretical and empirical writing oriented by the concept of an industry life cycle (see, e.g., Utterback, 1987, 1994; Klepper and Graddy, 1990; Klepper, 1997; Klepper and Simonis, 1997). Under that theory, new industries come into existence as a result of the emergence of primitive versions of a new kind of product for which strong demand might be anticipated if it is perfected, or more broadly by a new technology that promises to have a range of possible valuable uses. Industry life cycle theory aims "to capture the dynamic processes that take place both within an industry and within its member firms over time" (Utterback, 1994: 92) as the industry evolves. Some of the more important dynamic patterns highlighted in that theory are depicted in Figure 4.1 (Pyka, 2000: 28).

As this description indicates, in some of the treatments the life cycle of an industry is viewed as associated with the life cycle of a product or a class of them. In other treatments the orientation is to a particular technology. In either case there is a certain arbitrariness about the boundaries of the industry, and about how its history should be described. Thus should the invention and ascendancy of the transistor over the vacuum tube be regarded as starting a new industry, or the transformation of an established one producing components for electronic devices? Should firms that started producing personal computers after these became technologically feasible be regarded as starting a new industry, or as initiating a new branch of a more broadly defined computer industry? Differences in the breadth or narrowness of the industry definition certainly have been an important factor behind the differences across industries in life cycle characteristics we will consider shortly. (We note that these

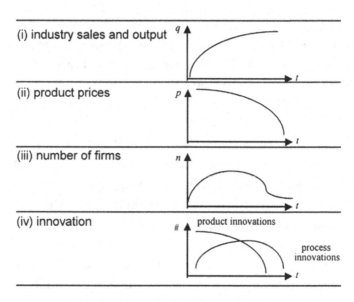

FIGURE 4.1   Stylized facts of industry life cycles

same kinds of issues arise regarding the cross section time series data on industries discussed in the previous section.)

As indicated above, there now are a substantial collection of studies of the histories of different industries, some focused on developments in a particular country, some seeing the industry more globally, that have been oriented by the life cycle framework. Despite their heterogeneity, a large fraction of these studies of industry dynamics show a number of similar patterns.

Consistent with the studies using industrial census data just described, these patterns include prominently high rates of entry and exit in the early stages of an industry's life cycle. In a large share of the industries studied most of the entering firms are small ones, some migrants from another industry which used some of the same skills, some new firms; the automobile industry is a good example. However, in some new industries there is considerable entry by large established firms that start branches working in the new area; mainframe computers and transistors are examples. Early in the life cycle the products designed and produced by different firms tend to vary considerably reflecting different notions of what customers will buy, as well as different competences among firms. In the early stages of the development of a new product or technology, paradigms tend to be loose. With the products still primitive, few firms sell very much, and many firms do not sell enough to stay in business for very long. As noted, at this stage of the industry life cycle exit rates are high.

In the industries that ultimately became important, sooner or later product designs are developed that are able to attract a significant number of customers. Firms producing these products grow. Firms that on their own have not been able to develop and market an attractive product try to learn from their more successful competitors, and some succeed and some fail, and drop out of the industry. In the early stages of industry "take off" entry of new firms may be accelerated. But as firms in the industry grow in size and strength, entry becomes more difficult. The number of active firms tends to stabilize and then to decline. And average firm size tends to grow larger.

Alongside, and strongly influencing, these developments in industry structure, the range of product variation offered by firms in the industry tends to decline, and product innovation tends to focus on improving existing designs. Both as a result of and a spur to the growth of firm size, process R&D and innovation tend to increase.

In virtually all of the cases studied, industry structure became more concentrated as the industry matured. In a number of these cases, strong concentration was associated with the emergence of a "dominant design" (Utterback and Abernathy, 1975; Anderson and Tushman, 1990; Suarez and Utterback, 1995). A dominant design may emerge when there is considerable similarity among the needs and tastes of the potential customers of a broadly defined product, and a design is developed that meets those wants particularly well and attracts the lion's share of demand. When this is the case, a monopolized or highly concentrated market then may come about if aspects of that design are proprietary or for other reasons hard to imitate, or if there are significant economies of scale in the production of particular products. The latter influence may be augmented dynamically if the presence of a dominant design induces significant and successful effort to develop more effective production equipment and processes suited to its production.

Klepper (1997) has argued that these latter factors often are very important, and lead to a monopoly or highly concentrated industry, even in contexts where there is no dominant design, except in the sense that it is the product the dominant firm produces. As firms come to produce larger volumes of output, the benefits to them of improving their productivity increases. Klepper's argument is that, in the industries he studied, the initial shakeout which led to firms of at least medium size induced a significant increase in their process R&D, and the firms that were more successful here grew even larger. It is implicit in his argument that when there are significant economies of scale in production of particular products, one design may come to dominate the market (often with a dominant firm producing it) even though that particular product design may not be particularly well suited to particular customer wants.

But then there is the question of what models consumers want and their preferences for particular products. It is clear that in many cases what particular buyers want is strongly influenced by what they have bought before, and by what other customers are buying. The product design that users have learned to operate effectively may well be the preferred design when they want to add to their stock or to replace items that have run their course. In their study of the forces that led to concentration in the early mainframe computer industry, Malerba et al. (2016) argue that such a "lock in" was an important factor at work. Alternatively, potential customers may be attracted to a design that a good proportion of other customers have bought, because there are advantages of compatibility, or simply because the fact that other customers have bought one is treated as a sign that quality is good. Malerba et al. (2016) propose that this "bandwagon" effect also was important in generating the dominance of IBM in the early mainframe computer industry.

These theories of why one often sees the emergence of a highly concentrated industry also give insight into reasons why in some cases this does not happen. One condition is that the market has very diverse customers with quite different needs. Here the pharmaceuticals industry is a good case in point. If one considers the pharmaceuticals industry as a whole, it is a mature but still innovative high tech industry that is not very concentrated. An important reason is that, while markets for treatments of particular ailments may be dominated by one or a few pharmaceuticals, if one considers the market for pharmaceuticals in general, no dominant design can emerge, because people with different ailments require very different kinds of pharmaceuticals (see the analysis in Malerba et al., 2016).

Another factor that can hold off the evolution toward high concentration in a new industry is vertical disintegration. A separate specialized industry may emerge of firms designing and producing production equipment or key components for the downstream industry that produces the product in question. Potential entrants to the downstream industry then are not faced with the barrier of extant firms that have superior production or component technology compared with what they are able to develop quickly on their own. Rather, state-of-the-art production technology is available to all firms in the industry. Malerba et al. (2016) argue that an important part of the reason why the personal computer industry never has become as concentrated as the mainframe industry relates to the fact that a separate component industry emerged relatively early in the former.

It is possible that, as a result of the remarkable advances in information and communication (IC) technology that have been occurring, the range of markets where there is a particular dominant design is diminishing. These new technologies greatly enhance the ability of companies to tailor their products to the diverse needs of their customers, and competition is forcing them to do this rather than trying to sell one basic product to a variety of customers with somewhat different needs. And these technologies also enable more design flexibility to be built into production machinery, and thus reduce the importance of scale in the production of particular designs. Thus the phenomena that Klepper flagged as very important in a number of the industries he studied may be becoming less so.

An implicit assumption of industry cycle theory is that, after an industry takes off and goes through a period of rapid technological advance and rapid growth, sooner or later there are diminishing returns, as opportunities for further advances become exhausted. This pattern does fit many of the industries that have been studied, but not all of them. Where it does fit the industry may continue to be an important part of the economy, but producing a relatively constant range of products with relatively stable technologies. Automobile tires would appear to be an example. Or the industry may be superseded by a new industry using new and different technologies but producing products that meet the same needs. The disappearance of the vacuum tube industry and its replacement by a new semiconductor industry is a prime example.

In most cases when a new technological regime replaces an older one, the firms that were dominant in the old regime tend not to be effective in the new, and decline and go out of business, while a whole new set of firms becomes prominent in the new industry. The management literature (e.g., Tripsas, 1997) is rich with case studies of firms that had been very strong, but failed to recognize that a new technology was coming in (in some cases because of a "not invented here" syndrome), or did adopt it but could not manage it well. But not always. Thus many of the early designers and producers of transistors were firms that had been prominent in the vacuum tube business. It is interesting, however, that as the new semiconductor industry took off, new firms, like Microsoft, became dominant, and the older established firms declined or dropped out of the business. A substantial literature has developed concerned with what has been called "competence destroying" technological advance (Tushman and Anderson, 1986), changes in the base technologies of an industry, which causes firm capabilities that had been built up around the older technology to become obsolete. An important management literature has developed exploring what enables a firm to learn to operate effectively when the relevant technological base changes. A portion of this literature was surveyed in Chapter 2.

4.4 THE BROADER EVOLUTION OF INDUSTRY "WAYS OF DOING THINGS"

We highlighted earlier that the "ways of doing things" in economic activity include much more than what customarily are thought of as "technologies." We argued in Chapter 2 that the technologies used by a firm are a prime determinant of what that firm can do. However, those technologies – the design of its products and the methods it uses to produce them – constrain but do not determine how the work is done, the division of labor involved, the methods of coordination and control, the way decisions regarding these matters are made and enforced. A number of empirical studies have shown that different firms employing the same basic technologies can differ significantly in the quality of the products they produce and the costs of production, and that an important factor behind these differences lies in the ways the work is organized and governed.

Learning how to organize and manage effectively the operation of a new technology, making the kinds of changes that are needed when the technology being used changes, is a difficult challenge for management. Many firms simply resist dealing with the problem by ignoring the new technology. And of those that decide to adopt, some firms clearly are better at learning to master it than others, and the differences here may matter as much to the ability of a firm to survive as the technology it is using. As the technology used in a field begins to settle down and become more standard across firms, as product cycle theory suggests it will sooner or later, the learning process can be more cumulative, and firms also can try to learn from what they can discern about what other firms are doing. We will come to some institutional developments that facilitate that process shortly. But here we note that, in industries like those studied by Klepper, as product technology settles down there actually may be a speed-up in the rate of change of process technology.

Klepper highlights that these developments in process technology very often require that the firm operate at larger scale. While growth of sales may justify this move, the process of reorganizing and restructuring governance modes to enable effective operation at significantly larger scale may be a significant challenge. Major restructuring of firm organization and routines may be required. Alfred Chandler's (1977) great study of the development of mass production firms in the United States, provides details on the struggle of these firms to find and implement modes of organization and management that could cope with the challenges associated with large scale operation. Among the more important of the organizational innovations he identifies was the development of the multidivisional firm. More on this shortly. But more generally the management literature clearly shows that Chandler's "economies of scale and scope" are not easy to achieve.

There also are questions that must be resolved as an industry evolves regarding the scope of the different firms participating in it. If the product or service involved has a number of different components, a firm must decide which ones of these to produce itself and, if it wishes to sell a complete product, which ones to buy from other firms. Some firms may specialize in producing one or a few components, and sell these to another firm who assembles the complete system. In some industries specialized assemblers have developed who produce none or only a few of the components themselves.

There are similar issues regarding the extent of vertical integration of firms. As noted earlier, in some industries there originally are or there develop firms that specialize in production equipment. There may emerge firms that specialize in interacting with customers and doing marketing. Some other firms, however, may prefer a significant degree of vertical integration, doing their own customer relationships and marketing, and designing and producing their own production equipment.

Many years ago Adam Smith (1776) proposed that "the division of labor depends on the extent of the market." Years later, George Stigler (1951) gave a number of examples of industries where this dynamic pattern was followed. Contemporary economists doing research and writing on industry life cycles have paid little attention to the aspects of industry structure and behavior that we have been considering here. But we would bet that Smith's proposal is broadly correct. As industries come out of their early formative stages and the basic technologies and other ways of doing things become more stable, and the overall market gets larger, there is a strong tendency toward increasing horizontal and vertical specialization of firms. Firm networks become better established and more important.

The organization of production in modern economies is marked by extensive division of labor among heterogeneous actors with different areas of technological knowledge and expertise (Teece, 1987). But to be effective, this division requires strong mechanisms of communication and coordination. No single firm can keep up with the changes going on in all the technologies relevant to its operation. Therefore firms seek access to external knowledge sources. Innovation networks (Pyka, 2002) involving a number of firms and other actors are increasingly important aspects of industrial R&D. These networks were first recognized and studied by scholars in the 1990s as a new development in pharmaceuticals, in which large diversified pharmaceuticals firms cooperated with smaller specialized biotech firms, often new, and often closely connected with universities (e.g., Powell, Koput, and Smith-Doerr, 1996). At that time it often was argued that this type of arrangement was temporary and that sooner or later the large pharmaceuticals companies would build their internal capabilities in the new field, and some of the specialized biotech research companies would grow to become full fledged pharmaceuticals companies. To some extent this has happened, but the network arrangements remain prominent in this field, and have spread to others.

Innovation networks evolve with industries and adapt to the way the technologies employed by the industry develop. In young industries, particularly before a dominant design has emerged, one often can see the firms in the industry engaging in explorative research with a variety of external specialists. During this stage innovation networks can grow fast but tend to involve relatively loose connections among the actors. As the technology becomes more mature, firms increasingly become engaged in exploitative research, aimed at fine tuning of products and cost reduction. The networks become more compact and durable.

Most of the evidence we have regarding these kinds of patterns is in the form of case studies. There is little general data on networks of these kinds, and how they vary across industries and over time. And ability to document the temporal patterns suggested above empirically is made specially difficult by the fact that in many industries large firms tend to operate a number of different quasi-independent divisions, a phenomenon noted and studied by Alfred Chandler. In a number of cases these separate divisions operate as if they were independent firms.

In any case, both R&D and other transactions between a firm assembling a complete product system and a separate firm from which it buys some of the components, or between a firm producing a product and a separate firm that designs and produces production equipment tailored to the needs of the downstream firm, seldom proceed through the kind of anonymous buying and selling depicted as what market transactions are in the standard economics textbooks. They generally will involve a considerable amount of discussion as to just what is wanted and just what that will cost, and some bargaining about the details, and often some explicit cooperation in getting what is needed provided and transferred. It takes time and learning for these kinds of relationships to develop effectively. The underlying structures can be described as fully articulated and partly connected networks.

More generally, the way textbook economics tends to describe "markets" glosses over the fact that many markets involve quite complex institutional structures, that differ significantly from sector to sector, and which evolve over time. Consider product markets, the institutional structures that link customers or users more generally of a good or service to those that produce or provide it. As noted above, in many industries there are a set of firms that lie between the producer and the users: car dealers in the automobile industry; grocery stores for the vegetables bought and consumed by households; theaters which provide the stage for plays and concerts the production of which usually is under the control of another company. For many products there are wholesalers as well as retailers. It generally takes a different kind of expertise to market and distribute a product or service than to make it, and this usually is reflected in different companies doing the jobs, although here too the existence of multidivisional firms may blur the distinction. And product markets evolve over time as the industry evolves.

The same is so on the upstream side. Above we mentioned that in many industries a set of specialized equipment suppliers emerges, often with quite complex market relationships with their downstream customers. We also have noted the difficulties firms operating in new and emerging industries often have in getting finance. As the industry matures financial institutions come to know it better and patterned arrangements for making and dealing with financial operations get worked out.

We have highlighted the uncertainties, and the enthusiasms, that tend to mark efforts to form a new industry. Some of the entrepreneurs bring their own finance, or are able to convince family and friends to put up money. A good portion need to go to outside persons or financial organizations and plead their case. Banks generally are not in the business of financing ventures like these. Reliable expertise they can tap to judge the likelihood of success of a proposal just is lacking at this stage in the development of a new industry, and for many years banks have not seen themselves as sources of finance for highly speculative ventures. The new entrepreneurs generally are not in a position to convince financial institutions that sponsor new security issues to work with them to finance what they have in mind. In earlier eras rich individuals, or collections of them, with an enjoyment for gambling were, along with the friends and relatives of some of the entrepreneurs, important sources of capital to finance ventures in new industries.

Since the end of World War II, the institution of "venture capital" has emerged in many countries, and is an important source of funding for new firms in new industries. However, various studies have shown that venture capitalists often are reluctant to support new things, before there is good evidence that a commercial product is on the way. In recent years many countries have put in place government programs to provide finance (directly or indirectly) for the development of new industries, but generally their funds are quite limited. Financing highly uncertain ventures, and this is what ventures are in a brand new industry, remains a highly chancy business in most countries.

However, once products are produced that sell and promise to be profitable, the situation changes drastically. Financial institutions and the stock market are open to new public offerings. Bank finance for certain kinds of activities becomes feasible. If the industry takes off, financial institutions develop expertise in evaluating projects and requests for funding.

As new industries develop industry associations tend to form, first informally, but later often as formal organizations. These organizations provide a mechanism for addressing internal conflicts and shared interests, and also for interacting with and lobbying external industries and groups that matter.

Not all industries need workers with special skills, but many do. Again, as the industry develops a specialized labor market often develops bringing together potential employers of people with those skills, and the pool of skilled labor. Alfred Marshall (1890, 1892) gave great importance to the labor market that developed around

Manchester during the nineteenth century as a factor explaining why firms in Manchester were leaders in the textile industries for such a long period of time.

A very important aspect of the evolution of some (certainly not all) industries is the emergence of programs at schools (if the skills are very sophisticated at universities) that provide training in the special competences needed to perform effectively certain of the tasks that need to be done. In some cases a new profession may emerge, with the standard trappings of a profession: meetings, journals, awards, etc. In a few cases a new scientific discipline may emerge oriented to the scientific underpinnings of the industry's technology, and universities may begin to do research in that field. The emergence of chemical and electrical engineering as fields of university training and research are good examples. The development of computer science is a more recent case that illustrates vividly the co-evolution between the development of an industry and the development of external institutions that support it.

And government policies and programs bearing on an industry evolve as the industry develops. When the industry is emerging, the firms in it have to operate in the context of a body of regulation, and public policy more generally, that was put in place in an earlier era, but which can influence significantly what they are and are not allowed to do. As the industry takes shape and begins to get attention as an entity in its own right, there are pressures for the law to change. Some of those pressures come from those within the industry, often working through their industry association, to get rid of constraints not meant for them, and to lobby for more supportive government policies. Some pressure may come from external parties, who are affected by the new industry's products and presence more generally. And these pressures, and the regulations and laws they induce, tend to evolve as the industry matures, and more is learned about the problems and needs associated with the industry and its products.

The automobile industry is a good example. As the number of automobiles on the roads increased, it became clear that there was a need to regulate driving practice. A whole new body of traffic law came into existence along with new tasks for the police. Later, a collection of regulations on automobile design as well as driver practice came into existence to protect people in cars from injury. Still later, environmental concerns led to the development of another body of law. While the automobile case is particularly vivid, a similar emergence and development of new bodies of law and regulation can be seen in the histories of a large number of industries. Pharmaceuticals is a good example. And more recently innovators pushing the development of nanotechnologies have struggled with a body of law, some old and some new, that is constraining and molding what they can do.

And both of these industries, as well as aircraft and air travel, are good examples of the fact that in many cases for a new industry to develop effectively, new government programs and investments may be required. The growth of automobile ownership led to increased demands for governments to provide paved roads, and road building and maintenance became an important government budget item. The rise of the pharmaceuticals industry, and lobbying by the industry, was an important reason why since World War II many governments have spent a significant amount supporting biomedical research. Governments are responsible for designing and operating the air traffic control systems that make today's high density flight patterns feasible, and in many cases governments are responsible for building and maintaining airports.

Clearly industry evolution is a very complex process involving many interdependent aspects. Very few treatments of how industries evolve bring in the aspects of an industry's structure that we have discussed in this section, and no study that we know about has studied systematically the co-evolution of supporting institutions (see also Hanusch and Pyka, 2007). But we believe that without considering these aspects of the evolution of an economic industry or sector, the analysis is seriously incomplete.

4.5 TOWARD A WIDER ADHERENCE TO AN EXPLICITLY EVOLUTIONARY PERSPECTIVE

The evolutionary perspective on industrial behavior, performance, and dynamics, which has been developed in this chapter, differs significantly from the view of these variables that would be seen through neoclassical theoretical glasses. However, as we suggested at the start of this chapter, there long has been within the mainline discipline a tradition of research and analysis of industrial economics that sees industrial behavior and performance in relatively pragmatic and dynamic ways. Partly this reflects the influence of Schumpeter, but the tradition goes back much farther in time, and was manifest prominently in Alfred Marshall's *Industry and Trade* (1919). A significant number of the studies reported in this chapter were the work of economists with a home in an economics department.

But we think it fair to say that a major advantage of an explicit evolutionary perspective on economic activity is that this enables the different strands of research we have treated in this chapter to be fitted together coherently. Some of our fellow economists whose work we have described have that orientation, but a number do not, at least as yet.

The point we are making here is that the orientation of evolutionary economics is at once roomy, capable of taking aboard a wide range of phenomena identified by empirical research as associated with the subject matter being studied, and theoretically broadly constructive, capable of making sense of how those phenomena relate and how they influence or are influenced by the evolutionary processes that generate them. Put another way, an evolutionary theory certainly does focus attention ex-ante on certain phenomena and processes, but is quite open to recognizing that a wide range of factors and mechanisms may be operative, and thus has the capability for developing a theoretical understanding of what is going on that is broadly responsive to what has been learned empirically.

We believe that this characteristic, clearly visible in the description we have given of research from an evolutionary perspective on industrial behavior, performance, and dynamics, is a highly desirable one for studying the kind of phenomena and asking the kind of questions that mark economics as a field of study. We have noted that today many economists are operating and thinking quite pragmatically, and many of these recognize explicitly that the economic world needs to be understood as constantly changing. We want to argue that for economists inclined this way, an explicit evolutionary orientation would be very helpful.

Appendix to Chapter 4: History-Friendly Modeling

Sidney G. Winter

This appendix to Chapter 4 offers a summary account of history-friendly modeling, a flexible approach to formal modeling designed for the analysis of industry dynamics. This approach takes into account the particular considerations bearing on how a specific industry evolves, as well as more general forces. As the discussion in Chapter 4 highlights, the factors shaping the dynamics of industrial development are quite different from one industry to another. These differences are documented in historical studies and policy-oriented analyses, and are recognized also in fields like technology studies and organization studies. The differences extend to matters that are clearly central to the story of long term growth, such as the nature of innovative opportunities and the character of firm behaviors that seek to exploit those opportunities.

Interpretations of the dynamics of a particular industry necessarily involve an element of "theory" – although it may not be stated in formal terms. Because the industry stories are so diverse collectively, the question arises as to how much similarity is appropriate in the theoretical frames adopted in the different cases. There are clear similarities in the phenomena that allow, or call for, similar treatment – but on the other hand, the differences call for adaptation to important differences in context. In the pharmaceutical industry, for example, it is well established that the patent system is an important influence on innovation incentives. Therefore, ideas about how the patent system works form an important subset of the ideas about how the industry's dynamics work. To leave the patent system out of the pharmaceutical industry story – or to introduce it in a simplistic way, uninformed by study of the actual case at hand – would clearly put the analysis at risk of grave error. It does not follow, however, that careful attention to the patent system is an indispensable ingredient of *every* analysis of the dynamics of a particular industry. Thus, there is a need for some sort of rough cost-benefit analysis concerning the incorporation of individual elements of the overall situation in a particular industry, and such analysis will imply different choices in different industries.

The history-friendly art form provides a flexible, context sensitive approach to the analysis of the diverse realities of industry dynamics. This approach is explained here in terms of its particular response to a threefold challenge confronted by all forms of theorizing that aspire to support empirical science. Following the characterization of these challenges as a group, the method's responses to the three challenges are discussed individually.

The threefold challenge. First, there is the challenge of selecting the particular real phenomena that are to be theorized about. Second, there is the choice of representation for those phenomena – the concepts, variables, axioms, and tacit premises that will collectively "stand in" for the phenomena, for the purpose of the theorizing. And third, there is the selection of a mode of manipulation for the representations – the tools that permit the process of theorizing to arrive at destinations that are something other than a simple restatement of its starting point. In the context of "science" or aspiring science, the response to this third challenge is guided by norms of logical argument, and also by extra-logical norms that reflect ideas about what "science" means – or what the particular science in question *should* mean in the specific context. The specific forms that "theory" takes are, however, strikingly diverse.

There are tradeoffs presented by the three challenges. A decision to limit analysis to a small number of variables and causal mechanisms can facilitate or justify a simple representation. A simple representation offers the particular advantages of mathematical or logico deductive tools for the exploration of the implications of those representations. This is the path that has been taken, overwhelmingly, by economic theorists at least since the middle of the last century. The consequences are ubiquitous in theoretical literature; an imposing illustration is the large corpus of international trade theory with two factors and two goods – but no geography, transport costs, or technological change. Simplicity is valued highly, especially the kind of simplicity that creates a puzzle that the theorist can address with his or her limited repertoire of mathematical skills.[1] Conversely, choices that favor broad scope and engagement with complexity have traditionally been reflected in a greater use of verbal arguments to explore the logic of the situation; such choices are more prevalent in policy-oriented or historical work. History-friendly modeling is a mode of formal theorizing that offers an alternative to the simplicity-dominated view of the tradeoffs among the three basic challenges; it is a new contender in the intellectual terrain contested by existing approaches that respond particularly to one or another of those challenges.

On the first challenge, selecting the phenomena demanding theoretical attention, history-friendly modeling draws inspiration from economic history, and particularly from the history of specific sectors that seem significant in the grander story of economic growth. More specifically, it looks to the histories of individual sectors that are of interest in the larger picture. Still more specifically, it looks to the history of particular, time limited episodes that seem critical in that larger history.

Regarding the second challenge, history-friendly modeling largely incorporates the same basic representations used elsewhere in evolutionary economic theory. Thus, business firms are the focal actors, and their innovative behaviors (or lack thereof) are seen as key causal mechanisms. Firms are characterized by their capabilities and typically shape those capabilities by extended efforts over time. The environments of these focal actors are, as represented, neither simple nor passive. Severe constraints on the effective agency of individual

---

[1] Of course, the repertoire of the typical theorist advances over time, though always remaining – for good reasons – well within the frontier that existing mathematical understanding would support.

actors arise from familiar mechanisms of competition, but also from exogenous sources, such as the appearance or disappearance of particular sources of demand.

Above all, the representations adopted in the history-friendly approach honor the causal importance of the time dimension. For example, firms are not born large, nor do they reflect equilibrium conditions of optimal scale. Rather, some firms become large by growing, typically over extended periods. Size matters for a number of reasons, but particularly because informational economies of scale support the appropriation of gains from innovation. Industry structure (understood roughly as the size distribution of firms) evolves, and industry structure matters. Technology changes over time both endogenously (through firm R&D) and exogenously (through trends in opportunity). Because of the link through R&D, the evolution of technology is causally intertwined with the evolution of firm capabilities, profitability, growth, and the firm size distribution.

Given the need to respect the complexity of historical phenomena (challenge one), and to reflect (challenge two) judgments about key representations (business firms, innovation, time itself), what is the theorist to do about challenge three? How can the representations of complex processes be manipulated in a style that aspires to a high standard of logical accountability? *Computer simulation* is the answer offered in the community of history-friendly modelers, but also, today, in response to similar challenges across the sciences. For example, the modestly helpful medium term weather forecasts we have today are built on the foundation of an effective, *computational* aggregation of an enormous amount of local, time specific, data, within a theoretical frame built on physics.[2]

Following the spirit of such examples, history-friendly modelers seek to represent the key dynamics of significant historical episodes, opening the door to relatively complex representations of the

---

[2] See Auerswald (2017, Ch. 4), for a concise history of numerical weather forecasting.

considerations at work, and relying heavily on computers to produce the interesting results that were not obvious from the start – thus honoring (in principle at least) the demand for logical accountability. They are not oblivious to the case for simplicity and the related need for some limitations of scope (challenge one). However, they do not enshrine these constraints, but rather try to push against them, in the interest of engaging complexity.[3]

Historical grounding. Focus is needed to guide theorizing, but the question arises as to what guides the choice of focus. In history-friendly modeling there are many criteria, some of which are no doubt operating at the subconscious level. Among the avowed criteria, relevance to the grand story of modern economic growth holds first place. We (history-friendly modelers) hold to the particular view of that story that sees it as involving strong causal interactions between the development of modern economic institutions (imperfectly labeled as "capitalism" or "the market system") and the advance of knowledge (particularly technological and organizational knowledge). We do not hold with the idea that knowledge has causal primacy in this story (as in some versions of the "linear model") nor with any view that sees economic development as a miracle that the market system worked by itself – or perhaps with the help of "entrepreneurship." In holding to the emphasis on the interactions, we are aligned with a vast array of contributions ranging at least back to Adam Smith. Among these are many detailed studies of particular industries and technologies, which interpret histories with the aid of well-considered judgments at the theoretical level (i.e., "appreciative theories," as discussed in Chapter 1 and also below). Rarely indeed do

---

[3] See Rodrik (2015), for a thoughtful apologia for simplicity in modeling. Yet Rodrik's case seems to rest, like others before it, on an undefended assumption that the world's complexity *can* be adequately treated in a model simple enough to accommodate the restrictive modeling preferences of today's mathematical economists. Similar preferences do not constrain other sciences, or engineering, which manage to find ways to find ways of coping when the intrinsic complexity of the phenomena is inconveniently high.

such studies offer compelling support to a knowledge only or a capitalism only view of major episodes.[4]

At this date, only a modest number of history-friendly models have been built. The focal episodes in these efforts are obviously important ones in the history of economic progress. Thus, Malerba et al. (2016) model roughly fifty year episodes in the histories of the US computer, semiconductor, and pharmaceutical industries. That general economic growth has been powerfully impacted by progress in semiconductors and computers is quite obvious. As for pharmaceuticals, the German synthetic dye industry stands out in the historical record as the first truly science-based industry (Murmann, 2003), and as a precursor of today's research-based pharmaceutical industry. Its causal dynamics have been explored with history-friendly simulation methods by Garavaglia, Malerba, and Orsenigo (2006); Brenner and Murmann (2016) and others. In all of these cases, and elsewhere in the history-friendly literature, the interactions between the domain of productive knowledge and the domain of profit seeking enterprise are seen as causally central. Each is marked, however, by major influences from structures and forces that are particular to the case. Thus, the specific approaches taken to modeling the interactions should be quite different.

Representations. As noted above, the representations chosen in history-friendly modeling have much in common with those favored across the whole span of contemporary evolutionary economics, and indeed, beyond. We posit populations of stylized business firms, competing in stylized environments that define conditions of cost, demand, and technological opportunity. These model firms are not designed via detailed matching to real firms; they do not have names that reference historical firms.[5] In most cases, the firms (or large

[4] A good start on a contemporary reading list on this point is offered by the works that have won the biannual Schumpeter Prize. See the list at www.issevec.uni-jena.de/Schumpeter+prize.html.

[5] In expounding the results of their model of the US computer industry, Malerba et al. (2016) sometimes refer to a model firm as "IBM." That model firm (which

subsets of them) are actually represented as identical *ab initio* – that is, before the stochastic elements and cumulative dynamics of the model have had a chance to produce differences. The first small doses of those elements establish heterogeneity in the population, and it is a strongly path dependent heterogeneity that only tends to get more pronounced as simulated time goes on.[6]

Model firms can be seen as either very simple or very complicated, depending on where one looks for a comparison. If one looks to economic reality, or even to the accounts of reality found in the literature, then model firms are extremely simple by that standard. If, however, one finds the comparisons in the textbooks and papers of mainstream economics, then history-friendly firms are very complicated. They are entities of much higher dimensionality. In the computer industry model of Malerba et al. (2016), there are about twenty-five variables that are distinguished by firm and time, and often by other things such as market segment or technology type. Others are distinguished, or potentially distinguished, by firm but not by time – including the initial values of many of the time varying variables. Many other parameters appear in the routines and decision rules that shape model firms' behavior, and could quite reasonably be treated as firm specific as well, but (for the sake of simplicity) that is not done in the modeling work reported.

The domain of firm decisions offers the starkest contrasts between the spirit of history-friendly modeling and the spirit of contemporary mainstream theorizing. In the latter, rational agents with high-level influence on firm behavior make decisions only after they "think it all through" very carefully – and often with sophisticated attention to the fact that rival firms are also trying to "think it through." In the history-friendly representation, the firm choice

is identified one run at a time) has a relation to the historical IBM – but it is only that, thanks to the model dynamics, it has come to take on a role in that model run that is reasonably analogous to that of the historical firm in the real history.

[6] It is too often forgotten that very simple but *cumulative* random processes, epitomized by the game of matching pennies, will reliably generate extreme heterogeneity as time goes on.

problem is viewed as decentralized, or "nearly decomposable," in parallel to the realistic decentralized control of the action variables in most firms of substantial size. Further, key firm choices are driven by decision rules that respond to available current data on the firm and its environment, one question at a time – not to elaborate, rationalistic prognostications of the future, and not remotely in response to "thinking it all through."

Here, the phrase "available current data" has two closely linked meanings: First, the data that are input to a model decision rule at a particular simulation time step must have gotten into the model somehow, either as parameter values input at the start, or variable values generated by the model at an earlier time step. Second, it is the guidance of the empirical evidence and attendant interpretive efforts that is invoked in settling larger questions about the parameters and variables that are included in the model, thus determining what data are ultimately "available" in it. From that guidance derives an element of future-oriented "wisdom" in the assumed decision rules: While model firms do not engage in detailed projections of simulated futures, the rules they follow can be partly rationalized as efforts to adapt to a complex and changing environment.

Consider, for example, the decisions of a specialized computer producer about whether to take up the production of the semiconductor components for its computers. In the formulation adopted by Malerba et al. (2016), the choice is governed by a "propensity" model. The probability of integrating in a particular time period increases with the age of the component technology, on the presumption that the reduction of technological uncertainty over time makes the move less risky. The probability also responds positively to the ratio of the firm's computer output to the output of the largest component supplier,[7] reflecting the notion that scale economies in R&D

---

[7] A units choice in the background determines that one semiconductor component is needed for each computer produced, so the ratio described is the fraction of the component firm's output that the computer firm buys if it met its needs from that source.

favor reliance on the external specialist when that ratio is small. The effective magnitudes of these two influences are determined by parameters specific to the integration submodel. This example provides a good indication of the typical characteristics of evolutionary/history-friendly formulations, such as the fact that while the posited rule is interpretable as "profit seeking," it responds to considerations of uncertainty, strategic position, and firm heterogeneity that are typically suppressed in mainstream models – and is not plausibly interpretable as "profit maximizing."

Modelers make their choices, imperfectly informed as they may be, in their attempts to guess the nature of these structures and the character of the variables that are likely to be influential – and the character of the strong simplifications that can bring these judgments within the scope of computational modeling. As in many parallel cases, such modelers uphold the idea that these approaches, though still under development, are much more consonant with observable reality than are the narratives about firms as "unitary rational decision makers."

In addition to these basic representational features, which are commonplace in evolutionary economics, a particular history-friendly model includes representations that are grounded in the specifics of the segment of history addressed – such as the role of the patent system, or of government funding of R&D. Those specifics do not, of course, speak for themselves regarding their effective representation. As discussed in Chapter 1, evolutionary economists generally rely quite heavily on the "appreciative theorizing" put forward by scholars who have focused intently on a particular subject matter and grappled with the problem of characterizing the principal mechanisms at work in it. This approach is adopted in history-friendly modeling, especially in regard to the "subject matter" defined by a particular industry in a particular time period.

Appreciative theorizing is usually expressed verbally, rather than in symbols and formalisms. It often has the character of persuasive storytelling, and certainly a reader may experience it as more descriptive than theoretical. But it is *interpretive* description, and that is where the theoretical elements inevitably come in. Appreciative theory is a key resource in addressing the explanatory challenges of complex subject matter – such as an episode in the history of a major industry. The stock of insights developed by appreciative theorists in the past – theorists who operated under diverse flags such as industry expert, business historian, policy economist – is taken as valued intermediate product by history-friendly modelers. They then seek to recast the logic of the received narrative in the more formal terms of computer code, thus opening new opportunities for analysis – including close scrutiny of the explanatory logic, and exploration of counterfactual cases.

Consider, for example, the case of the US computer industry. A prominent feature of its history is the dominant position that IBM held over the bulk of the first half century. A number of questions exist concerning IBM's dominance: Why did it happen? Why did it ultimately come to an end? Why was it particularly characteristic of the market for mainframe computers, while the personal computer market had a very different history? The several scholars who have explored such questions reached conclusions that depended partly on the specific historical circumstances, as well as on generic economic mechanisms.[8] In particular, both the innovative character of the product and IBM's strategy underpinned the phenomena of "bandwagon effects" and "lock-in," – the former being the cumulating effect of IBM's favorable reputation, and the latter, the tendency of customers to return to IBM when expanding or upgrading their computing facilities. A success-breeds-success dynamic, deriving from informational scale economies in R&D and its application, also favored IBM's sustained strength – in spite of the turbulent technological environment. These "appreciative" insights were incorporated in the history

---

[8] See Malerba et al. (2016: 43) for specific references.

friendly model developed by Malerba et al. (2016), and play a key role in that model's reliable tendency to produce IBM-like dominance patterns (see the figure reproduced below). In this sense, the formal model provides support for the explanatory power of the appreciative theory; it also points to areas where that theory might be refined.[9]

Manipulation. Advances in information technology over recent decades have transformed the craft of simulation modeling. Computational requirements *per se* have become almost a negligible consideration, except in cases where the system modeled is very large (as in weather forecasting), or the interactions involved are particularly subtle (protein folding). Though not unknown in social science applications, such challenging conditions are comparatively rare in that domain. In particular, efforts at history-friendly modeling have been pursued (thus far) well within the frontier of the computational possibilities.

As illustrated in Malerba et al. (2016), a typical model might involve the interactions of some tens of firms, each characterized by perhaps twenty-five time-varying variables, plus other parameters. Then there are the equations specifying the environments and the interaction processes among the firms. The story is played out in a "run" consisting of 200 time steps, conceived as corresponding roughly to calendar quarters. Along the way, the stochastic elements of the model are instantiated in random number draws, implementing a variety of distributional assumptions. There are a few of these per firm/per time period – implying a total over a run of some thousands of draws. Multiply all of this by the number of runs over which results are averaged in the interest of discovering the systematic tendencies of the model; in Malerba et al. (2016) this number is typically 1000.

This mass of computation – which was unthinkably challenging in its magnitude as recently as the early days of evolutionary

[9] And more fundamentally, it makes the case that the phenomena can be explained without invoking unique attributes of the historical IBM, an observation related to the naming issue discussed in note 5 above.

modeling – is not the "hard problem." Thanks to the computer, its challenges are modest compared to those that come before the actual computation, the design and programming of the model, and those that come after – the assessment, analysis, and interpretation of the results.

In the assessment of results, a prominent role is played by descriptor variables that reveal interesting features of the industry state at a point in time. In the model's logic, these variables play no active role. For example, conventional measures of the concentration of the firm size distribution, such as the Herfindahl Index, or its numbers equivalent, or the four-firm concentration ratio, make frequent appearances in the analysis but rarely appear in causal roles. In analysis, such measures are an alternative to examining the actual value of size (meaning sales, typically) for each individual firm. Further compression is achieved by averaging over a large number of runs, such as 1000, and then by plotting the evolution of the averaged variable over time. The sort of message that results is illustrated in Figure A.4.1 below, drawn from the Malerba et al. (2016) modeling study of the US computer industry.

This is an extremely compressed message compared to the underlying data, the firm sizes taken firm by firm and period by period. The compression obviously affords enormous advantages in ease of interpretation. That act of interpretation is, however, conditioned on substantive guidance from a theoretical framework in which concentration matters and is appropriately measured by the Herfindahl Index. Perhaps a different descriptor would afford more insight – but if so, it would have to arise from an alternative theoretical frame, which the model itself cannot supply, and then be implemented.

Although simulation runs and their interpretation are the most characteristic approach to manipulating a history-friendly model, there are other methods, which are mostly complementary to the core method. Some are informal, such as asking "what if?" questions about the implications of possible changes in the code or the parameter values, and then simply trying to think it through,

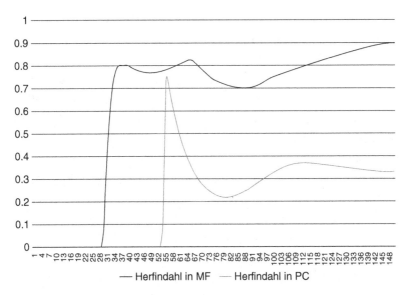

FIGURE A.4.1 Herfindahl in PC and mainframe markets (standard set)

and possibly checking that conclusion with simulations. Some are formal, involving mathematical scrutiny of a particular relationship, or side calculations made in a spreadsheet. These sorts of analysis make an important but ultimately largely invisible contribution to the design of the model and to the modeler's confidence in it.

The future of history-friendly modeling. A rich opportunity set awaits scholars who are attracted by the potential of the history-friendly approach. That potential rests fundamentally on the ability of the approach to engage the challenge that complexity presents to our understanding of social phenomena. Such ability rests, in turn, on the value of the large but limited objective of explaining particular historical episodes, and on the method's ability to absorb and exploit insights from diverse sources. There is an inviting path to more compelling models through better matching of model details to the available information about the focal episode. Not all of that information is necessarily specific to the episode; for example, new insights about the general character of firm behavior should shape model representations of it.

Whatever is available in the way of quantitative description of the focal episode is a resource that can be drawn upon both to suggest model formulations and to assess their adequacy. Key trends at the level of industry aggregates should ideally be reproduced by the simulation model when it is used in full "history-friendly" mode (as opposed to "counterfactual history" mode). Inability to achieve such matching could be regarded as a disconfirmation of the model. To posit this principle, of course, is implicitly to raise questions that the descriptive data cannot answer: What does "key" mean and how are the key trends to be distinguished from those that are inconsequential or accidental? What degree of quantitative accuracy in trend matching should be aspired to? How can the causal interactions of the key trends be uncovered and reflected in the model? These questions underscore again the point that there is an indispensable component of theoretical thinking in the art of simulation; the priorities for the modeling effort can only be determined by the application of such thinking to the specifics of the case.

In the representations of firm behavior, it would be good to build in better information on firm routines and decision rules. Advances in history-friendly modeling could be much more compelling if they were complemented by new research on firm behavior, a research program that would amount to a resurrection of the Carnegie School approach to that subject (Cyert and March, 1963).[10] In that regard, it is a long road that beckons to us. More incremental improvements are, fortunately, closer to hand, and can be explored in the context of a wider range historical cases, as Malerba et al. (2016) also suggested in their concluding chapter.

---

[10] While the Carnegie view of organizations and decisions has been broadly influential, there has been very little effort to follow the Carnegie lead toward empirically grounded simulation modeling of firm decisions and routines.

5 Evolutionary Perspectives on Long Run Economic Development

Andreas Pyka, Pier Paolo Saviotti, and Richard R. Nelson

5.1 INTRODUCTION

Adam Smith's *The Wealth of Nations*, published in 1776, begins with a description of the economic development then going on in the United Kingdom. With the vision of hindsight it is clear that much of what he is describing demarks an historical watershed. Prior to the mid to late eighteenth century, while the standards of living achieved in the different countries of the world tended to vary and rise and fall, there is no earlier record of continuing sustained rise in living standards of the sort that began then in the United Kingdom, and then somewhat later in some of the countries of northern Europe, and the United States, and later more broadly. In the introductory chapter of this volume, we proposed that perhaps the most widely shared goal of evolutionary economists is to understand the economic development process better.

Understanding economic development clearly was a central challenge for Adam Smith. And most of the great classical economists that followed Smith dedicated at least as much of their research and writing to the sources and prospects for economic development as they did to the determinants of the allocation of resources and prices at any time. However, with the rise of neoclassical economics the focus shifted more sharply to analysis of conditions of economic equilibrium and, with the exceptions of heretical writers like Schumpeter, interest in the determinants of long run economic development seemed to fade.

That interest and writing came back strongly in the years after World War II. The refreshed view on long run economic change was shaped by two new intellectual developments. One was the emergence of neoclassical growth theory. As discussed in Chapter 2, neoclassical growth theory, as oriented empirically, highlighted technological advance as the key driving force behind economic growth, a point of view modern evolutionary economists have embraced. On the other hand, in accord with the neoclassical perspective more broadly, neoclassical growth theory treated the process of economic growth as one of moving equilibrium with economic actors modifying their behaviors to continue maximizing their profits and their utilities from consumption as productivity and incomes rose smoothly. We note that this was not a characteristic of the views on economic growth put forth by the earlier classical economists. And Schumpeter, of course, in characterizing the economic growth process as one of continuing "creative destruction" put forth a position very different from that of neoclassical economics. The perspective of modern evolutionary economists on economic development is much more in tune with Schumpeter than with neoclassical growth theory.

It also is important to recognize that the explanatory orientation of neoclassical growth theory, and its cousin "growth accounting," is focused on the variables in a "production function": labor and capital and other inputs of different sorts adjusted for their qualities, and how these have changed over time. Technological advance is treated as a (not well defined) force that increases the productivity of these inputs. Moses Abramowitz called these the "proximate" sources of economic growth. There is no explicit recognition of changes in the ways economic activities are organized, for example the rise of the factory system and later the modern corporation and mass marketing, or the stock market and other modern financial institutions, or the rise and decline of labor unions, and the continuing advance of science, or the changing roles of government, as factors influencing the growth process, although these may be recognized as factors behind changes in the proximate sources. Again, we note that this is very different from analyses of the determinants of growth by earlier economists.

The second intellectual development shaping the post World War II renewal of interest in economic growth was the new availability of national product and income statistics, which provided previously unavailable aggregate measures of a country's economic output and income and how these had changed over time. As a result, the principal task of analysis of economic growth came to be viewed as explaining the time paths of real GNP in total or per worker.

While there are severe problems regarding just what is included in GNP and what is not, and how the different included components are measured, we agree with our colleagues in neoclassical economics that GNP or a related number provides a useful broad summary measure of a country's economic output, and that following these numbers over time in different countries tells us a considerable amount about the course that economic development has taken. However, a single minded focus on aggregate measures, to the point of defining economic development in those terms, blinds analysis to the extraordinary diversity and continuing change in what an economy produces. It represses that the economic development process as we have experienced it has been marked by the periodic rise of new industries and decline and disappearance of older ones.

We have noted that today there is consensus that technological advance has been the principal driving force behind the economic progress we have experienced. Some of the technological advance that has occurred can be reasonably well characterized in terms of how it has enabled higher productivity in the production of relatively standardized products; advances in technology used in coal and corn production are good examples. But new technologies also have enabled us to do things, and meet wants, that could not be satisfied before. Consider the telegraph and telephone, the electronic computer, the internet. The effect of these advances on how people live and interact cannot be characterized adequately in terms of the ability of the economy to produce "more output." Similarly regarding medical advances that have eliminated or provided cures for many diseases that used to be mass killers and sources of human misery.

There also have been dramatic changes in the way people earn a living, and in how various needs are met. Among other things, production to meet one's own needs, which was an important part of economic activity in Adam Smith's day, and until the close of the nineteenth century, has diminished greatly. On another front, since the middle of the twentieth century government programs of a great variety have become an important part of the economy.

The use of the term economic "growth" rather than economic "development" to denote the processes through which an economy's ability to meet human wants through the production of goods and services is advanced reflects the narrow view of most of the post WWII orientation to long run economic progress. Most evolutionary economists believe that we need to characterize the increases in the economy's ability to meet wants more broadly than simply by measuring increases in real GNP, and that a focus on the proximate sources of economic development is far too shallow.

5.2 A VARIETY OF PERSPECTIVES

This broader perspective on what economic development is all about clearly calls for analysis that treats a wide range of variables and processes. The notion that our scientific aim should be to develop a sharp compact theory that illuminates all the relevant aspects would seem extremely dubious, indeed impossible. Rather, it would seem more reasonable to try to develop a collection of perspectives, each focused on an important and coherent subset of aspects, each one in a sense separate, but together providing a reasonably coherent overall picture of what is going on. The scientific goal is not to develop a tightly integrated evolutionary theory of economic development but rather a variety of perspectives and an understanding of how they relate to each other.

We note that much of natural science about complex phenomena is of this sort. Consider for example our understandings of the causes and effects of global warming, or the dynamic ecology of a forest, or to shift to the domain of the social sciences, our understandings of how a city develops over time. In none of these cases do we rely on one theory or model, and in none of them is our characterization of the phenomena expressible simply in terms of a small set of numbers. Our argument is that this is the case with respect to our developing understanding of economic development as an evolutionary process.

While there is some overlap, we can identify three clusters of research by evolutionary economists concerned with different aspects of the economic development process. One, which includes some of the earliest writings by modern evolutionary economists and continues to be an important arena of research and writing today, in effect explores how an explicitly evolutionary process of technological advance, of the sort described in Chapter 2, could drive the process of long run economic development, and generate the kinds of time series of aggregate output and inputs that have been the focus of much of the work guided by neoclassical growth theory. Much of this work involves formal modeling. As we will elaborate shortly, the conclusion of this body of research is that an explicitly evolutionary theory of economic development can generate the kinds of macroeconomic time series that have occurred, and at the same time be compatible with the great variation in economic activity that one observes at any time, and phenomena like diffusion curves depicting how new and more productive ways of doing things enter and come to permeate the economy. But in terms of what happens over time to the output of an economy, this body of evolutionary research treats economic growth as a macroeconomic phenomenon, and its explanatory orientation is to the "proximate" sources of growth.

A second body of analysis and writing by evolutionary economists, which includes both qualitative studies and, more recently, formal modeling, breaks away from the characterization of economic growth in terms of a macroeconomic variable like real GNP. It is concerned, explicitly, with changes over time in the composition of output produced by the economy, and in particular with the emergence and rise of new product classes and the decline and disappearance of older ones, and the associated rise and fall of industries in the economic development process. The industry cycle literature described in Chapter 4 is an important part of this body of research. The way economic development is viewed is not simply wider but different from the more macroeconomic-oriented evolutionary growth literature.

A third body of research by evolutionary economists on economic development is focused on institutions and institutional change and on how institutions co-evolve with the technologies in use and economic structure. The origins of the contemporary interest in this broad subject were the emergence of research and writing on innovation systems, which was described in Chapter 2. The key understanding here was that one could not effectively analyze the factors behind the technological innovation that was driving economic development without recognizing the wide range of institutions, non-market as well as market, that are involved in the process and the division of labor among them and their modes of interaction. This perspective gradually was extended to explicit recognition that the range of institutions operative in an economy reflects, induces, and co-evolves with the principal technologies in use and with industrial structure.

In the following three sections of this chapter we will describe these strands of research and writing in more detail. In the concluding section we propose that each of the different views of the long run economic development process are valuable, and they should be viewed together.

5.3 EVOLUTIONARY GROWTH MODELS

The early evolutionary growth models were developed under the sway of the neoclassical growth theory that was dominating the conceptions of most economists at that time regarding the nature of economic growth, and followed their focus on increases over time of

GNP and GNP per worker as the phenomena a good growth theory ought to explain. As noted in Chapter 2, reflection on the processes involved in technological advance, widely understood to be the key driving force behind economic growth, that empirical research was bringing to light led a number of economists to try to develop an evolutionary theory of economic growth driven by technological advance that would explain the patterns of GNP growth that had been experienced, but with a characterization of technological advance that was more consistent than neoclassical theory with what was coming to be known about the process. Many of the developers of evolutionary growth theory recognized that their formulation was Schumpeterian in some important respects. The evolutionary/Schumpeterian growth models they have developed over the years differ in certain respects, but all have a similar basic format. (For a sample of these models see Nelson and Winter, 1974; Chiaromonte and Dosi, 1983; Soete and Turner, 1984; Metcalfe, 1998.)

All of these models are of a one sector economy. (We will consider multisector evolutionary growth theory in the following section.) The models bring into the picture a diversity of practices being used at any time by different firms, and differences among firms in terms of how well they are doing, but assume that all technologies and all firms are producing the same kind of thing, so that their outputs can be added up and the total treated as like GNP.

Since the models differ in certain details, the discussion below largely relates to the Nelson–Winter 1974 model, although in many aspects it fits most of the models in this class. In the Nelson–Winter model, firms operate in a perfectly competitive market setting. Each firm produces at full capacity, which given the technology it is using is determined by the size of its capital stock. The amount of other inputs needed by a firm – in the Nelson–Winter model this is only labor – is determined by its output and its technology. The unit variable production costs of a firm then are determined, given its technology, by factor prices. The models described in this section differ in terms of how factor prices (in most cases the wage rate) at any time are determined, but in the Nelson–Winter model the wage rate is sensitive to the total amount demanded by the industry, but with the supply curve shifting to the right as population grows.

Because they differ in the technologies they are using and hence in their unit production costs, profit rates – rates of return on their capital stock – differ among firms. Profitable firms (those that are employing the more productive technologies) use their profits to expand their capacity and unprofitable ones contract. At the same time, some firms not using the most profitable technologies learn about and adopt the technologies of their more profitable rivals. Thus the relative importance in use of different prevailing technologies is changing both through differential firm growth and firms switching technologies. And as this is happening, some firms are innovating and introducing new technologies to the economy.

The process continues. In the Nelson–Winter model these dynamic processes result in an expansion of aggregate output, capital, and employment, and in most periods a rise in the wage rate. Because of the sensitivity of capital growth to the rate of return on capital, in this model the aggregate rate of return tends to be relatively constant over time.

These evolutionary models have been able to generate and hence "explain" a variety of different phenomena that have marked economic development as we have experienced it. The Nelson–Winter model is able to generate time series of aggregate output, and capital and labor inputs, and the prices of labor and the returns to capital, that have the broad characteristics of the historical record. In Figure 5.1 below the lower line shows the time path of output per worker hour generated by one of the runs of the Nelson–Winter model, and the upper line the path of the actual time series of real GNP per man hour. It is clear that an evolutionary theory of economic growth is consistent with the macroeconomic time series data.

At the same time, these models generate distributions of firms that differ significantly in sizes, productivities, and profitability, phenomena repressed by neoclassical growth theory. The models also

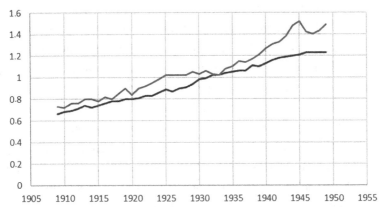

Output (1929 dollars per man hour)

FIGURE 5.1 Output per worker hour generated by the Nelson–Winter model (lower line) and actual time series of real GNP per man hour (upper line)

generate S-shaped diffusion time paths of the growing use of productive new technologies after they have been introduced to the economy, and their decline as still better technologies emerge and the associated changes in industry structure. If one reflects on it, this is a quite remarkable achievement for relatively simple models.

Within these models, as in neoclassical growth theory, growth of output per worker and rising living standards are associated with technological advance which increases the productivity of the inputs used in production, and also with increases in capital stock per worker. However, while in neoclassical theory these two sources are regarded as independent, in evolutionary growth theory they are tightly intertwined. The ability to operate in a more capital intensive way than under the present regime of technology is assumed to require the development of new technologies that are more capital intensive. In the Nelson–Winter model the rising wage rates induced by rapid growth of output and rising demand for labor induce technological advance to be labor saving and to enable a rising capital–labor ratio as well as higher worker productivity.

Thus to a much greater extent than neoclassical growth theory, but in the spirit of Schumpeter's general orientation, the conception, creation, and implementation of new ways of doing things are at center stage in evolutionary growth models. And the basic determinants of the pace of economic growth are those that determine how technology, in the broad sense of that term, advances.

Earlier we argued that in economics formal models are useful primarily to explore and test the logic of qualitative but richer theorizing regarding what is going on in an arena of economic activity, and to suggest extensions of that logic. Viewed that way, while obviously the models we are describing miss a lot of what is going on and treat much of the relevant activity in highly abstract form, they certainly have provided support for a broad evolutionary perspective on how economic productivity has risen so much over the years.

On the other hand, the treatment in these theories of economic growth as the increases in a measure of aggregate output totally represses the fact that the economic growth we have experienced has been marked by the introduction of new products and services and the disappearance of others, by the rise of new economic industries and the decline of others, phenomena that cannot be recognized in a macroeconomic treatment of the subject. We now turn to more recent evolutionary approaches to understanding growth where the diversity of the goods and services produced by the economy and the transformation of what is produced over time is central, and what economic growth is all about.

5.4   MULTISECTOR EVOLUTIONARY GROWTH MODELS

We have highlighted the influence of Schumpeter's writings on the orientation of evolutionary economics. The evolutionary growth models described in the preceding section were the result of early efforts by evolutionary economists to build an analysis of economic growth that incorporated important elements of the Schumpeterian perspective, and to show that such an analysis was at least as capable as neoclassical growth theory in explaining the macroeconomic pattern of growth. However, nothing in those models recognizes that growth as we have known it has centrally involved the birth of new products and industries and the decline and death of others, a perspective incompatible with thinking about and measuring growth simply as an aggregate phenomenon. In recent years evolutionary economists have built in more of the Schumpeterian perspective in their modeling as well as in their more appreciative characterization of what is going on in the economic growth process.

We have stressed that, to a much greater extent than economists working in the neoclassical tradition, evolutionary economists tend to build their theoretical conceptions from observation of what is going on empirically, rather than starting from abstract principles. There are several "stylized" empirical facts that evolutionary economists increasingly have been building into their analysis of the economic growth process.

First, as Schumpeter stressed, economic growth as we have experienced it since at least the middle of the nineteenth century has been marked by the emergence of broad new product classes and, often, new industries producing them, and the erosion and sometimes the disappearance of older ones. Second, at the same time, within many broad product classes and industries there have been significant advances in the quality of the products produced and the variety of the versions of the goods produced and offered to customers. As a result of both of these developments, the late nineteenth and the twentieth centuries have been marked by a dramatic increase in the variety of goods and services offered to households, and in the range of items bought and used by customers.[1]

At the same time productivity, in the sense of output per worker employed, has increased continuingly and greatly, and this growth of productivity has been associated with significant increases in the capital intensity in many industries. These are the features of economic

---

[1] Hidalgo et al. (2007) and Hidalgo and Hausmann (2009) have shown that in a cross section of countries the higher income ones tend to have a more varied mix of output and consumption.

growth on which neoclassical growth theory is focused. But measures of the advance of productivity do not show the increasing range of goods and services that economies have been producing, and totally miss the fact that many of the new goods and services enable users to do things and meet needs that they simply could not achieve before, no matter how many of the older goods they were able to buy and use.

The advance of living standards enabled by these developments certainly was not even across groups in the population. Hobsbawm (1968) has argued that well into the twentieth century working class families in the UK could not afford to purchase more than the traditional necessities. But as growth continued in the second half of the century, the real incomes of working class families rose significantly, and they began to join the middle classes in buying and using a wide variety of goods.

Alongside these advances in what the economy was able to produce there were significant increases in the resources allocated to education as well as to new physical capital. In economies where economic growth occurred, a growing fraction of the population came to get at least a primary education, and then somewhat later the fraction completing high school rose significantly. Particularly in the years after World War II there have been large increases in university attendance and degree completion. These increases in "human capital" clearly were a major factor enabling the increases in the ability of economies to produce goods and services that have been achieved, and we would propose that they also were an important factor associated with the widened and enriched patterns of consumption. From the mid nineteenth century rising literacy rates were associated with a large increase in the faction of the population reading newspapers and magazines which told of what was going on beyond the physical and social confines of individuals. At the same time there was a significant gap between the educational attainments of the middle and lower classes and this almost surely was an important reason for the lag in the rise of living standards of the latter that Hobsbawm has described (Saviotti and Pyka, 2013b; Jun, Saviotti, and Pyka, 2017).

The causal mechanisms involved in the economic growth processes we have been describing are many and complex. We evolutionary economists find it useful to recognize the advance of educational attainments, the rise in the capital intensity of production, the increases in productivity, and in the range of goods and services the economy is capable of providing, as a co-evolutionary process, with the ultimate driving force the increases in know-how that have been achieved and which are continuing. And we recognize, as another aspect of this co-evolutionary process, the continuing structural change going on in a growing economy – Schumpeter called it creative destruction – with at any time more resources flowing into some sectors and decreasing in others. Those with a stake in the latter can and have been seriously hurt by what is going on. But from an evolutionary point of view, creative destruction is an essential aspect of the economic growth process.

Another striking characteristic of economic growth as we have experienced it is that the process has not been smooth over time. Growth by any measure has been more rapid in some eras than in others. And in a number of cases a slowdown of growth has been associated with recession or even deep depression, and on occasions an acceleration of growth has been accompanied by inflation. It has been proposed that economic growth proceeds in "long waves" (Schumpeter, 1939; Freeman, Clarke, and Soete, 1982; Freeman, 1983, 1984, 1987, 1994; Perez, 1983, 2002; Silverberg and Lehnert, 1993, 1994; Silverberg and Verspagen, 1995, 2005; Freeman and Louça, 2001; Silverberg, 2007). Under this perspective, upswings and rapid growth are associated with the emergence and development of important new technologies and industries. Growth slows down and recession sets in as these new industries mature. A new upswing is associated with the emergence of a new cluster of industries. These patterns clearly reflect the workings of financial institutions, as well as the irregularities that are innate in the way technological progress proceeds.

It also is important to recognize that the economic growth we have seen has been marked by a significant and continuing change in the institutions bearing on economic activity. The structure of firms and of markets has changed greatly over the years. School systems have expanded greatly, and there have been major changes in how they were organized and financed. The financial system changed dramatically. Particularly in the twentieth century the roles played by government expanded greatly. We will deal more extensively with institutional change and economic growth in the following section.

The focus of this section is on some basic implications of the fact that economic growth has involved an expanded range of goods and services and the emergence of new industries and the decline of older ones, along with productivity growth. Perhaps the most dramatic proposed implication is that economic growth cannot continue over a long period of time if technological advance only enabled more effective production of a given set of goods and services, and that the continuing (if uneven) emergence of new or better goods and services is necessary if growth is to be sustained.

Pasinetti's writings (1981, 1993) provide the best known argument of this sort. The basic proposition is that consumer demand for a particular good or service tends to get saturated after a certain amount is procured and used, and that after a point neither declines in the price of that good nor higher income levels will induce consumers to buy more. Thus if no new or better goods are introduced, but productivity continues to grow in the production of existing goods and services, sooner or later spending increasingly will fall short of the rising incomes made possible by productivity growth, and Keynesian demand insufficiency problems will emerge. This problem has been averted in the economic growth we have experienced because new goods and services have continued to emerge, and hence spending out of growing incomes continues to be high. Recently Saviotti (1996) and Saviotti and Pyka (2004, 2008a, 2008b, 2013b) have developed this argument further.

A considerable part of their analysis has been presented in the context of a formal model of multisector economic growth. In that model economic growth proceeds both through the emergence and development of new economic sectors and through advances in the quality and variety of the goods produced by firms in any given economic sector, along with advances in their productivity. An economic sector is defined in terms of a class of goods within which there can be considerable variation. At any time firms in the different existing industries, and perhaps other organizations, engage in R&D, some of which is oriented to enabling advances in the economic sector where the firm resides, and some more generally oriented and which can enable the emergence of a new product class and a new industry.

When there is successful R&D of the latter sort, this opens possibilities for entrepreneurs to seize the new opportunities and to establish firms producing a new type of good and defining a new industry. If potential customers are attracted and the new firms do well, other entrepreneurs will move into the industry, and something like an industry product cycle (of the sort described in Chapter 4) will occur, except that in the Saviotti–Pyka model no dominant design will emerge, and indeed the variety of products offered by the industry will continue to grow even though industry growth will slow down and ultimately stagnate.

In their model consumer demand for a product in a particular class depends on the quality of those products and their variety, as well as on prices and the incomes of potential customers. And the demand saturation effect, as proposed by Pasinetti, is built into the model. Thus in this model a sector is doomed to ultimate stagnation after it has achieved a high level of productivity (and hence low prices), and quality, and product diversity. And continued growth depends, as Pasinetti proposed, on the continuing introduction to the economy of new product classes and new industries.

As the authors note, this characterization of the long run economic growth process fits the pattern of production and consumption that was experienced in rapidly growing economies after the mid nineteenth century. Part of the advance in economic capabilities that was going on was taken up with greater per capita production and consumption of particular broadly defined traditional consumption goods, like food and clothing. Some was taken up in improved quality of such goods. Thus after the turn into the twentieth century at least middle class people lived in larger and better apartments or houses, that contained central plumbing and running water. Municipalities built better sewage systems and systems to provide clean water.[2] But much of the benefits of growth were associated with the new products and services that became available, and which often enabled their users to do entirely new things. The availability of electricity in living quarters changed the way people lived in many respects. The ability to travel long distances quickly and cheaply, and instantaneous long distance communication, are other obvious examples. The advances in medical knowledge and technology wiped out or provided cures for many diseases that long had been the scourge of humankind. As we have stressed, virtually none of this shows up in increases in GNP measures of economic growth.

As we have noted, the Saviotti–Pyka model tends to generate booms when a new class of goods and a new industry comes into the economy, and recessions as that industry matures and there are no other industries just emerging, and then a new boom as a new product class comes into existence. However, most of the writing on "long waves" in the economic growth process done by economists of an evolutionary persuasion appears in other places.

Schumpeter's *Business Cycles* (1939) is the primary source most economists recently writing in the field refer to. Schumpeter himself was strongly influenced by the Russian economist, Kondratieff, who proposed years before that economic growth was marked by long waves, and these waves were connected with the timing of entry into the economy of important new technologies and industries. In more recent years Freeman (1983, 1984; Freeman et al., 1982) and in particular his work with Louça (2001) and Perez (1983, 1985, 2002) have been the most prominent writers on the general subject.

---

[2] Robert Gordon (2016) has provided an excellent description of many of these developments.

As economists grew interested in the long wave concept, there was considerable argument about whether long waves in fact existed, and if so in what sense (see Silverberg and Lehnert, 1993, 1994; Silverberg and Verspagen, 1995, 2005; and Silverberg, 2007). There is now general agreement that while the pace of growth tends to vary over time, and there are booms and busts, there is no regular timing to these developments. On the other hand, most economists who have studied the matter empirically would agree that the emergence of important new technologies and industries tends to be associated with subsequent rapid economic growth, and that with time the associated booms tend to peter out. This is basically what the Saviotti–Pyka model generates.

The recent writings by Carlota Perez (2014) on long waves has brought to the fore the workings of financial institutions. Her argument is that the way financial systems work causes the instability that is innate in the fact that the introduction of important new technologies and industries is jerky rather than continuous. The emergence of new product classes and firms producing them that seem to promise high profits down the road causes much more entry and speculation than in fact is justified, and leads later to many entrepreneurs and investors going bankrupt. Similarly, the slowing down of progress as an industry matures is associated with much more withdrawing of finance than is appropriate, thus leading to sharper depressions than would be the case if financial markets were not so volatile.

And the recent writings of Perez (1983, 2002) and Freeman (particularly in Freeman and Perez, 1988, and Freeman and Louçã, 2001) have elaborated the argument that new technologies and new industries often require new institutions if they are to be effective. Perez has called the package of a cluster of technologies and the institutions appropriate for their effective development a "techno-economic paradigm," and Freeman clearly has a similar set of ideas.

The role of institutions and institutional change in the economic growth process will be the subject of the next section.

5.5 INSTITUTIONS, INSTITUTIONAL CHANGE, AND THE EVOLUTION OF ECONOMIC STRUCTURES

The belief by economists that a nation's institutions were the primary factor influencing its ability to advance economically goes way back in the history of economic thought. This clearly was the position taken by Adam Smith. But with the rise of neoclassical growth theory, analysis of institutions became at most a background consideration. This also is true of the early evolutionary growth models we discussed in this chapter. But recently institutions and how they evolve has become a top item on the agenda of evolutionary economics.[3]

As we have noted, the term" institution" is used by economists in a variety of ways. Today, following Douglass North (1990), the most common specific definition is that institutions are generally accepted "rules of the game" operative in an arena of economic activity. But North himself, and other economists, have used the term broadly to encompass governing structures more generally that channel economic behavior, deterring certain kinds of actions and supporting other kinds, thus inducing a certain degree of standardization and predictability of action in that domain. Thus how firms are organized and managed, the way financial markets are structured, and the presence or absence of labor unions in a field of activity, would be considered institutional facts of life, influencing what economic actors do in an arena of economic activity. And of utmost importance for economic development, the creation and diffusion of new knowledge in an economy is structured by a set of institutions that support and channel interactions among firms, universities, government agencies and regulatory authorities, and other involved agents. The "innovation system" concept discussed in Chapter 2 is about institutions.

To say something is an institution often carries the connotation that it is durable and hard to change, and scholars who study

---

[3] For a broad analysis, see Nelson and Sampat (2001).

institutions generally assume that characteristic. Economists who conceptualize economic growth as proceeding through a series of economic eras tend to write as if an era is marked by a particular set of institutions that emerge and then persist over the course of that era. This point of view tends to play down the fact that institutions are always evolving; however, a case can be made that the pace of change tends to be slower later in a particular economic era than when the new era is just coming in.

The range of institutions bearing on economic activity at any time, molding how work is done and the nature and distribution of economic benefits, is enormous and varied. As we highlighted at the start of this chapter, over the past two centuries there have been extraordinary changes in the way the economy is structured and operates, and in the ways people obtain their livelihood, and live their lives. These changes have both induced and been supported by institutional changes. But while in many cases well described by historians, these developments have received only modest explicit analysis from modern economists, evolutionary or otherwise.

As we noted earlier, one exception is the attention evolutionary economists have been paying to innovation systems. And in more recent years, the arguments by Carlota Perez and Christopher Freeman, to which we briefly referred at the close of the last section, that the key technologies and industries driving economic development in different eras need different sets of institutions to be effective, have received increasing attention. We turn now to a number of empirical cases that support that argument. While evolutionary economists have largely drawn on the research of other scholars for their empirical descriptions of how particular new technologies induced the development of new institutions, we believe that those descriptions clearly show evolutionary processes at work.[4]

Our first example is Alfred Chandler's (1962, 1977) description of the rise of mass production during the last quarter of the nineteenth

---

[4] The following discussion follows along the lines of Nelson (2008a).

century first in the United States and then in Europe, which shows dramatically the interaction among the emergence of new technologies, the development of new ways of organizing and managing work, and institutional evolution more broadly. Chandler proposes that the development of several new technologies set the process in motion. The key technologies were those that enabled the railroad and the telegraph, and hence made it possible for firms to market their products over a much larger geographical area, together with the development of machinery that enabled significantly enhanced productivity at large scales of output.

To exploit these enhanced "economies of scale and scope" (Chandler's term) firms had to be much larger than what had been the norm, and larger size raised significant problems for both organization and management. The organization problem was partly solved by the emergence of the modern hierarchically organized company and, later, by the multidivisional firm (sometimes called the M form). We note, with Chandler, that the railroad and telegraph companies themselves pioneered in this organizational evolution.

New modes of business organization were only a start on what was needed. To manage these huge corporations required many more high-level managers than an owner could garner by canvassing family and friends, which had been the usual practice. The notion of professional management came into being, and business schools emerged as the institutional mechanism for training professional managers. The financial needs of the giant companies were beyond what could be met through existing financial institutions, and both modern investment banks and modern stock markets emerged to meet the needs.

All these developments raised complicated issues of corporate, labor, and financial law. Gradually these were worked out. At the same time the market power of the new large firms and their tendency to collude gave rise to new regulatory law and anti-trust.

Another important case in which the emergence of new technological capabilities led to the development of new institutions is that of synthetic dyestuffs, occurring in the latter part of the nineteenth century initially in Germany, and then more widely. Murmann (2003) has recounted the story in considerable detail.

The initiating events here were breakthroughs in understanding and research techniques in science concerned with organic chemistry. As a result of these advances, persons with advanced training in the field had a special capability for creating and developing new synthetic dyes. In order to take advantage of this new capability business firms had to develop the concept and the structure of industrial research laboratories as places where university trained scientists could work with their peers in discovering and developing new products, relatively insulated from the day to day activities of production and marketing going on in the firm. German patent law also was revised to better enable firms to profit from the new dyestuffs they created. And labor law needed revision to deal effectively with the new kind of employment relationships involved.

Also, the German university system had to both expand and reorient its educational programs to train the growing number of student chemists who would find their work in industry. The various German governments provided significant funding to support this development and along the way developed Technical Universities where the engineers of the emerging industries were trained.

The institutional changes set in train by the development in the early twentieth century of automobiles and their rapid expansion of use is another striking example of how a new technology induces institutional change. As was described in Chapter 4, the rapidly growing number of automobiles on the road led to a need for the development of a body of traffic law, and its enforcement soon became one of the major functions of police departments. The building and maintenance of roads became an important duty of government, and a significant budgetary item. In the post World War II era, concern for the safety of those in cars increased, and a body of law, including the requirements that all cars have seat belts as well as meeting other safety standards, came into existence. And more recently, of course, environmental issues have been prominent in generating new regulation of the product and the industry.

A more recent example is the rise of biotechnology. Like the emergence of technology for making synthetic dyestuffs a century earlier, the initiating development here was new scientific knowledge and technique, this time in molecular biology, which appeared to open a new road to pharmaceuticals development. At the start at least, existing pharmaceuticals companies had no internal competences here. Therefore, university researchers, and their students, came to the fore as potential sources of breakthroughs that could be highly profitable for a company that commercialized them.

In the biotech case, particularly in the United States the result was the establishment of a number of new biotech firms staffed by university researchers and their students, with plans to develop new pharmaceuticals and either license the results to established pharmaceutical companies, or themselves to go downstream into the pharmaceuticals business. Several prevailing broad institutional factors enabled and encouraged these developments. One was, in the US at least, a culture at many universities of encouraging faculty entrepreneurship. A second was an established venture capital industry, which quickly came to see the finance of biotech startups as a potentially profitable business.

And several institutional developments, spurred by the emergence of biotech, supported these developments. One was a key legal decision that indicated that outputs of biotech research could be patented, a matter where there had been some doubt. A second was the passage by the US Congress of what came to be called the Bayh–Dole act in 1980, which encouraged universities to take out patents on their research results.

As matters have turned out thus far, not as much in the way of new pharmaceuticals have come out of the biotech revolution as had been anticipated by the optimists. And only a few of the biotech research firms have been profitable. But the case certainly does illustrate the intertwining of the emergence of new technologies (often accompanied by the birth of new industries), and the development of new institutions designed to make them effective, that we have been stressing in this section.

As these different examples show, the emergence and development of new institutions may be the result of private initiative, or new public policies and programs. A number of different actors and mechanisms may be involved, and while these may be formally separate, there often is strong interaction. And we would argue that the processes through which new institutions come into existence and change over time are evolutionary in the sense that, while actions tend to be taken in response to felt needs and opportunities, and often with considerable reflection, what happens over time generally is not predictable in any detail, and generates new challenges inducing new responses deemed appropriate in the light of experience. At the same time, different variants almost always co-exist at any time, sometimes in extant form, and more generally in different perceptions about what is the best way to proceed.

In the cases we have considered thus far, the evolution of institutions clearly was induced by the emergence of new technologies and the birth and expansion of new industries (or a transformation of older ones) linked to them. But also, these new institutional structures clearly influenced the subsequent evolution of those technologies and industries. In turn, these developments often lead to further institutional change.

In some cases institutional developments preceded and to a good extent supported the generation of new technologies and economic structures based on these. In the United States the establishment after World War II of the National Institutes of Health, the National Science Foundation, and the Defense Department's ARPA (Advanced Research Projects Agency), was an important cause of the surge of US R&D in the biomedical sciences and in electronics, and the rapid development of new technologies in those areas.

The emergence of new institutional structures may be associated broadly with the economic development going on, rather than with particular new technologies and industries. The rise of unemployment insurance and social security are cases in point. More generally, in many countries there has been a significant increase over the past half century in the range of goods and services provided or subsidized by government, under the rubric of "the welfare state."

We think it fair to say that, while economists certainly recognize these developments, neither evolutionary economists nor those of more orthodox persuasion have built an understanding of them into their characterization of the nature of the processes involved in long run economic growth. We evolutionary economists have a start on this, oriented by our increasing recognition that long run economic growth should be understood as being driven by the co-evolution of technologies, economic structure, and institutions. But we clearly have a long way to go.

5.6 SEEING ECONOMIC DEVELOPMENT FROM DIFFERENT ANGLES

The perspectives on long run economic development that have been described in the preceding sections are different. All see economic development as an evolutionary process. However, the evolutionary analysis described in Section 5.3 is oriented to explore the relationships between technological advance and the rising capital intensity of production and of labor productivity that have been striking features of economic growth particularly when viewed at a macroeconomic level, while the evolutionary analysis described in Section 5.4 focused on the changing mix of industries and products produced and consumed that also are salient features of the economic development we have experienced. The analysis discussed in Section 5.5 was focused on the changes in economic institutions that has been another striking feature of the economic development process, and how this has been related to the evolution of technologies and economic structure that have occurred.

We would argue that all of these perspectives are valuable, and that a good understanding of economic development as an evolutionary process requires looking at the phenomena from all of these angles.

An obvious question is why not put all of these different perspectives together in a unified, if very complex, but coherent theory? Our response is that to try to do so for a subject as broad and rich as long run economic development leads either to a theory that is too complex to understand, or to a theory so simplified and abstract that it sheds little light on the phenomena one is trying to understand.

We note that, while not recognized as well as it should be, the use of several different perspectives to provide a more complete picture of what is going on is characteristic of how scientists understand many complex phenomena, like earthquakes, hurricanes, the effect of drought on the ecology of a region, global warming. The scientific understanding of what is going on regarding phenomena like these is not in the form of one coherent theory, but rather combines different bodies of knowledge and theory concerned with different aspects of the phenomena. Economists need to recognize that the same is true regarding theorizing about a complex subject like long run economic development.

Appendix to Chapter 5: The Pyka–Saviotti Growth Model

Andreas Pyka and Pier Paolo Saviotti

In this appendix to Chapter 5 we discuss in more detail the multisector model TEVECON, developed by Pyka and Saviotti. In TEVECON long term economic development depends fundamentally on the emergence of new sectors. In the model new sectors are created by radical and pervasive innovations capable of giving rise to large markets. Each new sector is created by a Schumpeterian entrepreneur induced by the expectation of a temporary monopoly. A bandwagon of imitators following the initial successful innovation expands the market and gradually reduces the extent of the temporary monopoly transforming the innovative sector into a part of the Schumpeterian circular flow. For the number of firms in this sector, this means, after a period of massive entries, a consolidation process characterized by firm exits, mergers and acquisitions, and an increase in average firm size follows. The declining profit rates in this industry triggers again entrepreneurial activities and eventually a new industry emerges. Thus, the evolution of past economic activities induces the emergence of new ones. This interaction of intra-sector and of intersector dynamics generates aggregate economic growth from the sectoral level of an economy. The simulation model creates a sequence of industry life cycles in a setting that resembles the principal ideas of Schumpeterian competition.

An important feature of TEVECON is its ability to generate an increasing output variety. The above described life cycle combines intra-industry dynamics transforming an emergent sector into a mature one with the inducement to create new sectors which will renew the potential for a temporary monopoly. With this combination of intra- and inter-industry dynamics TEVECON is both an endogenous growth model and a model with increasing variety.

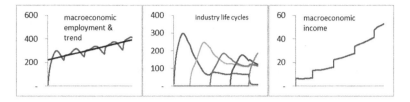

FIGURE A.5.1 Emergence of new industries in a multisector model (TEVECON), aggregate employment, and income growth. Number of firms, aggregate employment, and macroeconomic income are plotted as a function of time.

A detailed formal description of the model can be obtained from Saviotti, Pyka, and Jun (2016). The sectorial dynamics are created by the following central TEVECON equation (1):

$$dN_i^t = k_1 \cdot \underbrace{FA_i^t \cdot AG_i^t}_{entry\ terms} \underbrace{-IC_i^t - MA_i^t}_{exit\ terms} \tag{1}$$

The entry of new firms into an industry depends on financial availability FA_i^t and on the adjustment gap of the industry AG_i^t, which describes the size of the potential market for a new industry. The adjustment gap is widened by the search activities of firms, which focus on increasing efficiency in production as well as product differentiation and quality improvement. The exit of firms increases with increasing intensity of competition IC_i^t, which is composed of both intra-industry and of inter-industry competition. The latter arises when different industrial sectors supply comparable services and is an example of market contestability. Furthermore, failure, as well as mergers and acquisitions, captured in MA_i^t, decrease the number of firms in an industry in maturing industries. The interplay of financial availability, of the exploitation of technological opportunities, of demand as well as of competition and failure gives rise to the behavior of the economic system some aspects of which are shown in Figure A.5.1. In the central part, the number of firms in each sector tends to follow a life cycle increasing first, reaching a maximum, and then declining. Such a life cycle is not programmed in the model but results from the interaction of innovation, demand, and competition. The left part of Figure A.5.1 shows the aggregate employment trend and demonstrates that despite decreasing employment in individual sectors overall employment can have a positive trend as long as new sectors emerge.

In TEVECON search activities can be of two types: sectoral search activities, aimed at improving productive efficiency, product quality, or product differentiation, within a sector, and fundamental search activities which explore more basic knowledge and can increase the probability of emergence of new sectors. The discovery process for transferring this new knowledge into techno-economic opportunities is triggered by entrepreneurs who search for a radical innovation, which is capable of opening up a new industry when they start to feel – in a Schumpeterian fashion – uncomfortable about declining profit opportunities in existing industries.

TEVECON models a complex economic system in which most variables can interact with any other variables. The sequence of industry life cycles generated by the TEVECON model resembles those of real development as e.g. are depicted in Figure A.5.2 for the case of South Korea. The interactivity matters in real economic systems, but makes modeling considerably more difficult. TEVECON allows us to study important forms of co-evolution, such as the one between innovation and demand (e.g., Saviotti and Pyka, 2013a). Innovation could not have affected economic development unless a demand and a market for the corresponding products had been created. Thus, the economic system needed to create both new technologies and the disposable income required to purchase them. Co-evolution creates a positive feedback between demand and innovation, or in general between interacting variables, and can accelerate the emergence of and growth of new industrial sectors.

The TEVECON model offers a flexible framework, which can be applied to a broad set of questions about long term economic development. For example, Saviotti and Pyka (2013b) analyze the long term implications of the co-evolution of demand and innovation

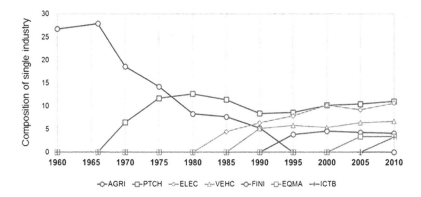

FIGURE A.5.2 Emergence of new industries in South Korea (Yeon, Pyka, and Kim, 2016)

to explore the complex interactions between increasing efficiency, variety, and product differentiation. With the help of the model the conditions for the transition "from necessities to imaginary worlds," which occurred in capitalist economic development starting from the beginning of the twentieth century, are identified. In Saviotti et al. (2016) the model's employment representation is extended to include blue and white collar workers in order to investigate the impact of education on long term economic development. In current work, the co-evolution of income growth and income distribution is analyzed in a similar framework. This analysis reveals that both the curve proposed by Kuznet (1955), involving a first increasing and then decreasing income inequality, and the long term development toward increasing income inequality proposed by Piketty (2014) are observable in an evolutionary multisector model with structural change, coevolving demand, and education systems.

6 Economic Catch-up by Latecomers as an Evolutionary Process

Keun Lee and Franco Malerba

6.1 INTRODUCTION

From the times of Adam Smith, many economists who were interested in economies around the world recognized that there were great differences among national economies in their productivity levels, the standards of living they could support, and their speed and level of economic development more generally. However, research on the factors behind these differences, and on how the economic development of countries significantly behind the economic frontiers could be encouraged, did not emerge as a recognized field of economic study until after World War II. In the early days of this research, most of the attention was directed to two different variables. One was the low levels of physical and human capital in the poor countries, a condition that the emerging neoclassical growth theory proposed was directly related to low levels of productivity and low incomes. The other was aspects of the institutional structures of these countries that seemed to be holding back development.

A striking aspect of the analysis of the sources of underdevelopment contained in the early studies was that the technologies and practices that were used in economies closer to the economic frontier were not viewed as difficult to master, if the capital was in place (Nelson and Pack, 1999). "Technology transfer" itself was regarded as no problem, although some analysts were concerned that the process might be blocked in some instances by holders of intellectual property rights. There was very little attention paid to the processes of learning and capability building that those attempting to employ technologies that were new to them might need to go through.

In recent years, this has changed, especially with the rise of new academic community like Globelics.[1] This chapter will survey the body of research and writing, strongly influenced by the perspective of evolutionary economics (Nelson and Winter, 1982), that has emerged and developed over the past quarter century, concerned with the processes of learning and capability building and catch-up in countries initially far behind the economic and technological frontiers. This chapter defines economic catch-up as a narrowing of a firm's or country's gap vis-à-vis a leading country or firm. It will then focus on the role of the national and sectoral systems in supporting capability building by national firms aiming to catch up. The final emerging message of this chapter will be that successful catch-up cannot be done just by doing cloning but eventually by creating a new path or trajectory different from the forerunning countries or firm although it starts from learning and imitating at the initial stage.

The body of analysis we describe here has been built largely from the pioneering works of Martin Bell, Charles Cooper, Jorge Katz, Linsu Kim, and Sanjaya Lall. These five giants in the analysis of technology and economic development have extensively discussed the role for economic development of learning and appropriate technologies for domestic firms (Bell, 1984; Katz, 1984, 2001; Bell and Pavitt, 1993); science and technology (Cooper, 1973); the variety of technological capabilities and public policy (Lall, 1992, 2000; Lall and Teubal, 1998); and the link between imitation and innovation (Kim, 1997). Their contributions are at the base of this chapter, although we do not quote them continuously in order not to be too repetitive.

Building upon the existing work of the early pioneers, this chapter further extends their ideas by reflecting the more recent literature in the following ways. First, we explicitly adopt the innovation systems perspective, thus extending our analysis beyond the firm level to the level of sectors and nations, such as sectoral and national

[1] The key research theme of this group (www. Globelics.org) is innovation and development, with a specific goal of promoting catching up and inclusive development by the latecomer economies and their firms.

innovation systems, so that we may deal with the concept of not only market but also system failure. Second, we consider the catch-up as a matter of not only learning and building capabilities but also of finding niches and sectoral specialization for latecomers because latecomers are "late entrants" in the already established international division of labor. Third, we propose that successful catch-up in a longer term requires not only gradual enhancement of capabilities but also sometimes radical jump or leapfrogging taking advantage of diverse windows of opportunity opening for late entrants. Fourth, we take a longer perspective in understanding catch-up cycles including the situation in which latecomers take industry leadership from incumbents but then later on latecomers give their leaderships to new latecomers.

After discussing briefly the literature and the theoretical perspectives on catching up (Section 6.2), the chapter proposes that for catching up domestic firms' capability building must go hand in hand with system factors (national and sectoral). The chapter then proceeds to examine these three main levels of analysis. We discuss, first, the role of firms' learning and capabilities as central for the catching up process (Section 6.3). We then move on to the role of country factors and national innovation systems in affecting catch-up, a topic highly discussed in the literature (Section 6.4). Because countries' economic development has been uneven across economic sectors, we make the point that economic development and catch-up proceeds to a considerable extent at the sectoral level, and sectors vary significantly in terms of the conditions required to spur successful catch-up. Viewing economic development in the aggregate obscures this important fact. Therefore Sections 6.5 and 6.6 deal with the dimensions of sectors and technologies. Finally, Section 6.7 briefly discusses successive changes in industry leadership and the catch-up cycles. The perspective advanced in this chapter has been developed in close intellectual contact with the evolutionary writing on technological advance, and on firm capabilities and behavior, that have been described in other chapters in this volume.

6.2 PERSPECTIVES ON ECONOMIC CATCH-UP

We would like to start with the statement that catch-up does not mean just cloning. What is actually achieved by successful catching up invariably diverges in certain ways from practices in the countries serving as benchmark models. In part, this divergence reflects the fact that exact copying is almost impossible, and attempts to replicate at best get viably close. In part it reflects modifications required to tailor practice to local circumstances. The organizational, managerial, and institutional aspects of productive practices often are the most difficult to replicate, and the most in need of adaptation to indigenous conditions, norms, and values. So, each developing country does things in a different way, as a result of an indigenous process of learning and capability building. The development process involves innovation in the basic sense of the term (a break from traditional ways of doing things).

In the process of catching up, the practices brought in are certainly not new to the world. They are new to the country, however, and bringing them in involves considerable risk and requires a lot of trial and error for learning to be effective. Adopting this view of catch-up as a learning process and capability building, the countries involved in the process may follow different trajectories of technological and product advancements and be positioned in different ways along the catching up ladder. However, countries cannot catch up by trying rigidly to emulate and replicate economic practices of the forerunning economies but only by taking a different path from them (Lee, 2013a). This implies that apart from the cases in which countries have reached a clear position of international leadership in some industries and technologies (such as in the case of Korea or Taiwan, and, more recently, China), it is often difficult to rank a country as unequivocally successful or unsuccessful in catching up.

The analysis of catching up has a long intellectual history which goes back to the work of Gerschenkron (1962). In his book, *Economic Backwardness in Historical Perspective*, the author described the economic growth catch-up of continental Europe in the late nineteenth century with the United Kingdom as the forerunning country. Later on, it is with Abramowitz (1986), "Catching-up, forging ahead and falling behind," that the concept of catch-up has become a standard vocabulary in economic development literature. Since then, building on the pioneers in the field that we identified earlier – Martin Bell, Charles Cooper, Jorge Katz, Linsu Kim, and Sanjaya Lall – major advancements have been made by Schumpeterian and innovation economists, such as Fransman (1985), Freeman (1987), Amsden (1989), and Mathews (1996). In parallel, following the evolutionary tradition opened by Nelson and Winter (1982), another set of contributions linked catching up to learning, knowledge, and capabilities.[2] We will examine the main points and results of this literature in the following pages.

A first major distinctive feature of this literature is the emphasis on technological capabilities as enabling factors of catch-up, and the move away from the view that sees capital accumulation as the main driver of catch-up as in the early literature in the 1960s and 1970s. It has to do with recognition that learning is not automatic upon transferring of foreign technologies but is highly uncertain, and learning failure tends to be common in developing countries attempting to "modernize." So only countries that have invested heavily in the formation of skills and R&D, as well as organizational and managerial capabilities, seem to be capable of catching up, while those who did not have fallen farther behind.[3]

Moving away from the traditional development literature that did not pay enough attention to the fact that technological knowledge is a very special input, the new evolutionary and Schumpeterian approach to catch-up indicated that technological knowledge has

---

[2] See for example Verspagen, 1991; Nelson, 1995, 2008d; Nelson and Pack, 1999; Fagerberg and Godinho, 2005; Lee, 2005; Mazzoleni and Nelson, 2007; and Malerba and Nelson, 2011.

[3] In the late 1970s and early 1980s scholars such as Jorge Katz emphasized the importance of acquiring "indigenous" technological capabilities for catch-up.

some basic characteristics of imperfect imitability and tacitness that should be taken as normal than rather exceptional. And this has major implications for technological transfer, as we will discuss later on.

In addition, innovation in the sense above has been considered a key factor for a successful catch-up. However, in a Schumpeterian fashion, innovations do not include only technological ones, but also organizational and institutional innovations.

In order to catch up, learning and capability building by domestic firms has to be complemented by the presence of a working innovation system. Innovations systems are composed by a variety of different actors that affect the innovation and production of domestic firms (suppliers, users and consumers, universities, public research laboratories, government, and financial organizations), by specific institutional settings (education system, norms, regulation, standards, and so on) and by links and interactions among the actors that compose the system. The large literature on innovation systems has discussed the relevance of national systems (Lundvall, 1993; Nelson, 1993), regional systems (Cooke, 2001), and sectoral systems (Malerba, 2002) in affecting innovation and growth. It must be noted that the concept of innovation system can be linked to the discussion of the role of institutions in economic development.

In the next pages, we will concentrate on the topics just mentioned. Here we first want to expand the discussion from learning, capability, and innovation systems to the types of "failures" that may interfere with catch-up, and that are quite different from the neoclassical "market failure."

In the traditional neoclassical approach, "market failure" stems among other things from the fact that knowledge is a public good, and thus R&D subsidies are necessary due to possible under-investment in learning when there are flaws in the capital and risk markets, as well as market failures associated with imperfectly competitive industries and a spillover in learning. From this perspective, the actual amount of R&D is often less than the optimal amount that would prevail without the presence of market failure. Therefore, government subsidies to support R&D are suggested given the externality involved in the production of knowledge. However, in an evolutionary framework, two other failures may be more important in blocking economic development and catch-up: "capability failures" and "system failures" (Lee, 2013b).

In the "market failure" approach the common and hidden presumption is that the firms and other economic actors are already capable of producing and innovating and that the government may simply try to modify the extent of their activities. Thus, in the market failure view the reasons for failures are sought outside the firm: these are the areas where the government's corrective action is suggested (Lee, 2013b). However, the stark reality in developing countries is that economic actors, especially firms, have extremely weak levels of capability. In a number of developing countries, private firms are unable to pursue and conduct in-house R&D, which they consider as an uncertain endeavor with uncertain returns. Thus, the problem is not one of less or more R&D, but of "zero" R&D. Therefore, in contrast to the concept of market failure, in dealing with catch-up this chapter emphasizes the issue of "capability failure" and the need to raise the capabilities of firms, sectors, and nations in broad areas of innovation beyond formal R&D. According to this view, learning failure happens because of a lack of opportunity for effective learning and capability building. Thus, the capability failure view essentially stresses the importance of raising the level of capabilities of the firms by providing learning opportunities, as has been discussed in this volume.

In addition to capability failures, "system failures" may also be present for catching up because a key element – a node in the system – is missing, or has limited competences or has low absorptive capabilities. As a consequence, virtuous cycles related to the workings of dynamic complementarities cannot take place. Rather, agents remain trapped in vicious cycles of low interaction and low learning. Failures may also occur because connections among heterogeneous agents and complementary activities are not present. This may be due to lack of information about the presence of other actors or because of bounded rationality which constrains the actions of agents. In this case an innovation system cannot fully develop, and the overall level of exploration and exploitation of the system may be limited. Finally, failures may occur in the change of existing innovation systems or in the emergence of new ones. Here the policy may intervene because there are mismatches or misalignments among actors within an established system which is undergoing transformation or because a new innovation system may fail to emerge and develop.[4]

In sum, catching up is basically a process of capability building and institutions and innovation system creation. The difference in industrial performance across countries comes basically from the differences in capabilities and system development, including the capability to produce and sell internationally competitive products for a prolonged period of time. Neoclassical economics cannot be "good development economics" because it simply assumes optimization and optimal uses of (existing) resources, with an implicit assumption that all resources are already there and we only have to think about how to utilize them most efficiently with markets that function well. In reality, most of the developing countries do not have to worry about the optimal use of the resources, simply because they do not have them at hand. For us, as far as catch-up is concerned, the more critical issue is how to build up such capabilities and how to develop the innovation systems – including a broad institutional setting – that support firms' catching up.

6.3   CATCHING UP AT THE FIRM LEVEL

This section is concerned with business firms in developing countries, centered around the key question of what are the factors

---

[4] For a discussion of capability failure see Lee (2013b) and for a discussion of evolutionary failures and system failures see Metcalfe (2005), Bergek et al. (2008), Malerba (2009), and Dodgson et al. (2011).

that, at least initially, limit their capabilities relative to those of firms in countries at the frontier, and how firms that catch up are able to do so. Regarding this issue of catching up firms, three recent contributions are relevant.

One concerns capabilities, and how they are accumulated and change over time. Here the concept of absorptive capacity (Cohen and Levinthal, 1989) and of dynamic capabilities (Teece et al., 1997 and Teece, 2012) discussed in Chapter 3 by Constance Helfat occupy a central position. Helfat and Peteraf (2003) introduced the concept of the capability life cycle, which articulates general patterns and paths in the evolution of organizational capabilities over time, and incorporates the creation, development, and maturity of capabilities in a manner that helps to explain the sources of heterogeneity in organizational capabilities. The second concerns the presence of entrepreneurship and the rise to market leadership. Often catching up firms emerge because there are entrepreneurs that launch new companies which enter niche segments of the domestic market, learn, accumulate capabilities, and grow (Malerba et al., 2016). The third concerns business groups (Amsden and Hikono, 1994; Guillén, 2000; Kock and Guillén, 2001) and their diversification as a way to utilize their own unique capability or resources.

The acquisition of initial capabilities by firms in developing countries, in particular in East Asia, has to do with the unique origins of the firms themselves. Having started often in simple labor intensive sectors, these latecomer firms in developing countries faced severe barriers to entry and growth based on first mover advantages in many of the new, capital intensive industries (Chandler, 1990). In the absence of proprietary technology to exploit in related industries, their pattern of diversification tended to be in the area of several key sectors identified by the government's industrial policy (Amsden and Hikino, 1994) up to the early 1990s. Through repeated, often unrelated, diversification, they had been able to learn and accumulate knowledge, which can be called project execution capability. Only during the later period or after the 1997 Asian financial crisis, did some high tech oriented new firms start to emerge as some big businesses went into trouble with the crisis.

In this context, several authors, such as Hobday (1995), Mathews (2002), and Bell and Figueiredo (2012) define "latecomer firms" from emerging economies as "resource-poor late entrants." In other words, lack of resources and late time of entry are the two essential aspects to define the firms from developing countries, unless they are affiliates or subsidiaries of multinational corporations (MNCs). In what follows, we discuss these two aspects in sequence.

First, the aspect of "resource poor" implies that one of the most fundamental differences between firms in the advanced and developing economies is that for the former diverse resources are available within the firm or from other firms, whereas for the latter these critical resources are not easily available either within the firm itself or from other neighboring firms. Thus, the main task for catch-up is not only to learn how to utilize existing resources effectively but also, and more importantly, how to acquire the critically lacking resources and improve their availability over the course of the firm's life. Profits are sought not just to be distributed back to owners of the firm but to be used for further expansion of the firm's resources. To put it another way, accounting profitability might be lower owing to the additional "growth costs" borne by the firms from developing countries, which is actually confirmed by empirical analysis in Lee (2013a) of the Korean versus American firms with the former representing the catching up (latecomer) firms and the latter representing advanced firms. Growth costs would include the costs incurred to increase the capabilities of workers, managers, R&D team, brand power, and so on. While these are of course borne by all firms (including those from advanced economies), they will be heavier for developing countries firms because these firms are faced with more imperfections in the markets and other constraints in the business environment or investment climate (as pointed out by Tybout, 2000; World Bank, 2005; and Lee, 2013a).

The resources that affect firm performance and growth are diverse: they include social capital (network and connections), physical capital, human capital (embodied in workers employed by the firm), managerial capital, R&D capital (capability to conduct R&D independently), and brand capital. The relative importance of human capital and learning by doing has long been pointed out as one of the determinant factors for economic growth in developing economies.

The key resources may be different across firms within a country or across countries. Actually, using the World Bank survey data of eight developing countries in the 2000s – Peru, Indonesia, Bangladesh, Ethiopia, China, Brazil, Tanzania, and India – Lee and Temesgen (2009) indicated that for firms in general, and specifically for those with low levels of capabilities in developing countries, growth is mainly due to relatively basic resources such as physical capital and basic human capital, whereas for the high growth capability firms in developing countries, growth is, in a relative sense, more driven by higher level resources such as managerial capital and R&D capital.

The second aspect of the firms in developing countries is about the time of entry in the global economy. These firms are late entrants in the sense that when they begin their manufacturing activities, the value chain of production is already well established in the market segment they enter and is already occupied by firms from advanced countries or other developing countries (Ernst and Guerrieri, 1998; Sturgeon and Gereffi, 2009). Given their late entry, the latecomer firms had no choice but to inherit some segments left free from the firms from the advanced economies or to start from original equipment manufacturing (OEM) (Amsden, 1989; Hobday, 1995). OEM is a specific form of subcontracting under which a complete, finished product is made to the exact specifications of contracting firms. Some OEM firms evolve into own design manufacturing (ODM) firms, which carry out most of the detailed product design, while the customer firms of ODM companies continue to carry out marketing functions. Meanwhile, the original brand manufacturing (OBM) firms carry out manufacturing, design of new products, R&D for materials, processing of products, and conduct sales and distribution for their own brand. The path from OEM to ODM to OBM has become the standard upgrading process for the latecomer firms.

Another stage-based theory of the latecomer firms is that of Kim (1997), which proposed the three stages of duplicative imitation, creative imitation, and innovation. However, there is really a rare incidence of the latecomer firms reaching the final stage of OBM or innovation, because there are several entry barriers to OBM (Chu, 2009). The transition to OBM status is not possible if a firm stays on the given path of subcontracting or collaboration; rather, the transition is possible only when a firm makes a structural break by adopting its own path creation strategy. But creating one's own path requires innovation capabilities, as exemplified by successful small and medium enterprises (SMEs) from Korea which made the transition to OBM (Lee, Song, and Kwak, 2015). Thus, how to build up innovation capabilities is also a key issue for latecomer firms from a long term dynamic perspective.

This brings us to the issue of firm level knowledge and capabilities in latecomer firms, compared with those in advanced country firms. We can consider several variables able to measure in an approximate way the knowledge base of firms, the nature of such knowledge, and the changes in the underlying technologies. One obvious and extensively used variable refers to patents.

Examining the technological characteristics of the catching up firms represented by the Korean firms, Lee (2013a, Ch. 5) finds that they are inferior to US firms in many aspect, such as the number of patent counts, quality, originality, self-citation ratio (high in the US), and diversity (more diverse in the scope of patenting in the US firms), except that Korean firms tend to have more patents with shorter cycle times, compared to US firms (this issue of cycle time will be discussed further in Section 6.6).[5] We find the self-citation a useful measure of firm level technological capabilities. Higher self-citation means that US firms rely relatively more on their own pool of knowledge accumulated over time, which can be treated as an attribute of advanced firms. Firm level regressions show that higher self-citations are statistically significant in explaining firm value of the US firms, whereas the level of self-citations is too low to be significant in the Korean firms where more patents with short cycle times are correlated with higher profitability. Given that firm growth is significantly related to investment ratio in the Korean firms, the interpretation is that the catching up firms pursued growth by borrowing and investing more, while specializing into short cycle technology based sectors was a way to seek a minimum level of profitability (Lee, 2013a, Ch. 5).

The last part of this section is dedicated to a discussion of some limitations of the resource based theory of the firm growth in the context of catching up. As is well known, one important criticism of the resource based theory of firm growth (Penrose, 1995) is that many modern firms tend to rely on outsourcing rather than trying to do everything themselves. International networking and integration are particularly important for firms in developing countries, as many of the critical resources are not available within the national territories. One of the key factors of growth of Korean firms is getting connected to reliable international and domestic firms' pool of knowledge. In contrast, integration of several firms (or plants) within the business groups or conglomerates is an effort to cope with scarcity of resources by sharing of resources within a given territory (Amsden, 1989; Chang and Hong, 2000). One may consider diverse networking or integration strategies, such as networking with foreign buyer firms in exporting arrangement (export orientation), being a joint venture partner (FDI) of foreign firms, being integrated as a part of conglomerates, doing

---

[5] Cycle time of technologies is measured by the mean citation lags, and short cycle times means that the old technologies tend to be soon outdated.

subcontracting with other big firms, or being in connection with the government by selling to state owned enterprises. As forms of intra-national networking, integration within the business groups has received more attention in the literature.

The advantages of being a member firm of the conglomerates or business groups have been discussed in the context of market failure (Leff, 1978; Goto, 1982) or "institutional voids" (Khanna and Palepu, 1997, 2000). The basic argument is that since many of the institutions that support business activities are absent in many parts of the world, the business groups emerge to fill the institu-tional voids. For example, in capital markets, without access to information, investors refrain from putting money into unfamiliar ventures. In such context, established and diversified groups have superior access to capital markets. In labor markets, given the lack of well trained business people and educational facilities in devel-oping countries, the groups can create value by developing promising managers within the group, and can spread the fixed costs of profes-sional development over the businesses in the group. From the view of the resource based view, an obvious advantage of conglomerates is sharing and coordinating the use of scarce resources, whose benefits has been confirmed in the case of the Korean chaebols (Chang and Hong, 2000; Choo et al., 2009).

In a similar context, the limitations of strategies of attracting FDI have also been pointed out. Whereas FDI may benefit local firms and economy by bringing in new knowledge through imitation and learning (Findlay, 1978; Blomström, 1986), introducing more competition in local markets, facilitating human capital mobility (Fosfuri, Motta, and Rønde, 2001), and/or promoting vertical linkages (Rodriguez-Clare, 1996), these positive effects of FDI are not well confirmed by the empirical analysis (Gorg and Greenaway, 2003). For example, Aitken and Harrison (1999) were not able to establish any positive linkage of technology spillover from MNCs to local firms in Venezuela in the 1980s. In the case of FDI firms owned by foreigners, transfer of knowledge might be limited or learning is not really automatic. Actually, FDI contributes to economic growth only when a sufficient absorptive capacity is available in the host country (Borensztein, Gregorio, and Lee, 1998).

While the literature is more divided with regard to the impact of FDI arrangements it seems less divided with regard to the benefits of exporting. Exporting can help resource scarce firms to the extent that exporting is a way to learn from foreign buyers in the forms of blueprint, designs, quality control, and technical advice (Rhee et al., 1984; Dahlman, Westphal, and Kim, 1985). In general, export orientation and conglomeration are found, by Lee and Temesgen (2009), to be the most important strategies for firm growth, compared to other networking or integration strategies (including FDI strategy, subcontracting, and connection with government).

So, it is possible to sum up the preceding discussion as follows. First, firms from countries with different stages of economic development focus on different resources for firm growth. At an earlier stage, they focus on building physical and human capital based on primary and secondary levels of education. As their economy develops and they want to upgrade their production process, a gradual shift is needed to upgrade managerial and R&D capabilities/resources. Second, catching up firms may well try to be export oriented as exporting serves them as a window of opportunity to learn from buyers and worldwide competition and discipline. However, given the significant correlation between export orientation and FDI, we can say that a specific type of FDI would work better when it is oriented toward production for exports rather than for local markets (as in the case of China during the 1980s and 1990s). This observation on the role of the FDI does not mean that the latecomer countries should not "invite" foreign firms. Many Korean chaebols, including Samsung Electronics' affiliates, used to have an FDI or OEM relation with MNCs.

Finally, once arrived at the higher stage of technological development, the catching up firms might want to form international alliances or even joint ventures to cope with the increasingly fierce global competition and to keep ahead. However, the alliance or networking strategy is possible and can work only after the latecomer firms have become able to command a certain level of technological capability, which affects their bargaining positions. Nowadays we are witnessing the cases of the latecomer firms taking over the industry leadership, as analyzed in Lee and Malerba (2016). This is possible as the latecomer firms reach a higher level of technological capabilities by taking advantage of some exogenous windows of opportunity. We will turn to this issue in the last section.

6.4 CATCHING UP AT THE COUNTRY LEVEL

In this section, we consider research and writing by evolutionary economists on this broader national picture, and in particular their development of the concept of a national innovation system.

Nelson and Pack (1999) distinguish between what they call an "accumulation" and an "assimilation" theory of development using the example of Korea and Taiwan. In the former, the problem of development tends to be the issue of higher or lower rates of physical investment leading to higher or lower capital–labor ratios. In the latter, development is more than simple capital accumulation: rather it is linked to innovation and learning to master technologies and other practices that are new to the country. So, in the assimilation theory (which is in the spirit of this chapter) development is basically an evolutionary process: learning and innovation which often starts with technology transfer from abroad and involves a high degree of uncertainty. In this framework, countries' success or failure in learning and innovation depends upon diverse factors: an increasing level of formal education; a growing supply of well trained technical people; the existence of entrepreneurial firms; and an appropriate policy regime from the government.

However, learning and capability building take place in specific institutional settings (broadly defined) which can be related to national innovation systems (NIS). As mentioned in Chapter 2, NIS are composed of a broad set of actors and institutions (Nelson, 1993) and by the interaction and relationships among all these actors

(Lundvall, 1992) that shape catch-up. In evolutionary terms, NIS affect the production, diffusion, and use of new and economically useful knowledge. Several actors are major components of a NIS and affect the generation of knowledge, innovation, and catch-up. Universities and public research organizations may play a key role in catching up because they do basic research and applied research and supply advanced human capital (Mazzoleni and Nelson, 2006). Financial organizations (such as banks, stock markets, as well as internal funding) are major sources of support for technology diffusion, innovation, and catching up. Vertical linkages with suppliers and users may provide catching up firms with inputs and the relevant knowledge and information for production and innovation (Lundvall, 1988; Von Hippel, 1988). The broader institutional setting is also quite relevant. The educational system proves to be a key element in stimulating learning and creating advanced human capital (Nelson, 1993). Public policy plays a major role in catching up by actively supporting basic research, the educational system, firms' industrial R&D, specific sectors, entrepreneurship, and regulation (Kim, 1997; Amsden and Chu, 2003; Bretnitz, 2007; Cimoli, Primi, and Rovira, 2011).

The book by Freeman (1987) presents an excellent example of the working of a national system in terms of firms, links, and relationships among actors and institutions in the catching up of Japan during the 1980s. Here the government and public policy have played a major role in diffusing knowledge and supporting and directing the efforts of private firms in a systemic and forward looking way.

A quantitative analysis of the role of technological capabilities and institutions in affecting catch-up has been conducted by Fagerberg, Srholec, and Knell (2007), Fagerberg and Srholec (2008), and Fagerberg, Srholec, and Verspagen, 2010). Examining the growth of more than a hundred countries, they find that technological capabilities and national systems do affect the growth of GDP per capita, while unit labor cost and openness of the economy play a relatively minor role. Here national innovation systems and institutions are considered in a broad way in terms of higher education, the legal system, norms, technological cooperation, public policy, and so on.

More recent discussion on the role of national innovation systems, institutions, and catch-up can be found in Arocena and Sutz (2000), Cimoli et al. (2011), Malerba and Nelson (2012), Muchie and Baskaran (2013), and Lundvall (2016). Three major points emerge from these works centered on the experience of Latin American, African, and Asian countries: institutions defined in a broad way play a major role in the process of catching up; an active public policy rather than hands off policy is necessary for growth and development; and the features and structure of national systems as they have emerged over time differ extensively across countries so that "one type does not fit all" when they are linked to catch-up.

Two interesting findings regarding knowledge and catch-up can be added to the previous discussion. The first finding regards the role of the creation and diffusion of indigenous knowledge versus a reliance on foreign knowledge (Lundvall, 2014). Knowledge localization measures how much knowledge is created domestically. According to Lee (2013a), Korea and Taiwan showed a low degree of localization in knowledge creation in the early 1980s, which was similar to that of other middle income countries, but much lower than that of advanced countries. However, the degree has increased rapidly since the mid-1980s, and reached the level of the average advanced country by the late 1990s, indicating a significant catch-up in this regard.

The second finding regards the type of knowledge most needed for catch-up. An interesting difference between the East Asian and the Latin America experience is that it is not scientific knowledge but technological knowledge that matters most for economic growth, and that generating scientific knowledge does not automatically lead to the generation of technological knowledge. Kim and Lee (2015) have conducted country panel econometric analysis with a focus on the different roles of scientific and technological knowledge on economic growth and on the knowledge production functions.

They link technological knowledge to corporate R&D efforts, which is more lacking in Latin American countries compared to East Asia. In Korea and Taiwan, policy makers preferred technology policy to science policy by putting emphasis on technological development in private industrial sectors. In contrast, based on the belief that science is an important input for industrial technology, Latin America placed an emphasis on science (which can be measured by scientific articles) rather than on technology (which can be measured by corporate patents). Such a policy choice isolated academia from the private sector and its technological activities. In Latin America, the science community and academia tended not to reflect industrial needs and was oriented toward more academic research. Without this interaction, both sectors began to lag behind. In contrast, domestic firms in East Asia have invested in their own in-house R&D activities after adapting and assimilating the foreign technologies. In turn, the increasing demand to academia for research in applied science from the industrial sectors enabled an effective interaction between university and industry.

Up to now we have not mentioned another major factor that has been found to affect catch-up at the country level: local demand. The specificity of local demand with respect to global demand in terms of income per capita, consumer preferences, local industrial requirements, and public procurement, may provide a test bed for local firms and shelter them from international competition long enough to allow them to survive and then grow. When such demand is also large, as was the case in China, India, and Brazil, it provides the economies of scale needed to set off virtuous cycles of learning, capability building, and growth (Malerba, Mani, and Adams, 2017). One type of large local demand refers to price sensitive, low end markets, as in the case of auto in China or India or pharmaceuticals in India (Guo, 2017; Mani, 2017). For these markets, local firms may provide low price solutions to low end market segments different from the ones in more advanced economies. Given the size of the population, especially in countries such as China and India, these markets also offered local firms the possibility to benefit from economies of scale in production and marketing and, if successful, to grow. A second type of demand is related to specific groups of users that require customized products tailored to their specific needs, such as in software in large countries such as Brazil (Araujo, 2017). While these markets were smaller than the undifferentiated markets for low end products, they were still large enough to provide local firms with the volumes necessary to reach competitive economies of scale in their operations (Malerba et al., 2017).

Most of the previous analysis on catch-up refers to emerging countries catching up in manufacturing and services. It has not addressed catch-up through the use and transformation of natural resources. The "resource curse" hypothesis proposed by Sachs and Warner (1995) has been discussed among others by Katz (2006), Iizuka and Soete (2011), and Lundvall (2016). Most of these authors have pointed out that, in contrast with the North European countries which developed a competitive and diversified economy from a strong presence of natural resource, the reason of failure to catch up in several developing countries in Latin America or Africa is due to the fact that these countries had limited investments in knowledge and weak institutions that did not support processes of learning, upgrading, and diversification in related manufacturing and services which could have led these countries to move away from operating in purely isolated enclaves (Lundvall, 2016). The case of Chilean salmon farming discussed by Iizuka and Katz (2011) indicates that countries that have natural resource industries need to develop a set of appropriate institutions that can monitor and manage the exploitation of the common pool of resources under conditions of long term sustainability and that can maintain a close and effective interaction with the natural resource industries in order to foster environmental sustainability.

Recently the concept of the middle income trap has also come to the forefront in the development research community (World Bank, 2010). Such a trap is described as the success of developing countries to grow and attain middle income status, but the failure of these countries to achieve high income status as real growth stagnates. Examples of countries that have suffered from the middle income trap are Brazil and Argentina, whose growth stalled during the 1980s and the 1990s. Other similar cases are Indonesia and Thailand. There seems to be only a very small number of former middle income economies that moved beyond the middle income status to join the advanced country club. Examples of these include Korea and Taiwan, whose per capita income tripled in the 1980s and the 1990s after staying at par with those of Latin American countries in the early 1980s. This growth divergence justifies a growth diagnostic in order to identify the binding constraints for growth in each country. Whereas bottlenecks or binding constraints may be different not only for each country but also for different groups of countries (Rodrik, 2006; Hausmann, Rodrik, and Velasco, 2008), it seems that innovation capabilities are the critically binding factor in the stage of middle income countries (as verified by Lee and Kim, 2009). In other words, middle income traps tend to occur because middle income countries get caught between low wage manufacturers and high wage innovators: their wage rates are too high to compete with low wage exporters and their level of technological capability is too low to enable them to compete with advanced countries (Yusuf and Nabeshima, 2009; World Bank, 2010, 2012).

6.5   CATCHING UP AND SECTORS

For a full understanding of catch-up in an evolutionary framework, we need a final level of analysis: the sectoral one. Catching up takes place in specific economic sectors, that often drive the growth of the whole economy of a developing country. India, for example, has been quite successful in catching up in pharmaceuticals and not successful in catching up in telecom equipment. Brazil has been successful in catching up in agro-food and less so in pharmaceuticals. China is moving quickly up the ladder in auto and telecommunications and more slowly in semiconductors (Lee, Gao, and Li, 2017). In an

evolutionary and system perspective, the notion of a sectoral innovation system is useful for illuminating the firms and system factors
affecting the catch-up process in different industries. A sectoral
system framework considers the sector as a system, and focuses
on the knowledge underpinning innovation and production, firms'
learning and capabilities, the other non-firm actors involved in innovation and production, and the institutions – broadly defined – that
characterize a sector (see Malerba, 2002, 2004). There is ample evidence that the sectoral system dimension proves quite important in
the explanation of the differences in catching up processes among
countries (Mowery and Nelson, 1999; Malerba, 2004; Malerba and
Mani, 2009; Malerba and Nelson, 2012; Lee, 2013a).

A broad comparison across industries of the factors affecting
catch-up point to some major similarities across sectoral systems.
One common factor refers to firms' learning and capability building,
and another to firms' access to foreign know-how (as already discussed
in Section 6.4 and as illustrated also by the firms' cases studies in
Malerba et al., 2017). A third factor relates to the supply of skilled
human capital (already discussed in Section 6.3), which has proven
particularly relevant in sectors highly dependent on skilled labor and
on high tech entrepreneurship.

Empirical research on several industries however has identified
major cross industry differences in the sectoral system factors that
led to catch-up.

A first difference is the type of knowledge base underpinning
innovation in the sectoral system. In some sectors innovation is
based on advances in technologies with a rather insignificant link
with advancements in science (the machinery sector is an example).
Of course, in almost all technologies engineers working to advance
them need to be knowledgeable in certain fields of science but in these
sectors the science they need to know is a somewhat established one.
On the other hand, in other sectors understanding and advancing scientific knowledge is very important for catching up. Pharmaceuticals
and biotechnology are cases in point. And as will be discussed below,

this difference among these two types of sectors implies also a different role of universities.

A second difference relates to industry structure. In Schumpeter Mark I type sectors, with small firms and high entry rates of new firms (Nelson and Winter, 1982; Malerba and Orsenigo, 1996), such as software and agro-food, new firms played a major role in the catching up process (Gu et al., 2012; Niosi, Athreye, and Tschang, 2012). In Schumpeter Mark II sectors, with large firms and high industrial concentration, such as auto and telecom, large firms have been key drivers of the catch-up process (Lee, Mani, and Mu, 2012). At the very general evolutionary level this difference depends to a large extent on the working of different technological regimes (in terms of technological opportunity, cumulativeness, and appropriability conditions) and demand regimes (in term of homogeneous or segmented demand) (Malerba et al., 2016).

Also, the role of multinationals has differed across sectors. In those sectors with a vertical division of labor and knowledge specialization – such as software, semiconductors, and agro-food – multinationals have governed the innovation and production processes within global value chains. In this case the catch-up process has started from the local production for global value chains and for the international outsourcing of the leading firms in advanced countries (as in the case of software firms in India and the Philippines; Chinese, Taiwanese, and Malaysian semiconductor firms; and most of the coffee producers in Costa Rica) and then has moved to the building of technological and marketing capabilities, leading to an upgrading and to moving up along the value chain (Gereffi, 2005; Ernst, 2002; Lee, 2005; Morrison, Pietrobelli, and Rabellotti, 2008; Gu et al., 2012; Niosi et al., 2012; Rasiah et al., 2012). As discussed above in the section on catching up at the firm level, the path from OEM to ODM to OBM has been a common upgrading process for catching up firms. In other sectors, MNCs have been active within a developing country but the evidence on catch-up is mixed. In some industries, such as pharmaceuticals, local branches of multinationals did not have a positive effect on knowledge diffusion and mainly produced for the global market or for their headquarters (Ramani and Guennif, 2012). In other industries, the establishment of joint ventures and alliances with a local subsidiary was a key tool for domestic firms to learn and accumulate capabilities, as in the case of Chinese automobile producers. As discussed previously, the alliance or networking strategy can be effective if the latecomer firms have a certain level of technological capabilities.

The third major difference refers to local clusters and to local vertical links between users or suppliers and producers. In some industries, such as software in India or semiconductors and computers in Taiwan, local clusters have triggered intense formal and informal interactions, knowledge sharing, and an intense division of labor (Niosi et al., 2012; Rasiah et al., 2012). In other industries, global value chains have allowed emerging countries to specialize in specific stages of production and then upgrade along the value chain, as in various segments of ICT and in pharmaceuticals (Ernst, 2002; Gereffi, Humphrey, and Sturgeon, 2005; Giuliani et al., 2005; Lee, 2005). What is interesting is the role of vertical links between local users and local producers, or between local producers and local suppliers. These vertical links proved quite effective for catching up in the case of the auto industry because they led to the rise and growth of an advanced domestic industry in auto parts. In other sectors, such as software, strong links with advanced international suppliers have provided new inputs and complementary knowledge to domestic firms and have enabled them to learn and develop capabilities (as in the case of Taiwan, China, and Malaysia – Niosi et al., 2012 and Rasiah et al., 2012). It must be noted that the presence of an upstream and a downstream local industry does not necessarily imply strong vertical links that may then drive catch-up.

In sectors where competition is intense and takes place on a world scale, domestic firms cannot be a source of large demand for local suppliers if these local suppliers are not advanced technologically. Because these domestic firms have to compete globally, and require advanced machinery and components to keep their capabilities and performance at the frontier, they demand state-of-the-art inputs and machinery that local suppliers cannot provide. When this happens, local links between downstream domestic producers and local suppliers cannot develop, and therefore local learning cannot take off. Thus, the presence of a strong and competitive downstream domestic industry may not always be a sufficient condition to generate an equally strong upstream local industry. Kim and Lee (2009) discuss this phenomenon in the Korean machine tool industries, and Lee et al. (2017) and Yu et al. (2017) examine the divergent dynamics of the telecommunication and semiconductor industries in China.

Finally, major differences across industries in the role and effects on catching up can be found also in the case of another component of the sectoral system – universities and public research centers – due, as mentioned above, to the type of knowledge needed for innovation in an industry. Because in some sectors science is very important for innovation while in others advancements in technologies, rather than science, are relevant, the role of universities, public research laboratories, or organizations aimed at diffusion of new technologies differ extensively across sectors. For example, in agriculture in China, Korea, and Taiwan, research and experimental stations had a pragmatic orientation and a focus on user needs, diffusing new information and new techniques to a large population of farmers and increasing their knowledge and capabilities (Hayami and Ruttan, 1985; Gu et al., 2012). In telecommunications, public research laboratories did advanced research and collaborated extensively in R&D with large domestic firms, positively affecting their research capabilities, as in the case of Korea and Taiwan (Mazzoleni and Nelson, 2006; Lee et al., 2012). On the contrary, in pharmaceuticals, both local and international universities played a major role in the rise of a domestic industry by conducting scientific research and doing joint projects with domestic companies, as in the case of India (Ramani and Guennif, 2012).

Finally, institutions broadly defined and specific industrial policy have differed across industries in the type and effects of catching up, depending on the characteristics of the sectoral system. In sectors where scale is relevant – such as telecommunication equipment – and where firms must carry out large R&D projects and technical change is cumulative and incremental, public policy has been designed to support the R&D of domestic firms, favor R&D consortia, use public research organizations, and promote product standardization as a tool for advancing the general knowledge and the capabilities of domestic firms, as in the case of Korea and China (Lee et al., 2012). Different is the case of sectors in which the knowledge base depends upon skilled individuals and new firms drive development and growth – such as software. Here governments have promoted education and the formation of advanced human capital, supported and funded the R&D of new and small enterprises, introduced favorable corporate tax rates, and established incentives to attract FDI (Niosi et al., 2012). On the contrary, in sectors in which empirical knowledge is important for production and the population of actors is quite atomistic and diffused – as in several crops of the agro-food sector – the development of a technological and scientific infrastructure, private-public partnerships in experimentation, regulation as well as the diffusion of market institutions proved quite successful, as in the case of Brazil, China, and Costa Rica (Gu et al., 2012). Finally, in sectors in which the knowledge base is related to science and research has a major scientific content (as in pharmaceuticals) the support of universities and university research was quite important for catching up, as in the case of India (Rasiah et al., 2012).

One final note regards the relationship between national systems (as discussed in Section 6.4) and sectoral systems in affecting catching up. This interplay is another explanation of why some sectors may emerge and catch up while others do not. National systems and institutional frameworks indeed affect positively the development and growth of those sectors whose dimensions correspond and fit the national ones. But the relationship may go also the other way. Sectoral actors or institutions which are effective in a specific sectoral system are often successfully replicated and diffused by public policies in another sector if the two sectoral systems have similar features, as in the case of Indian policies for university research, advanced human capital formation, and entry of new firms that from software were later adopted in pharmaceuticals. Similar is the case of Korean policies of access to foreign knowledge through licenses, support for national companies, and initial protection for the home market: these policies initially established in automobiles were later adopted also in telecommunications and semiconductors. However, if the characteristics of the sectoral system of two industries are quite different, any attempt to replicate actors or institutions of one sectoral system into the other one may be doomed to failure. Taiwan's attempt to replicate its success in ICT clusters by applying similar policies and institutions to biotechnology was a failure, because the sectoral system in biotechnology substantially differs from the one in ICT. What was required was a set of appropriate institutions and policies adapted to the innovation system that characterizes biotechnology (Dodgson et al., 2008).

6.6   CATCHING UP, SECTORAL SPECIALIZATION, AND LEAPFROGGING

The competitiveness in high tech sectors achieved by a number of firms based in Korea and Taiwan, and more recently China – countries that half a century ago were far behind the economic frontier – has impressed many observers, and has provided a goal that many other developing countries are trying to achieve. However, as discussed in the previous pages, the success of these firms in high tech sectors is the result of a long period of capability building by their home country followed by the ability to continue to be innovative as the technology changes.

As stated in the Introduction to this chapter, we consider catch-up as a matter not only of learning and capability building but also of finding niches and sectoral specialization. Latecomers are "late entrants" in the already established international division of labor: as they build more or new capabilities over time, latecomers may enter new and different sectors.

Given that many developing countries initially face labor (or natural resource) abundance, they have been advised to specialize in labor (or resource) intensive sectors. Thus capital–labor ratio becomes a key variable in sectoral specialization. In economies that are far behind the frontier of technological know-how and skills, and where labor is abundant and capital is scarce, market forces as well as traditions will generally support sectors that are labor intensive, and do not require high levels of technological or business sophistication to be effective (Kuznets, 1966). And there is very little that active government policies can do about this, at least in the short and medium run. Most of the previous discussion in this chapter has been about the recognition by economists that successful economic development beyond this low level of skills and technological know-how requires the development of stronger competences by firms and the presence of institutions supporting them.

Historical experience shows that, as these capabilities develop, the next stages of economic development occur as resources flow into sectors where capital intensity and labor productivity are higher. These industries may require a certain amount of technological know-how, skills, and managerial sophistication. Therefore the choice among different capital intensive sectors may emerge as a difficult issue of decision making. In other words, the simple criterion of capital–labor ratio no longer works because there are so many capital intensive sectors. The history shows that in the past latecomers have chosen the sectors in which technology is relatively constant or already mature and thus with a higher possibility of technology transfer available at low costs (see Viner, 1958, and Lin, 2012a, 2012b). For developing countries that have built up a reasonably strong capability for training labor, and have at least a cadre of reasonably sophisticated business leaders, a satisfactory competitive capability in sectors like these is within reach and has low entry barriers. Lower wages than those in high income countries will help. And the fact that technology is usually mature or not changing rapidly means that, once some competitiveness is achieved, the problems of keeping up with the technological advances that are occurring may be readily manageable. On the other hand, while getting into these industries is part of the way countries behind the frontiers climb the economic ladder, to climb even higher requires more.

High tech sectors, experiencing rapid economic advance, then become the next targets for developing countries that have built up relatively high levels of capabilities, along the lines we discussed earlier. South Korea and Taiwan reached this stage by the mid-1980s, and they had to upgrade their industrial structure to match that of the so called high tech sectors. The problem with moving into these sectors is that in order to do so it gets indigenous firms into direct competition with firms in countries at the technological frontier, who have much greater experience in the field. In these sectors lower wage rates do not bring much of a competitive advantage, and continuing international competitiveness is strongly tied to being able to stay up with other firms even as technology changes rapidly.

Analyses of the technological dynamics in the high tech sectors where Korean and Taiwanese firms have done well call attention to the fact that sectors differ in the extent to which the new technologies that are emerging require know-how and skills similar to those they are superseding, as contrasted with requiring different kinds of know-how and skills. The latter, which include many of the "information" technologies, have been called "short cycle" technologies, with the term referring to the fact that the particular knowledge and competences needed tend to change periodically in sectors associated with such technologies. Keun Lee and his colleagues (Park and Lee, 2006; Lee, 2013a) have argued that where firms from developing countries have achieved world class competence, the technologies usually are "short cycle," and therefore the advantages that firms at the frontier countries have because of their longer experience in the industry does not help them much when the frontier technology changes. One situation that makes technologies short cycled is the arrival of "competence destroying" innovations, proposed by Tushman and Anderson (1986).

The argument that firms based in a "catching up" country may do well in industries where technological advances tend to diminish the value of experience fits well with the concept of leapfrogging and windows of opportunity (Perez and Soete, 1988), in which the emerging generations of technologies, in particular competence destroying innovations, allow catching up countries to have a head start.[6] In the competition within a new techno-economic paradigm, both incumbents and latecomers (with a certain level of capabilities) start from the same starting line, but incumbents often stick with their existing technologies from which they derive their supremacy. Such leapfrogging is similar to the "long jumps" (Hidalgo et al., 2007) that economies must perform to shift themselves to those product spaces located far away from their current position and thus achieve subsequent structural transformation.

When combined with the latent comparative advantage concept of Lin (2012b), the idea of sectoral specialization along the cycle time of technologies may provide a comprehensive policy framework for the economic growth of developing countries. At lower middle income stage, latecomers target the mature industries (with easy technology transfer). After this step, developing countries can enter the next step, which means sectors with a shorter cycle technology (low entry barriers), or can leapfrog into new or emerging sectors. In other words, a sustainable catching up growth not only requires entering mature or neighboring industries (which are still new to the latecomers) but also leapfrogging into short cycle industries or into emerging industries that are new to both advanced and

---

[6] Replacing analogue technologies with digital ones provided a window of opportunity for some latecomers, especially South Korea and Taiwan. The digitalization of products and production processes entails fewer disadvantages for latecomers because the functions and quality of these products are determined by electronic chips rather than by the skills of engineers, who are more critical in analogue products.

developing countries. Without leapfrogging, they might be stuck in the middle income. The experience of East Asian "tigers" is close to this prescription.

The technological development of the Asian tigers over the last three decades (Lee, 2013a) reflects the increasing specialization of their industries into short cycle technologies. In the 1950s and 1960s, they specialized in labor intensive (low value added long cycle technology) industries, such as apparel or shoe industries. The economy then moved into the short or medium cycle sectors of low end consumer electronics and automobile assemblies in the 1970s and 1980s, to the shorter cycle sectors of telecommunication equipment in the late 1980s, and to memory chips, cellphones, and digital televisions in the 1990s. Their industries kept moving to shorter cycle technologies to achieve technological diversification.

The above discussion indicates the possibility of three alternative strategies for catching up: low, high, and middle road. The low road refers to the situation of low or lower middle income countries specializing in low value added activities or low end goods in longer technological cycle fields. This condition can be regarded as a choice that depends on their comparative advantage dictated by initial resource endowments. Thus, along this road, countries tend to achieve a certain degree of economic growth, which may be the phenomenon named growth spurt by Hausmann, Pritchett, and Rodrik (2005) and Jones and Olken (2008). This phenomenon was evident in Korea and Taiwan in the 1960s and 1970s, in China in the early 1980s, and in today's lower income economies, such as Bangladesh or Sri Lanka. However, these countries would find it difficult to move beyond the position they are in unless they are able to initiate upgrading and establish a different specialization. The high road is a strategy that aims to replicate directly the knowledge base of high income countries by specializing in hard science or highly original technologies. Several relatively advanced Latin American countries, such as Brazil and Argentina, seem to have been close to this road as they boasted a somewhat advanced level of academic research in science. But these economies have not been effective in becoming competitive in science based industries because their academic research has been poorly linked to the relevant business sectors (Kim and Lee, 2015).

The middle road is close to the path taken by the four Asian tigers in East Asia. However, not every East Asian economy has been as successful as Taiwan or Korea. For instance, consider several second tier catching up countries in East Asia, such as Malaysia and Thailand, that moved into short cycle time technologies like IT, but they have not made decisive success in upgrading (Rasiah, 2006). These countries are under the so called middle income country trap (Yusuf and Nabeshima, 2009), because they are still muddling through the middle road. Thus, although short cycles provide opportunity for catch-up for those who command a certain degree of technological capabilities, frequent changes in technologies may serve as an additional barrier for countries who do not have the appropriate level of absorptive and innovation capabilities as frequent changes interfere with learning and lead to the truncation of learning process, as discussed in Chapter 4 of Lee (2013a) in the comparison between the Asian and the Latin American economies. In this sense, the middle road is not a sufficient condition for eventual upgrading but something close to a necessary condition.

6.7 CATCHING UP IN THE LONG TERM EVOLUTION OF FIRMS, SECTORS, AND COUNTRIES

We conclude this chapter by considering the long run aspect of the processes involved in catch-up. If we do that, several changes in industrial leadership from an incumbent to a latecomer country are often observed. For example, in the steel industry, in the first half of the twentieth century, US firms dominated the production of steel, but were soon replaced by Japanese companies that emerged in the 1970s. Since the 1980s, however, Japanese firms have been challenged by Korean firms. More recently, Chinese firms have rapidly emerged since the early 2000s, supported by soaring domestic steel demand (Yonekura, 1994; Lee and Ki, 2017). The shipbuilding industry also experienced similar changes in industrial leadership. American firms were in the forefront of shipbuilding during World War II, but British firms caught up in the 1950s. From the 1960s to the mid-1990s, Japanese shipbuilders dominated this industry, and thereafter, Korean companies displaced Japanese firms as leaders (Lim, Kim, and Lee, 2017). Such successive shifts in leadership are also evident in the history of automobile industry, from Germany to the US, Japan, and possibly to Korea or China. Finally, in the mobile phone industry, Motorola invented the mobile phone and, as such, it is considered the pioneer in the industry. However, with the emergence of cell phones based on different standards (GSM digital technologies), Nokia gained control of the market. Then, in the era of smartphones, Samsung and Apple toppled Nokia (Giachetti, 2013; Giachetti and Marchi, 2017).

These phenomena of successive changes in industrial leadership have been examined in Lee and Malerba (2017). In these cases, the incumbent fails to maintain its superiority in terms of technology, production, or marketing, and a latecomer catches up with the incumbent. Subsequently, the latecomer that has gained leadership also relinquishes its position to a new latecomer. The reasons of successive changes in industrial leadership is due to the fact that in the long run sectoral systems evolve and change. Some of these changes are incremental and build upon previous characteristics and features, whereas other changes are more radical and represent some discontinuities with the past.

We refer to these discontinuities in the dynamics of a sectoral system as "windows of opportunity." Three windows of opportunity can be identified: a technological, a demand, and an institutional/public policy window. A "technological window" refers to major changes in technologies: see the pioneering discussion by Perez and Soete (1988) related to the introduction of new technological paradigms. For example, it can explain the advances of Korean producers in consumer electronics in the digital era against the incumbent Japanese leaders in the analogue era (Lee, Lim, and Song, 2005). A "demand window" refers to a new type of demand, a major shake-up in local demand, or a business cycle. For example, major increases in demand for certain products in China or a new set of consumers such as those demanding low cost cars in India have created the possibility for new domestic firms to enter the market and grow. Also a business cycle may create a situation in which the incumbents have difficulty during financial declines, whereas latecomers may have lower entry cost than in normal periods (Mathews, 2005). An "institutional/public policy window" can be opened through public intervention in the industry or drastic changes in institutional conditions. For example, public policy windows have been prominent in several catch-up cases, such as the high tech industries in Korea and Taiwan (Lee and Lim, 2001; Mathews, 2002), the telecommunications industry in China (Lee et al., 2012), and the pharmaceutical industry in India (Ramani and Guennif, 2012).

However, in order to have a successful change in industrial leadership, the opening of a window has to be coupled with a "response" by firms and the sectoral and the national systems of the catching up country. The response by firms depends on the level of capabilities of domestic firms and their learning processes. The response by the systems in turn depends on the level of education, the feature of the university and public research systems, the role of an active public policy, and the presence of appropriate institutions and financial systems.

With the opening of a window, the current leaders may fall behind because of the lack of an effective response due to an "incumbent trap" (Chandy and Tellis, 2000) and system misalignments or inadequacies in the new window. Firm leaders tend to be complacent and entrenched with the current success and often do not pay attention to the new technologies, disruptive innovations, or new types of demand or growing markets. And the system in which the current leaders are embedded may not be able to change or adapt to the new window, thus impeding or affecting the incumbents in a negative way.

During the long term evolution of sectors and countries, diverse combinations of windows of opportunity and responses from both incumbents and latecomers determine which pattern of successive catch-ups is most likely to emerge in the different sectors.

These remarks on continuous changes in industrial leadership that take place in the long run conclude our chapter on catch-up as an evolutionary process. This chapter has started by defining economic catch-up as the narrowing or the closing of a firm's or country's gap vis-à-vis a leading firm or country. It has pointed out that while catch-up may begin by imitating the forerunners, successful catch-up over a longer term cannot occur just by cloning existing products or technologies; rather it takes place by creating different products or technologies with respect to existing ones, or by opening completely new trajectories compared to ones of the leading countries or firms. This task of creating new trajectories requires not just production but also innovation capabilities which cannot be easily built by the efforts of the firms alone in the context of developing countries.

Consistent with an evolutionary view, this chapter has shown that in catching up firms' learning and capability have to be supported by effective national and sectoral systems. These systems complement domestic firms in various ways and with a variety of actors and institutions and they may greatly differ in structure and dynamics across countries and industries. It is the successful combination and integration of capable firms and strong national and sectoral systems that generates a catch-up. In this context public policy plays an active role by facilitating the learning and development of firms' capabilities and by creating the appropriate economic, technological, and scientific infrastructure at the base of catching up. The room for public policy exists in developing economies because there is a higher degree of not only market failure but also, more importantly, of capability and system failures.

Indeed, latecomer firms and industries are "resource poor late entrants" and that is why they can only start from low end segments in the international division of labor, which may serve as a niche for them. But when they reach the middle income stages, they may fall into a trap between low wage manufacturers and high wage innovators because their wage rates are too high to compete with low wage exporters and the level of their technological capability is too low to compete with high income countries. At this stage in order to continue the catching up process, they have to switch from endowment based specialization to technology based specialization. So, catch-up is not only a matter of building innovation capabilities but of seeking new room for entry into higher end segments, such as short cycle technology or low entry barrier sectors. Then, only after building even higher level of capabilities, they may target entry into long cycle or higher entry barrier sectors which represent the hallmark of the top tier high income countries. What has just been discussed represents a long term detour (Lee, 2013a), initially starting from specializing in low end segment (or low value added long cycle sectors, such as apparels), then moving into short cycle sectors (such as IT manufacturing or services) and finally entering long cycle sectors (such as science based or pharmaceuticals). In this detour, successive and upgraded entry into a higher end segment is not a smooth process, often requiring a strategy of leapfrogging and waiting for the opening of windows of opportunity related to new technological paradigms, new demand, or new institutional setting or public policy.

In sum, economic catch-up is an evolutionary, cumulative process of learning and capability accumulation which usually takes a long time, and often benefits from niches or windows of opportunities that open up for latecomers. In the long run, changes in economic leadership are going to happen again and are characterized by new firms and countries reaching the leaders but then falling behind to new latecomers who reach leadership, but then fall behind. And this process repeats over and over again.

7 The Evolution of Evolutionary Economics

Kurt Dopfer and Richard R. Nelson

The preceding chapters have provided a review of the fields of research where evolutionary economics has been concentrated. We propose that in each of these fields research oriented by an evolutionary perspective has led to recognition of important aspects of the empirical phenomena being studied that were not seen clearly in research not so oriented, and more generally to new understandings regarding what is going on in this arena of economic activity. Recently evolutionary economists have expanded the array of topics they are addressing, and in this chapter we will consider the broad range of economic phenomena and questions where we believe an evolutionary perspective would be fruitful. However, before we do that it is important to develop further the discussion started in the introductory chapter regarding the general perspective on economic structure and activity that an evolutionary orientation provides.

7.1 THE ORIENTATION OF EVOLUTIONARY ECONOMICS

The variation in the focus and style of analysis of the different subject matters considered in the foregoing chapters indicates clearly that evolutionary economics needs to be understood as oriented by a broad theoretical perspective but not tied to a particular narrowly defined set of analytic tools. We would propose that this is similar to the role of evolutionary theory in biology.

Many biologists will tell you that the basic understanding that life in general and all particular kinds of life have evolved through a long run continuing process involving variation and selection, as proposed by Darwin, with the formulation sharpened up and the mechanisms involved illuminated by subsequent analysis, provides the broad perspective that unifies biology as a field of science.[1] But this does not mean that explicit evolutionary theory is the dominant tool used by biologists to characterize or advance their scientific knowledge. In some fields of biology evolutionary theory is used centrally and explicitly; ecology is a good example. However, much of biological knowledge and research is basically about biochemistry. Research on "brain science" involves biochemistry and neurology and a number of subject specific biological structures, but generally not evolutionary theory explicitly. The situation is similar in many other subfields of biology. On the other hand, biologists and biomedical scientists working in these fields possess a background understanding that all living creatures, and the structures and processes that make them work, have come to be what they are through an evolutionary process. And in subfields of biology where there is little use of evolutionary theory in research, it often is useful to reflect on how the phenomena being studied could have evolved.

We propose that one ought to think about the roles that a broad evolutionary theoretical perspective can and should play in economic analysis in the same way. Most evolutionary economists do the research they do because they want to understand better certain economic phenomena and obtain better answers to various economic questions. They look at the economy as an evolving system because they believe that this perspective helps them to better understand the phenomena in which they are interested. Many of us, following Schumpeter, have a central interest in the processes driving and shaping economic change. This leads us to focus explicitly on the evolutionary mechanisms involved. But this orientation is not suited to all economic questions. Just as in biology, for many questions the basic understanding that economists seek is not so much the evolutionary processes that have shaped and continue to change the phenomena involved, but rather knowledge about their current structure

---

[1] Dobzhansky's statement is widely cited in the field: "Nothing in biology makes sense except in the light of evolution" (Dobzhansky, 1964: 449).

and how it works. However, evolutionary economists would argue that many of these economic questions can be understood much better if one recognizes that what is going on is the result of an evolutionary process, even if the details of that process may not be centrally relevant.

The point we are highlighting here is that an evolutionary perspective on economic activity is manifest in two different ways. One is explicit evolutionary analysis of particular economic phenomena or processes, particularly where an important aspect of the question being explored is how the current state of affairs came about and how it is changing. The other is in terms of a broad understanding that the economic structures and ways of doing things that one observes at any time are the manifestations of a continuing evolutionary process, an understanding that influences how one thinks about how they work but may not include an explicit evolutionary account. This perspective frames how one sees the structures and mechanisms that are operative in the economy at all levels of aggregation – micro, meso, macro – although the kind of analysis that is relevant obviously depends on the subject matter being studied.[2]

We argued earlier that a good case in point is how one understands what lies behind the current configuration of economic activity: the goods and services that are produced and consumed, their prices, the modes of production used and factor prices, the prevailing organization of industry... Economists looking at the picture through neoclassical glasses are drawn to see, at least as a first approximation, a system in general equilibrium, with economic actors doing what they are doing because they are optimizing, and with supply equaling demand on all markets, if perhaps involving some elements of "market failure." Evolutionary economists see nothing of this sort, but rather a configuration that has evolved to the state it is in now and which is continuing to evolve. They would

---

[2] For an elaboration of the micro-meso-macro framework see Dopfer, Foster, and Potts (2004).

expect to see some behaviors that appear inept in the current context and are not likely to be viable for long, along with some showing considerable prowess, both kinds generated by the evolutionary processes at work. More generally, an evolutionary context inevitably leads to firms in the same line of business differing in what they are doing, in some cases considerably, with some operating much more efficiently than others, some making money, and some taking losses and perhaps doomed for failure soon. One would expect that there would be some markets where supply and demand are in reasonable balance, but some marked by indications of considerable excess supply or demand.

We note that the evolutionary perspective here, while fundamentally shaping the way the current configuration of economic activity is understood, does not involve any particular detailed specification of the evolutionary processes that have led to it. However, if the question being explored was extended to consideration of what kind of changes to expect from the current configuration, a more explicit evolutionary analysis would be required. To get at this question requires one to consider explicitly factors like whether it is hard or relatively easy for firms, or economic actors more generally, who are significantly behind the frontier to adopt best practice, whether firms losing money are quickly forced from business or whether there are sources of funds to keep them alive, etc., and how these variables influence evolutionary dynamics.

The fields that were described in the earlier chapters differ in the extent to which explicit analysis of the evolutionary processes at work play a central role in research. For example, they clearly do in the research we described in Chapter 2 on technological advance as an evolutionary process. On the other hand, while the analysis of firm behavior and capabilities by evolutionary economists described in Chapter 3 sees the structure of firms and what they are doing as a result of an evolutionary process, the analysis of the details of firm behavior and of the efficacy of business plans and strategies that one finds in this work seldom involves explicit evolutionary analysis of what is going on. But of course such studies can be and sometimes are enriched by explicit evolutionary analysis of how changes in firm strategy and behavior come about, sometimes associated with analysis of the evolutionary dynamics going on in the sector where the firm lives.

In some ways the evolutionary perspective is broadly Marshallian.[3] Thus evolutionary economists, as our more orthodox colleagues, tend to see much (but not all) of economic activity going on in a market context. An important share of the analysis of evolutionary economists is concerned with illuminating the factors behind the prevailing quantities of outputs being produced and purchased in various economic sectors, and the prices at which transactions are occurring, and see these as reflecting the interaction of factors on the demand and the supply sides of the relevant markets. Like the rest of the economics community, evolutionary economists presume that whether a potential user will buy a product and, if so, how much of it, depends on its price, and also that what suppliers provide and, where they have pricing power, how they price, is sensitive to their views of the size and nature of the potential market. And evolutionary economists would argue that significant differences between supply and demand at any time tend to set in train changes in prices and in the quantities of production and purchase.

But the characterization by evolutionary economists of the nature of goal oriented economic behavior, and of the workings of markets, diverges in important ways from the theory that economic actors optimize and that the configuration of economic activity that one observes is one of equilibrium that marks much of contemporary neoclassical theory. In a nutshell, our argument is that "rational" economic behavior and the configuration of economic activity that one observes evolve. On the one hand this perspective enables us to recognize clearly the messiness that economic activity molded by the market almost always involves: failing firms, shoddy products,

---

[3] Marshall (1890); for an elaboration of this theme see Nelson (2013).

disappointed customers. On the other hand, an evolutionary view of economic activity also leads one to recognize learning by firms and users of their products regarding what works and what doesn't, and often highly creative innovation. While recognizing the continuing presence of economic action taking that is less than competent, it highlights much more than the neoclassical the striking effectiveness of what economic actors are doing in many fields of economic activity. And it attributes powerful effective action, where one sees it, to collective evolutionary processes that, often over many years, have generated and explored and winnowed a wide range of ways of doing things, rather than to the sophisticated goal seeking behavior of the present set of economic actors.

As we have stressed, evolutionary economists insist that the workings of the economy at any time need to be understood as a frame in the ongoing moving picture of economic history.

It has become standard to propose that, in this era of computer science and biotechnology, we have a "knowledge" economy in the sense that the state of knowledge is the principal factor determining the goods and services that can be produced. Some of that knowledge relates to how to do things. Some relates to what are the effective things to be doing. Evolutionary economists would strongly endorse the proposition that the state of knowledge, of both kinds, is the key determinant of the extent to which an economy can meet human wants. And while noting that throughout economic history the state of knowledge has been a principal factor influencing what could be produced, evolutionary economists would go on to argue that both the often incredible power and the rapid rate of advance of economically relevant knowledge, makes an evolutionary perspective an imperative if one is to understand what is going on in modern economies.

As we have argued earlier, while today's standard economics certainly recognizes the importance of the advance of know-how as a central driver of economic progress, it does so "off to the side" of its base analysis of how market economies work, which takes knowledge as a given. For evolutionary economists learning through science, through efforts focused on developing new and better technology, and as a result of what has been learned in practice and through observing what other actors are doing, are integral aspects of how modern economies work.

The examples of evolutionary economics that have been surveyed in the preceding chapters all have been closely oriented to empirical observation of what is going on in the arena being studied. We would argue that our kind of evolutionary perspective pulls one strongly toward a pragmatic realism. From an evolutionary perspective, there is nothing inevitable about the details of economic activity and structure today. The evolutionary processes, the economic history, that has generated them could have led to an economy that differs from the one we have in a variety of ways. Therefore the idea that there is some kind of an idealized economic form that, in some sense, involves the essence of what actually is there looks like nonsense. To understand how the economy actually works one needs to look carefully to try to see what actually is going on.

But of course the phenomena one sees and the shape they seem to have, and what one is blind to depend very much on the conceptual glasses one is wearing. Throughout this book we have been arguing that an evolutionary perspective leads one to see the economy and its workings in a different way than through the theoretical spectacles most economists trained over the past half century have learned to wear. Our argument is that, for a wide range of economic activities and questions, our view is the more informative one.

7.2   WHERE DO WE GO FROM HERE?

While most of the research and writing oriented by the perspective of evolutionary economic theory has been concentrated on the range of subjects surveyed in the previous chapters, an important part has been concerned with topics and questions outside of that domain, and in recent years that range of exploration has been expanding. We hope it will expand still further, since we believe that there are a number of important economic phenomena and policy issues where a significant increase in research oriented by an evolutionary perspective could yield high returns. In this section we highlight several of these.[4].

First of all, virtually all the analysis and writing of evolutionary economists has been concerned with the supply side of economic activity. There has been hardly any evolutionary writing concerned with factors affecting demand. More balance is needed.

While evolutionary economists have done some work on household consumption, the range of matters dealt with has been quite limited.[5] An evolutionary perspective on household purchases of goods and services is needed to illuminate several important matters. In particular, standard consumer theory presumes that potential customers are aware of the full range of goods and services they might purchase; however, in modern capitalist economies households, and individuals, face a continuing cascade of new goods and services. The question of how potential customers learn of new purchasing options, and the factors influencing whether and when they buy them, is treated to some extent in the literature on diffusion but is not considered at all in standard consumer theory. And households and individuals themselves are always changing, and as they change their wants change. Thus while the continuing introduction of new goods and services makes the consumer choice problem even more complicated, even in an economic world where the set of available goods and services was a constant, individuals and households often are in a position where they need to learn about and learn to evaluate new things.

Today many economists, not just adherents to evolutionary economics, understand that firms need to be understood as entities that change and learn over time, and often are challenged by changes in the context in which they operate. In contrast, there still

---

[4] Winter (2014) also is concerned with the question of how evolutionary economics should break out of its limited "beachhead."

[5] See for example Witt, 2001; Nelson and Consoli, 2010; Chai, 2017.

is a strong tendency in economics, including among evolutionary economists, to treat household behavior in a static framework. There clearly is a need for better treatment of how households respond to an economic world that is constantly changing around them, as they themselves change.

One fundamental question is how are preferences formed? What is the role of advertising? Of the influence of opinion leaders, or one's peers? One's own experience? There is nothing in the research tradition of evolutionary economics to date that indicates how to explore these questions. But a perspective that sees economic actors as boundedly rational, and often forced to make decisions in contexts with which they have had little or no experience, is far more open to their exploration than a perspective that starts with the presumption that economic actors somehow are able to optimize, although they may have to deal with incomplete information.

To turn to a second aspect where the range of evolutionary economic research needs to be broadened, the lion's share of the research and writing by evolutionary economists has been concerned, explicitly or implicitly, with manufacturing activity and manufacturing sectors.[6] Yet the service industries, which in high income countries account for more of output and employment than do manufacturing, tend to be different in certain important respects than manufacturing, for example in the nature of innovation. And many important aspects of what is going on in these sectors can only be understood, we would argue, if one takes an evolutionary perspective.

The medical care sector is a good case in point. Evolutionary economists would argue that one cannot understand what is going on in the medical care sector unless one recognizes that technological innovation there is rapid, and the efficacy of new artifacts and practices often highly uncertain. While much of the increases in life expectancy that have been experienced over the past half century in

---

[6] Evolutionary economists have studied a wide range of manufacturing industries, see for instance Frenken et al., 1999; Malerba et al., 1999; Perez, 2002; Graf, 2009; Grebel, 2010; Potts, 2011; Garavaglia et al., 2013, Strohmaier, 2014; Kudic, 2015.

high income countries has been the result of advances in medicine, these technological developments also are a major factor behind the rise in medical expenditures. And continuing technological innovation is a major factor behind the significant differences among hospitals in the treatments given for particular maladies and in the effectiveness of the treatments given. While health economists know this, to date there has been very little research treating the evolutionary processes at work explicitly and analyzing their effects on medical care.

To shift to a broader topic, as highlighted in several of the preceding chapters, evolutionary economists long have highlighted that there are important differences across economic industries and sectors in their structures and in the nature of the practices they use that influence the way they evolve. In particular, sectors have varied greatly in the rates at which their productivity and the efficacy of the goods and services they provide have improved. A number of our most pressing social problems stem from the stagnation or very slow progress that is occurring in particular economic activities and sectors, often (but not always) delivering services of various kinds; education is an obvious example. The payoffs could be considerable from coming to understand better what lies behind these differences in rates of progress, and what, if anything, can be done to boost progress in important sectors where it has been very slow. This is a major challenge for the research of evolutionary economists.

The issues here are very much germane to the concept of a "knowledge based" economy. Very few discussions of the topic point out that our knowledge is very uneven. It would seem important to recognize this better and to try to map out and understand how our knowledge of how to do things effectively varies greatly across fields of knowledge bearing on different human needs.

One of the most striking and disturbing phenomenon that has marked the evolution of high average income capitalist economies over the past half century is the growing inequality of the distributions of income and wealth. The questions of why this has happened, and whether these developments seem closely tied to the way the production systems of the capitalist world has evolved and cannot be significantly changed without eroding significantly the effectiveness of these economies in producing needed goods and services, or whether these trends can be stopped or reversed without such high costs, obviously are of the highest importance. And while these questions have been explored by many economists and other social scientists, very little of this research has been oriented by an explicitly evolutionary point of view.

How might an evolutionary perspective on this set of problems be manifest, in a way that differentiates it from the orientation of other scholars studying the issues? First of all, we suggest that research done with an explicitly evolutionary perspective could shed new light on the way labor markets work, particularly on the demand side of these markets. Thus there has been very little direct study of selection pressures on firms to keep wages from rising and to hire in ways that reduce labor costs, and on what makes these pressures strong or weak. It is apparent that these pressures have not been very strong regarding people in the managerial ranks, particularly high management. Why do the pressures to keep expenditures low on low or medium skilled workers outside of management seem to be much greater? How do these differences relate to the way firms are financed, and the beliefs and policies of people in the financial sector?

The rising inequality of incomes is strongly related to the significant increase in the share in National Income accounted for by non-wage and salary income, principally returns on financial assets, that has occurred over the same period. The gains in understanding could be considerable from an evolutionary analysis of what has been happening to the financial sector and the instruments it uses. More generally, evolutionary economists need to understand better the workings of financial institutions and mechanisms and build these understandings more richly into their analyses of how our economic systems work. Financial institutions and mechanisms are complex, and they affect economic activity in a variety of ways, many of which are poorly understood.

Most of the research and writing by evolutionary economists has been oriented by phenomena defined at the micro or meso economic level – firms and industries – and topics like technological advance have been studied largely at these levels of aggregation. The research described in Chapters 5 and 6, concerned with long run economic development, has been oriented to illuminating, among other things, phenomena defined at the macroeconomic level – the increase over time of GNP, and GNP per worker, and related aggregate measures. However, only a few evolutionary economists have done analysis focused on the determinants of aggregate employment and unemployment, and the rate of inflation, or the conditions needed for full employment and relative price stability, which, along with economic growth, are the standard subject matters of macroeconomics. But this is changing.

An evolutionary macroeconomics clearly is needed, for much the same reasons as an evolutionary micro and meso economics is needed. The fact that the economy never is still, always is changing, and technological change is the key driving force, clearly needs to be recognized in analyses of macroeconomic employment and inflation, just as in analyses of what is going on in firms and industries.

Macroeconomic variables like the overall unemployment rate, or the rate of change of the consumer price index, or GNP and its growth rate, are calculated by summing up figures for many different economic activities and sectors. But while much of mainline macroeconomic theory represses this diversity beneath the aggregate, evolutionary economists cannot since it is basic to our fundamental view of how economies work and change. For evolutionary economists macroeconomic variables are aggregates and, as in the evolutionary growth theory considered earlier, do not have a life independent of the micro and meso economic activity that is going on. But aggregate variables like the overall unemployment rate and changes in the index of consumer good prices certainly are very important to understand and explain. And a number of the important variables that determine these aggregate phenomena are broad influences on the economy as a whole, like the tightness of monetary policy, and income tax rates.

The perspective provided by evolutionary growth theory provides a basis for part of a more general evolutionary macroeconomic theory, but is focused almost totally on the supply side of economic activity, with an implicit or explicit assumption that somehow demand grows at the same rate and direction as does supply.[7] Many evolutionary economists are attracted to Keynesian or post Keynesian analysis of aggregate demand, and some have begun to try to marry Keynes and Schumpeter. And the long wave theories briefly discussed in Chapter 5 are other attempts to deal with fluctuations in the rates of unemployment and inflation that have occurred in the course of economic growth. There are various other contributions by evolutionary economists to the area of macroeconomics.[8] But we still are some distance from a persuasive evolutionary macroeconomics.

The complex and urgent set of issues about how to halt the trend toward global warming, and move more quickly toward an economy that is sustainable, of course is another topic of major interest to many evolutionary economists. Here, as in several other fields of economic analysis, the point of view taken by many economists in the mainstream has been implicitly evolutionary, and in some cases almost explicitly so. There is recognition that significant technological advance of particular kinds is needed, and that a variety of institutions need to be changed.

---

[7] The Saviotti–Pyka model does recognize demand side factors influencing the industry mix of economic growth, but does not deal with the question of what, if anything, operates to keep aggregate demand growing in pace with aggregate supply.

[8] Hanusch, 1988; Lundvall, 1988; Cantner and Pyka, 2001; Metcalfe, Foster, and Ramlogan, 2006; Aghion, David, and Foray, 2009; Castellacci, 2009; Mowery, Nelson, and Martin, 2010; Bleda and Del Rio, 2013; Mazzucato, 2013;Foster 2014; Metcalfe, 2014; Dosi et al., 2015; Peneder, 2016.

But evolutionary economists could add much to this body of research, particularly through their knowledge of the nature of the evolutionary processes involved in technological change, and in changing economic structures. While mainline economists recognize the importance of the development of new technology, they almost always assume that the source of new technology is R&D, which proceeds separately from ongoing economic activity. In contrast, evolutionary economists know that significant new technologies usually emerge and develop over relatively long periods of time, and that learning by doing and using is centrally involved in the process, as well as research and development, and that the process of development proceeds best when there is good communication between users of the technology and those doing R&D. These facts bear on the question of how R&D should be financed and who should be doing it, and also on the kinds of communication and information dissemination mechanisms that are important. Our reading of the studies being done by economists who do not have an evolutionary economics background is that these matters are not well understood. Thus research and writing by evolutionary economists could play a very constructive role here.

These are just a few of the areas of research where a significant increase in the attention given by evolutionary economists could yield high returns. There are many others.

7.3 THE ADVANTAGES OF AN EXPLICIT EVOLUTIONARY PERSPECTIVE

In each of the areas of research sketched above, as in those described in more detail in the preceding chapters, our argument is that understanding of what is going on is significantly enhanced if one recognizes that the phenomena involved are being generated by a continuing evolutionary process. The patterns of behaviors that are observed should not be interpreted as the result of well informed actors choosing the best actions available to them. Rather, although some of the actions being taken might be very effective, an evolutionary perspective leads the analyst to presume that many of the actions being taken fall far short of best practice. And the constellation of behaviors being observed are not interpreted as an equilibrium configuration, but as being in flux, with some ways of doing things expanding in use and others declining. At the same time an evolutionary theorist would presume that at least some innovation is going on, some of which will take while others will not.

This is a somewhat messy picture, not the clear clean one provided by neoclassical theory. But as the earlier chapters show, analysis oriented by an evolutionary theory can provide a very illuminating picture that has the advantage of being a much truer image of what really is going on.

As we proposed earlier, today many empirically oriented economists are doing their research and writing relatively unencumbered by the canons of neoclassical theory, and in some cases at least the framework they employ is implicitly evolutionary. But as we also argued, having that evolutionary perspective explicit greatly sharpens focus and brings into view phenomena that otherwise would not be seen or would be ignored as unimportant.

Beyond treating the subject matter being studied as evolving, evolutionary economics is quite eclectic. As the foregoing chapters show, evolutionary economists have tailored the details of their analysis to the particularities of the subject matter they are studying and the questions they are asking. In doing so, they have drawn extensively on the concepts and methods of traditional economics, and from social science more broadly.

But as suggested in the introductory chapter there is a particularly strong symbiosis between evolutionary economics and two other bodies of contemporary economic research that also are pressing for reform of the field. Recognized evolutionary economists are centrally involved in these fields, but many of the researchers are not usually considered to be in the evolutionary camp. These research areas are behavioral economics (broadly defined), and institutional economics.

There long has been a tradition of research and writing involving economists and other social scientists working to develop a characterization of purposive individual and organizational behavior that squares better than neoclassical theory with what is known about behavior empirically, and is better suited for analysis of various particular activities or contexts on which analysis is focused. Evolutionary economists clearly share this broad point of view. Earlier we discussed the similarities and differences between the theory of individual and organizational behavior that now is built into much of evolutionary economics and the orientation of what is today called behavioral economics. There is considerable overlap, but as we noted evolutionary economics draws much more on Simon,[9] and focus more on differences between behaviors in contexts that are familiar and those that are not or where the actor is trying to do something new[10] than does mainline behavioral economics. And many of the behaviors that most interest evolutionary economists are what organizations do.[11]

There also has been a long tradition of research concerned with the wide range of "institutions" that characterize modern societies and analyzing their effects on how economies operate. Institutional economists are united in their argument that standard economic analysis pays too little attention to economic institutions, beyond the stylized firms and markets treated in standard theory. The concept of "institutions" that has been employed over the years in economic analysis has varied greatly in its breadth. For Veblen, the institutions concept covered virtually all aspects of culturally transmitted and enforced common patterns of behavior and thought that one finds in a society.[12] Following the lead of North, many contemporary "new" institutional economists and social scientists have used the term to

[9] March and Simon, 1958; Simon, 1976, 2005.
[10] Lazaric and Raybaut, 2005; Muñoz, Encinar, and Cañibano, 2011; Gerschlager, 2012; Nelson, 2016, Becker and Knudsen, 2017.
[11] Cyert and March, 1963; Nelson and Winter, 1982; Eliasson, 1990; Winter, 2006; Teece, 2011; Johansson, 2009.
[12] Veblen, 1898.

refer to "systems of rules."[13] Other economists have used the term more narrowly to refer to particular organizational structures that are standard in a society, like the modern corporate form of business, or bodies of regulatory law, like that requiring the testing of new pharmaceuticals. Evolutionary economists clearly use the term flexibly, but almost always in reference to the governing structures, bodies of law and policy, and beliefs and norms that bear on activity in a field, and mold how things are done.

The arguments that economic analysis needs to be based on an empirically supportable theory of behavior, and that the role of institutions in molding behavior needs to be taken more into account, clearly are logically not the same. However, they often are presented together. The basic conceptual orientation of the American community of institutional economists, who were an important part of the economic scene during the first half of the twentieth century, involved both. And their writings often articulated an evolutionary point of view.[14]

As we noted in Chapter 1, the proposition that cultural, social, political, and economic structures and modes of operation should be understood as evolving predates Darwin.[15] We also highlighted that in recent years scholars in a number of different scientific fields have been developing and sharpening this perspective. There is now a substantial literature involving scholars from a number of disciplines arguing that human culture and social structures in general should be thought of as evolving.[16] Many evolutionary scholars focus on particular spheres of culture and activity. Evolutionary economics is part

---

[13] Crawford and Ostrom, 1995; North, 2005; Dopfer and Potts, 2008; Ostrom and Basurto, 2011; Blind and Pyka, 2014.

[14] Rutherford (1994) provides a broad review.

[15] See for example Mandeville (1714) regarding the evolution of ship design. Hume's description, in 1762, of how the British social structure and culture of his day came to be clearly is evolutionary in spirit, as is Smith's (1776) analysis of what is going on in the economy. It should be noted however, that the word "evolution" was not used in these accounts.

[16] See for example Richerson and Boyd (2005) and Mokyr (2017).

of this collection, and draws extensively on other bodies of evolutionary social science that bear on phenomena it deals with. Thus distinguished philosophers and historians are arguing that scientific knowledge evolves, and attempting to describe the mechanisms and structures involved.[17] Among empirically oriented scholars of technological change there is near consensus that the process should be understood as evolutionary.[18] Organizations are seen as evolving.[19] There are a number of different traditions of research on various aspects of economic activity and structure that take an evolutionary perspective. And much of economic history is written explicitly or implicitly as evolutionary.

Economic geographers increasingly are taking an evolutionary perspective on what goes on in different regions.[20] An evolutionary perspective now is prominent in ecological economics, the study of how human economic activity interacts with the physical environment.[21] And we would propose that much of the research and writing concerned with complex systems and how they work is implicitly and often explicitly evolutionary.[22]

Thus evolutionary economics certainly is not alone in arguing that what goes on in the economy must be understood as being driven by an evolutionary process. But in our view it is the most fully worked out of these perspectives. More generally, we propose that a key characteristic of evolutionary economics is that it combines, in a coherent way, all three of the strands of analysis considered above. We have stressed the evolutionary orientation. But the behavioral

---

[17] See, e.g., Campbell, 1960; Hull, 2001.
[18] Constant, 1980; Basalla, 1988; Mokyr, 1990, 2017; Vincenti, 1990.
[19] DiMaggio and Powell, 1991; Aldridge, 1999.
[20] Essletzbichler and Rigby, 2007; Boschma and Martin, 2010; Martin and Sunley, 2010; Schamp, 2010; Schroeder, 2011.
[21] Daly and Cobb, 1990; Daly, 2007; Rammel, Stagl, and Wilfing, 2007; Gerber and Steppacher, 2012; Safarzyńska, Frenken, and van den Bergh, 2012.
[22] Foster and Metcalfe, 2004; Allen, 2005; Holt, Rosser, and Colander, 2010; Arthur, 2014; Harper, 2014; Elsner, Heinrich, and Schwardt, 2015; Robert and Yoguel, 2016.

and institutional assumptions built into evolutionary economics are
fundamental aspects of its particular analytic structure.

7.4   REFORM MOVEMENTS IN ECONOMICS

Clearly none of the proposals we have described for reform of economic analysis is new.[23] From the time neoclassical economics
began to emerge as a significant movement of economic thinking,
economists resistant to that development have argued that neoclassical theory provided not just an oversimplified but a biased view of
what was going on in the economy, and regarding many policy issues.
The bias was in terms both of what was seen or interpreted that was
not accurate, and in terms of what was not seen or was ignored.

For the most part the defenders of neoclassical theory argued
that the attackers did not understand the nature of theory, which
innately simplified and abstracted from the buzzing complex reality.
A theoretical structure that did this was needed if economists were
to make any sense of the economic problem and how a market
economy dealt with it. Economists concerned with complex empirical phenomena or policy issues of course should pay attention to
the details, and in some cases their analysis might be able to draw on
broad theory to only a limited degree.

Actually the articulation of this point of view considerably predates the arguments about neoclassical theory, going back
to the writings of John Stuart Mill. In his *Principles of Political
Economy* (1848) Mill drew a sharp distinction between economics
as a "science," and economic analysis of particular empirical phenomena or policy issues. Regarding the former, Mill argued the need
for abstraction, which he proposed was the hallmark of a science. In
particular, he proposed that, in what later came to be called "pure
theory," economic actors should be assumed to be concerned only
with enhancing their wealth. More complex motivations, or recognition that economic actors may at times act ineptly, are to be

---

[23] The discussion which follows draws heavily on Mazzoleni and Nelson (2013).

abstracted away. But he also argued that when economists were trying to understand particular empirical phenomena, or analyzing a policy issue, a different orientation was appropriate. In this line of work it not only was legitimate to base analysis on detailed study of the relevant empirical phenomena, but this was necessary for good applied economics, and work of this kind should not be constrained to adhere to the assumptions built into the science aspect of economics.

Mill's point of view here was widely respected, and clearly conditioned the thinking of generations of economists who followed him. Thus a potential schizophrenia was built into our discipline early on. On the one hand there are the assumptions appropriate for abstract economic theory. On the other hand, empirical and policy research and analysis should not be bound by these assumptions but rather draw its perspective from close empirical study. Of course in principle these two different strands of economics can be complementary, if the abstract theory can provide a useful broad orientation for empirical analysis. But those who over the years have complained about the theory that was coming to dominate "scientific" economics have argued that much of theory has been at best unhelpful, and often a hindrance to empirical understanding.

We believe there is some truth to both sides of this argument, and some basic misunderstandings also. Mill, and the more recent defenders of neoclassical theory, are right about the need for broad theory in economics to be quite abstract and to repress many aspects of what actually is going on if that theory is to provide a coherent and understandable overview of the economic problem and how economies that make extensive use of market organization deal with it. Mill also is right that applied economic research needs to pay attention to the relevant details including those that are important in the context but ignored by broad theory, and that the causal analysis developed in such research may draw on broad general theory to only a limited degree. But economists interested in empirical phenomena and complex policy issues also are right that neoclassical theory often provides them with little useful guidance regarding how to see into the situation, and in many cases points them the wrong way. And good empirical research and policy analysis does require a broad general theory to help orient it.

Taking these propositions together, it is clear that the potential schizophrenia latent in Mill's argument about the appropriate difference between economic theorizing and applied economic research clearly is manifest today. But we would argue that it is not a necessary consequence of the abstract nature of theory in economics that Mill advocated and which in fact has characterized our discipline. It can be avoided if the basic background theory that is needed to provide broad structure to empirical research and policy analysis, and inevitably shapes that work to some degree, provides an appropriate broad orientation.

It is important to recognize clearly that the issue here is the fruitfulness of the orientation provided to thinking and research by a broad economic theory. The nature of theorizing in economics has followed the path argued for by Mill, and theory of that nature (unlike theory in physics) is too much abstracted from the complex reality of economic activity to be judged in terms of how well it explains it. Empirical inquiry, to be effective, inevitably is going to have to take into account aspects of the phenomena or question being explored that the broad theory does not consider, and to tailor its analysis to the particulars of the context. But on the other hand, that empirical inquiry is going to be oriented to a considerable degree by the broad theoretical perspective the researcher has in mind. And that orientation can be more or less fruitful.

It also needs to be recognized that, given the diversity of what is going on in the economy that we have highlighted, there is no way that a single highly simplified and abstract economic theory is going to provide good guidance to thinking and research regarding all aspects of the economy. The economics discipline recognizes this, in the form of models oriented toward focusing analysis of particular phenomena. We have a different body of theory for issues that are defined as macroeconomic than for microeconomics. Within macro, there are a particular collection of theories concerned with money and economic activity. Within micro, there are a number of theories specially oriented to issues in industrial organization and competition, and others concerned with the workings of labor markets.

As we proposed earlier, theorizing in economics proceeds at different levels of abstraction and generality. At the highest level of both are very broad theoretical orientations to what is going on in the economy in general. We might call these kinds of theory "master" theories, particularly if they influence strongly the orientation of theories focused more narrowly on particular phenomena and questions. General neoclassical theory is such a master theory. So is the broad evolutionary theory of what goes on in the economy that we have displayed in this book in various manifestations.

For the lion's share of today's professional economists general neoclassical theory is the only master theory they know. Therefore inevitably that theory influences strongly how they look at a variety of economic questions, and what they see and don't see, whether or not they believe that the theory provides a good abstract characterization of the economy and how it works.

As evolutionary economists we believe it very important to break this monopoly on high level economic theorizing. We do not deny that at least some of the research and understanding that modern neoclassical theory has engendered has been very fruitful. But we believe that for analysis of many of today's most interesting and important economic issues, the orientation provided by a broad evolutionary theory is likely to be much more fruitful. It is important to get a much larger fraction of the professional economics community familiar with it. We hope that this book contributes to that goal.

References

Abernathy, W.J., and Utterback, J. (1978). Patterns of innovation in industry. *Technology Review* 80(7): 40–47.

Abramovitz, Moses (1986). Catching-up, forging ahead, and falling behind. *Journal of Economic History* 46(2): 385–406.

Adler, P.S. (1993). The learning bureaucracy: New United Motors Manufacturing, Inc. In B. Staw and L. Cummings (Eds.), *Research in Organizational Behavior*, Vol. 15, JAI Press, Greenwich, CT, pp. 111–194.

Adner, R., and Helfat, C.E. (2003). Corporate effects and dynamic managerial capabilities. *Strategic Management Journal* 24(10): 1011–1025.

Aghion, P., David, P.A., and Foray, D. (2009). Science, technology and innovation for economic growth: Linking policy research and practice in "STIG systems." *Research Policy* 38(4): 681–693.

Aitken, Brian J., and Harrison, Ann E. (1999). Do domestic firms benefit from direct foreign investment? Evidence from Venezuela. *American Economic Review* 89(3): 605–618.

Akerlof, G., and Schiller, R. (2015). *Phishing for Pfools: The Economics of Manipulation and Deception*, Princeton University Press, Princeton, NJ.

Alchian, Armen A. (1950). Uncertainty, evolution, and economic theory. *Journal of Political Economy* 58(3): 211–222.

Aldridge, H. (1999). *Organizations Evolving*, Sage Publications, London.

Allen, P.M. (2005). *Understanding Social and Economic Systems as Evolutionary Complex Systems*, Cambridge University Press, Cambridge.

Allen, R.C. (1983). Collective invention. *Journal of Economic Behavior & Organization* 4: 1–24.

Amit, R., and Schoemaker, P.J.H. (1993). Strategic assets and organizational rent. *Strategic Management Journal* 14(1): 33–46.

Amsden, Alice H. (1989). *Asia's Next Giant: South Korea and Late Industrialization*, Oxford University Press, New York.

Amsden, Alice H., and Chu, Wan-wen (2003). *Beyond Late Development: Taiwan's Upgrading Policies*, MIT Press, Cambridge, MA.

Amsden, Alice H., and Hikino, Takashi (1994). Project execution capability, organizational know-how and conglomerate corporate growth in late industrialization. *Industrial and Corporate Change* 3(1): 111–147.

Anderson, P., and Tushman, M.L. (1990). Technological discontinuities and dominant designs: A cyclical model of technological change. *Administrative Science Quarterly* 35: 604–633.

Araujio, B. (2017). Market leadership in Brazil's ICT sector: The cases of Totvs and Positivo. In F. Malerba, S. Mani, and P. Adams (Eds.), *The Rise to Market Leadership*, Edward Elgar, Cheltenham, UK.

Argote, L. 1999. *Organizational Learning: Creating, Retaining and Transferring Knowledge*, Kluwer Academic Publishers, Norwell, MA.

Arocena, Rodrigo, and Sutz, Judith (2000). Looking at national systems of innovation from the South. *Industry and Innovation* 7(1): 55–75.

Arora, A., Cohen, W.M., and Walsh, J.P. (2016). The acquisition and commercialization of invention in American manufacturing: Incidence and impact. *Research Policy* 45(6): 1113–1128.

Arthur, B.W. (2014). *Complexity and the Economy*, Oxford University Press, Oxford.

Arundel, A., van de Paal, G., and Soete, L. (1995). Innovation strategies of Europe's largest firms. Results of the PACE survey. European Innovation Monitoring System, Report No. 23, European Commission, Brussels.

Auerswald, P.E. (2017). *The Code Economy: A Forty-Thousand-Year History*, Oxford University Press, New York.

Augier, M., and Teece, D.J. (2009). Dynamic capabilities and the role of managers in business strategy and economic performance. *Organization Science* 20(2): 410–421.

Basalla, G. (1988). *The Evolution of Technology*, Cambridge University Press, Cambridge.

Becker, C., and Knudsen, T. (2017). Heterogeneity of habits as a foundation for Schumpeterian economic policy. *Journal of Evolutionary Economics* 27(1): 43–62.

Becker, M.C. (Ed.) (2005). *Handbook of Organizational Routines*, Edward Elgar, Cheltenham, UK.

Becker, M.C., Lazaric, N., Nelson, R.R., and Winter, S.G. (2005). Applying organizational routines in understanding organizational change. *Industrial and Corporate Change* 14(5): 775–791.

Bell, Martin (1984). Learning and the accumulation of industrial technological capacity in developing countries. In M. Fransman and K. King (Eds.), *Technological Capability in the Third World*, Macmillan, London, p. 404.

Bell, Martin, and Figueiredo, Paulo N. (2012). Building innovative capabilities in latecomer emerging market firms: Some key issues. In Edmund Amann and John Cantwell (Eds.), *Innovative Firms in Emerging Market Countries*, Oxford University Press, Oxford, pp. 24–109.

Bell, R.M., and Pavitt, K. (1993). Technological accumulation and industrial growth: Contrasts between developed and developing countries. *Industrial and Corporate Change* 2(1): 157–210.

Bergek, Anna, Jacobsson, Staffan, Carlsson, Bo, Lindmark, S., and Rickne, Anneka (2008). Analyzing the functional dynamics of technological innovation systems: A scheme of analysis. *Research Policy* 37(3): 407–429.

Binswanger, H., and Ruttan, V. (1978). *Induced Innovation*, Johns Hopkins University Press, Baltimore, MD.

Bleda, M., and Del Rio, P. (2013). The market failure and the systemic failure rationales in technological innovation systems. *Research Policy* 42(5): 1039–1052.

Blind, G., and Pyka, A. (2014). The rule approach in evolutionary economics: A methodological template for empirical research. *Journal of Evolutionary Economics* 24(5): 1085–1105.

Blomström, Magnus (1986). Foreign investment and productive efficiency: The case of Mexico. *The Journal of Industrial Economics* 35(1): 97–110.

Bloom, N., and Van Reenen, J. (2010). Why do management practices differ across firms and countries? *Journal of Economic Perspectives* 24: 203–224.

Bonaccorsi, A., Giuri, P., and Pierotti, F. (2005). Technological frontiers and competition in multi-technology sectors: Micro evidence from the aero-engine industries. *Economics of Innovation and New Technology* 14: 23–42.

Borensztein, Eduardo, Gregorio, Jose De, and Lee, Jong-Wha (1998). How does foreign direct investment affect economic growth? *Journal of International Economics* 45(1): 115–135.

Boschma, R., and Martin, R. (2010). The aims and scope of evolutionary economic geography. In R. Boschma and R. Martin (Eds.), *The Handbook of Evolutionary Geography*, Edward Elgar, Cheltenham, UK.

Bottazzi, G., Dosi, G., Lippi, M., Pammolli, F., and Riccaboni, M. (2001). Innovation and corporate growth in the evolution of the drug industry. *International Journal of Industrial Organization* 19: 1161–1187.

Brenner, T., and Murmann, J.P. (2016). Using simulation experiments to test historical explanations: The development of the German dye industry 1857–1913. *Journal of Evolutionary Economics* 26: 907–932.

Breschi, S., Malerba, F., and Orsenigo, L. (2000). Technological regimes and Schumpeterian patterns of innovation. *Economic Journal* 110: 388–410.

Breznitz, Dan (2007). Industrial R&D as a national policy: Horizontal technology policies and industry-state co-evolution in the growth of the Israeli software industry. *Research Policy* 36(9): 1465–1482.

Campbell, D. (1960). Blind variation and selective retention in creative thought as in other knowledge processes. *Psychological Review*: 380–400.

Cantner, U., and Pyka, A. (2001). Classifying technology policy from an evolutionary perspective. *Research Policy* 30(5): 759–775.

Capron, Laurence, and Mitchell, Will (2009). Selection capability: How capability gaps and internal social frictions affect internal and external strategic renewal. *Organization Science* 20(2): 294–312.

Castellacci, F. (2009). The interactions between national systems and sectoral patterns of innovation. *Journal of Evolutionary Economics* 19(3): 321–347.

Chai, A. (2017). Tackling Keynes's question: A look back on 15 years of learning to consume. *Journal of Evolutionary Economics* 27(2): 239–250.

Chandler, A. (1962). *Strategy and Structure: Chapters in the History of Industrial Enterprise*, MIT Press, Cambridge, MA.

(1977). *The Visible Hand: The Managerial Revolution in American Business*, Harvard University Press, Cambridge, MA.

(1990). *Strategy and Structure: Chapters in the History of the Industrial Enterprise*, MIT Press, Cambridge, MA.

Chandy, Rajesh K., and Tellis, Gerard J. (2000). The incumbent's curse? Incumbency, size, and radical product innovation. *Journal of Marketing* 64(3): 1–17.

Chang, Sea Jin, and Hong, Jaebum (2000). Economic performance of group-affiliated companies in Korea: Intragroup resource sharing and internal business transactions. *Academy of Management Journal* 43(3): 429–448.

Chiaromonte, F., and Dosi, G. (1993). Heterogeneity, competition, and macroeconomics dynamics. *Structural Change and Economic Dynamics* 4(1): 39–63.

Choo, Kineung, Lee, Keun, Ryu, Keunkwan, and Yoon, Jungmo (2009). Changing performance of business groups over two decades: Technological capabilities and investment inefficiency in Korean chaebols. *Economic Development and Cultural Change* 57(2): 359–386.

Chu, Wan-wen (2009). Can Taiwan's second movers upgrade via branding? *Research Policy* 38(6): 1054–1065.

Cimoli, Mario, Primi, Annalisa, and Rovira, Sebastián (2011). National innovation surveys in Latin America: Empirical evidence and policy implications. In *National Innovation Surveys in Latin America: Empirical Evidence and Policy Implications*, ECLAC, Santiago, 7–14. LC/W. 408.

Cohen, M., and Bacdayan, P. (1994). Organizational routines are stored as procedural memory. *Organization Science* 5: 554–568.

Cohen, W., and Levin, R. (1989). Empirical studies of innovation and market structure. In R. Schmalensee and R. Willig (Eds.), *Handbook of Industrial Organization, Vol. II*, Elsevier, Amsterdam.

Cohen, Wesley M., and Levinthal, Daniel A. (1989). Innovation and learning: The two faces of R&D. *The Economic Journal* 99(397): 569–596.

Cohen, W., and Levinthal, D. (1990). Absorptive capacity: A new perspective on learning and innovation. *Administrative Science Quarterly* 35: 128–152.

Cohen, W., Nelson, R.R., and Walsh, J. (2000). Protecting their intellectual assets: Appropriability conditions and why U.S. firms patent (or not). NBER Working Paper, No. 7552.

Cohen, W., Nelson, R.R., and Walsh, J.P. (2002). Links and impacts: The influence of public research on industrial R&D. *Management Science* 48(1): 1–23.

Collis, D.J. (1994). How valuable are organizational capabilities? *Strategic Management Journal* 15(Winter Special Issue): 143–152.

Constant, E. (1980). *The Origins of the Turbojet Revolution*, Johns Hopkins University Press, Baltimore, MD.

Cooke, P. (2001). Regional innovation systems, clusters and the knowledge economy. *Industrial and Corporate Change* 10(4): 945–974.

Cooper, Charles (Ed.) (1973). *Science, Technology and Development: The Political Economy of Technical Advance in Underdeveloped Countries*, Routledge, New York.

Coriat, B., and Dosi, G. (1998). Learning how to govern and learning how to solve problems: On the co-evolution of competences, conflicts, and organizational routines. In A. Chandler, P. Hagstrom, and O. Solvell (Eds.), *The Dynamic Firm*, Oxford University Press, Oxford, pp. 103–134.

Crawford, S.E.S., and Ostrom, E. (1995). A grammar of institutions. *The American Political Science Review* 89(3): 582–600.

Cyert, R.M., and March, J.G. (1963). *A Behavioral Theory of the Firm*, Prentice-Hall, Englewood Cliffs, NJ.

Dahlman, Carl J., Westphal, Larry E., and Kim, Linsu (1985). Reflection on South Korea's acquisition of technological capability. In N. Rosenberg and C. Frischtak (Eds.), *International Technology Transfer: Concepts, Measures and Comparisons*, Praeger, New York.

Daly, H.E. (2007). *Ecological Economics and Sustainable Development*, Edward Elgar, Cheltenham, UK.

Daly, H.E., and Cobb, Jr., J.B. (1990). *For the Common Good: Redirecting the Economy Towards Community, the Environment and a Sustainable Future*, Green Print, London.

Danneels, Erwin. (2008). Organizational antecedents of second-order competences. *Strategic Management Journal* 29(5): 519–543.

(2012). Second-order competences and Schumpeterian rents. *Strategic Entrepreneurship Journal* 6(1): 42–58.

David, P.A. (1985). Clio and the economics of QWERTY. *American Economic Review* 75: 332–337.

(1989). A paradigm for historical economics: Path dependence and predictability in dynamic systems with local network externalities. Working Paper, Stanford University Press, Stanford, CA.

(2001a). From keeping nature's secrets to the institutionalization of open science. Discussion Papers in Economic and Social History, University of Oxford, Oxford.

(2001b). Path dependence, its critics and the quest for "historical economics." In P. Garrouste and S. Ioannides (Eds.), *Evolution and Path Dependence in Economic Ideas: Past and Present*, Edward Elgar, Cheltenham, UK.

(2004). Understanding the emergence of "open science" institutions: Functionalist economics in historical context. *Industrial and Corporate Change* 13(3): 571–589.

David, P.A., and Hall, B. (2006). Property and the pursuit of knowledge: IPR issues affecting scientific research. *Research Policy* 35(6): 767–771.

Deeds, David L., DeCarolis, Dona, and Coombs, Joseph. (1999). Dynamic capabilities and new product development in high technology ventures. *Journal of Business Venturing* 15(3): 211–229.

Diamond, P., and Vartainen, H. (Eds.) (2007). *Behavioral Economics and its Applications*, Princeton University Press, Princeton, NJ.

DiMaggio, P., and Powell, W. (Eds.) (1991). *The New Institutionalism in Organizational Analysis*, University of Chicago Press, Chicago.

Dobzhansky, Th. (1964). Biology, molecular and organismic source. *American Zoologist* 4(4): 443–452.

Dodgson, Mark, Hughes, Alan, Foster, John, and Metcalfe, Stan (2011). Systems thinking, market failure, and the development of innovation policy: The case of Australia. *Research Policy* 40(9): 1145–1156.

Dodgson, Mark, Mathews, John, Kastelle, Tim, and Hu, Mei-Chih (2008). The evolving nature of Taiwan's national innovation system: The case of biotechnology innovation networks. *Research Policy* 37(3): 430–445.

Dopfer, K. (Ed.) (2005). *Evolutionary Foundations of Economics*, Cambridge University Press, Cambridge.

Dopfer, K., and Potts, J. (2008). *The General Theory of Economic Evolution*, Routledge, London and New York.

Dopfer, K., Foster, J., and Potts, J. (2004). Micro–meso–macro. *Journal of Evolutionary Economics* 14: 263–279.

Dosi, G. (1982). Technological paradigms and technological trajectories: A suggested interpretation of the determinants and directions of technical change. *Research Policy* 11(3): 147–162.

(1984). *Technical Change and Industrial Transformation*, Macmillan, London.

(1988). Sources, procedures and microeconomic effects of innovation. *Journal of Economic Literature* 26(3): 1120–1171.

(2007). Statistical regularities in the evolution of industries: A guide through some evidence and challenges for the theory. In F. Malerba and S. Brusoni (Eds.), *Perspectives on Innovation*, Cambridge University Press, Cambridge.

(2014). *Economic Organization, and Development: Selected Essays*, Edward Elgar, London.

Dosi, G., and Nelson, R.R. (2010). Technical change and industrial dynamics as evolutionary processes. In H.H. Bronwyn and N. Rosenberg (Eds.), *Handbook of the Economics of Innovation, Vol. I*, Academic Press, Burlington, VA, pp. 51–128.

Dosi, G., Marengo, L., and Pasquali, C. (2006). How much should society fuel the greed of innovators? On the relations between appropriability, opportunities and rates of innovation. *Research Policy* 35(8): 1110–1121.

Dosi, G., Nelson, R.R., and Winter, S.G. (2000). *The Nature and Dynamics of Organizational Capabilities*, Oxford University Press, Oxford.

Dosi, G., Fagiolo, G., Napoletano, M., Roventini, A., and Treibich, T. (2015). Fiscal and monetary policies in complex evolving economies. *Journal of Economic Dynamics and Control* 52: 166–189.

Dosi, G., Faillo, M., Manara, V. Cecchini, Marengo, L., and Moschella, D. (2017a). The formalization of organizational capabilities and learning: Results and challenges. In D. Teece and S. Leih (Eds.), *The Oxford Handbook of Dynamics Capabilities*, Oxford University Press, Oxford. Forthcoming.

Dosi, G., Faillo, M., Marengo, L., and Moschella, D. (2011). Toward formal representations of search processes and routines in organizational problem solving: An assessment of the state-of-the-art. *Seoul Journal of Economics* 24(3): 247–286.

Dosi, G., Grazzi, M., Tomasi, C., and Zeli, A. (2012). Turbulence underneath the big calm? The micro-evidence behind Italian productivity dynamics. *Small Business Economics* 39(4): 1043–1067.

Dosi, G., Marengo, L., Paraskevopoulou, E., Valente, M. et al. (2017b). A model of cognitive and operational memory of organizations in changing worlds. *Cambridge Journal of Economics*. Forthcoming.

Dosi, G., Marsili, O., Orsenigo, L., and Salvatore, R. (1995). Learning, market selection and the evolution of industrial structures. *Small Business Economics* 7: 411–436.

Dutta, Shantanu, Narasimhan, Om, and Rajiv, Surendra. 2005. Conceptualizing and measuring capabilities: Methodology and empirical application. *Strategic Management Journal* 26(3): 277–285.

Eisenhardt, K., and Martin, J. (2000). Dynamic capabilities: What are they? *Strategic Management Journal* 21(10–11): 1105–1121.

Eliasson, G. (1990). The firm as a competent team. *Journal of Economic Behavior and Organization* 13(3): 275–298.

Elsner, W., Heinrich, T., and Schwardt, H. (2015). *The Microeconomics of Complex Economies. Evolutionary, Institutional, Neoclassical, and Complexity Perspectives*, Elsevier, Amsterdam.

Ernst, Dieter, and Guerrieri, Paolo (1998). International production networks and changing trade patterns in East Asia: The case of the electronics industry. *Oxford Development Studies* 26(2): 191–212.

Ernst, Holger (2002). Success factors of new product development: A review of the empirical literature. *International Journal of Management Reviews* 4(1): 1–40.

Essletzbichler, J., and Rigby, D.L. (2007). Exploring evolutionary economic geographies. *Journal of Economic Geography* 7(5): 549–571.

Ethiraj, S.K., and Levinthal, D. (2004). Bounded rationality and the search for organizational architecture: An evolutionary perspective on the design of organizations and their evolvability. *Administrative Science Quarterly* 49(3): 404–437.

Fagerberg, Jan, and Godinho, Manuel M. (2005). Innovation and catching-up. In D.C. Mowery, J. Fagerberg, and R.R. Nelson (Eds.), *The Oxford Handbook of Innovation*, Oxford University Press, New York, pp. 514–543.

Fagerberg, Jan, and Srholec, Martin (2008). National innovation systems, capabilities and economic development. *Research Policy* 37: 1417–1435.

Fagerberg, J., and Verspagen, B. (2009). Innovation studies: The emerging structure of a new scientific field. *Research Policy* 38(2): 218–233.

Fagerberg, J., Fosaas, M., and Sapprasert, K. (2012). Innovation: Exploring the knowledge base. *Research Policy* 41(7): 1132–1153.

Fagerberg, Jan, Srholec, Martin, and Knell, M. (2007). The competitiveness of nations: Why some countries prosper while others fall behind. *World Development* 35: 1595–1620.

Fagerberg, Jan, Srholec, Martin, and Verspagen, Bart (2010). Innovation and economic development. In B. Hall and N. Rosenberg (Eds.), *Handbook of the Economics of Innovation*, Vol. II, North-Holland, Amsterdam, pp. 833–872.

Fang, C., Lee, J., and Schilling, M. A. (2010). Balancing exploration and exploitation through structural design: The isolation of subgroups and organizational learning. *Organization Science* 21(3): 625–642.

Feldman, M.S., and Pentland, B.T. (2003). Reconceptualizing organizational routines as a source of flexibility and change. *Administrative Science Quarterly* 48: 94–118.

Felin, T., and Foss, N.J. (2011). The endogenous origins of experience, routines and organizational capabilities: The poverty of stimulus. *Journal of Institutional Economics* 7: 231–256.

Findlay, Ronald (1978). Relative backwardness, direct foreign investment, and the transfer of technology: A simple dynamic model. *The Quarterly Journal of Economics* 92(1): 1–16.

Foray, D. (2006). *The Economics of Knowledge*, MIT Press, Cambridge, MA.

Fosfuri, Andrea, Motta, Massimo, and Rønde, Thomas (2001). Foreign direct investment and spillovers through workers' mobility. *Journal of International Economics* 53(1): 205–222.

Foster, J. (2014). Energy, knowledge and economic growth. *Journal of Evolutionary Economics* 24(2): 209–238.

Foster, J., and Metcalfe. S.J. (2004). *Evolution and Economic Complexity*, Edward Elgar, Cheltenham, UK.

Franco, April M., Sarkar, M.B., Agarwal, Rajshree, and Echambadi, Raj (2009). Swift and smart: The moderating effects of technological capabilities on the market pioneering–firm survival relationship. *Management Science* 55(11): 1842–1860.

Fransman, Martin (1985). Conceptualising technical change in the Third World in the 1980s: An interpretive survey. *The Journal of Development Studies* 21(4): 572–652.

Freeman, C. (1982). *The Economics of Industrial Innovation* (2nd ed.), Pinter, London.

(1983). *Long Waves in the World Economy*, Butterworth, Kent.

(1984). Prometheus unbound. *Futures*, October, 490–500.

(1987). *Technology Policy and Economic Performance: Lessons from Japan*, Pinter, London.

(1991). Networks of innovators: A synthesis of research issues. *Research Policy* 20(5): 499–514.

(1994). The economics of technical change. *Cambridge Journal of Economics* 18: 463–514.

Freeman, C., and Louçã, F. (2001). *As Time Goes By, from the Industrial Revolution to the Information Revolution*, Oxford University Press, Oxford.

Freeman, C., and Perez, C. (1988). Structural crises of adjustment, business cycles and investment behaviour. In G. Dosi, Ch. Freeman, R. Nelson, G. Siverberg, and L. Soete (Eds.), *Technical Change and Economic Theory*, Pinter, London, pp. 38–66.

Freeman, C., Clark, J., and Soete, L. (1982). *Unemployment and Technical Innovation*, Pinter, London.

Frenken, K., Saviotti, P.P., and Trommetter, M. (1999). Variety and niche creation in aircraft, helicopters, motorcycles and microcomputers. *Research Policy* 28(5): 469–488.

Friedman, M. (1953). The methodology of positive economics. In M. Friedman, *Essays on Positive Economics*, University of Chicago Press, Chicago.

Garavaglia, C., Malerba, F., and Orsenigo, L. (2006). Entry, market structure and innovation in a history-friendly model of the pharmaceutical industry. In M. Mazzucato and G. Dosi (Eds.), *Knowledge Accumulation and Industry Evolution: The Case of Pharma-Biotech*, Cambridge University Press, Cambridge, pp. 234–265.

Garavaglia, C., Malerba, F., Orsenigo, L., and Pezzoni, M. (2013). *Technological Regimes and Demand Structure in the Evolution of the Pharmaceutical Industry*, Springer, Heidelberg, New York, Dordrecht, London.

Gavetti, G. (2005). Cognition and hierarchy: Rethinking the microfoundations of capabilities' development. *Organization Science* 16(6): 599–617.

Gavetti, G., and Levinthal, D. (2000). Looking forward and looking backward: Cognitive and experiential search. *Administrative Science Quarterly* 45(1): 113–137.

Gerber, J.-F., and Steppacher, R. (Eds.) (2012). *Towards an Integrated Paradigm in Heterodox Economics: Alternative Approaches to the Current Eco-Social Crisis*, Palgrave Macmillan, UK.

Gereffi, Gary (2005). The global economy: Organization, governance, and development. *The Handbook of Economic Sociology* 2: 160–182.

Gereffi, Gary, Humphrey, John, and Sturgeon, Timothy (2005). The governance of global value chains. *Review of International Political Economy* 12(1): 78–104.

Geroski, Paul A., Machin, Stephen J., and Walters, Christopher F. (1997). Corporate growth and profitability. *The Journal of Industrial Economics* 45(2): 171–189.

Gerschenkron, Alexander (1962). *Economic Backwardness in Historical Perspective*, Frederik A. Praeger, New York.

Gerschlager, C. (2012). Agents of change. *Journal of Evolutionary Economics* 22(3): 413–441.

Giachetti, Claudio (2013). *Competitive Dynamics in the Mobile Phone Industry*, Palgrave Macmillan, New York.

Giachetti, Claudio, and Marchi, Gianluca (2017). Successive changes in leadership in the worldwide mobile phone industry: The role of windows of opportunity and firms' competitive action. *Research Policy* 46(2): 337–534.

Giuliani, Elisa, Pietrobelli, Carlo, and Rabellotti, Roberta (2005). Upgrading in global value chains: Lessons from Latin American clusters. *World Development* 33(4): 549–573.

Gordon, R. (2016). *The Rise and Fall of American Growth*, Princeton University Press, Princeton, NJ.

Gorg, Holger, and Greenaway, David (2003). Much ado about nothing? Do domestic firms really benefit from foreign direct investment?, IZA Discussion Paper, No. 944. Available at SSRN: http://ssrn.com/abstract=475044 (last accessed November 7, 2017).

Goto, Akira (1982). Business groups in a market economy. *European Economic Review* 19(1): 53–70.

Graf, H. (2009). Inventor networks in emerging key technologies: Information technology vs. semiconductors. *Journal of Evolutionary Economics* 22(3): 459–480.

Granstrand, O. (1999). *The Economics and Management of Intellectual Property*, Edward Elgar, Cheltenham, UK.

Grebel, T. (2010). *Innovation and Health: Theory, Methodology and Applications*, Edward Elgar, Cheltenham, UK.

Greif, A. (2006). *Institutions and the Path to the Modern Economy: Lessons From Medieval Trade*, Cambridge University Press, Cambridge.

Griliches, Z., and Mairesse, J. (1997). Production functions: The search for identification. Working Papers from Centre de Recherche en Economie et Statistique, No. 97-30.

Gu, Shulin, Adeoti, John O., Castro, Ana Celita, Orozco, Jefferey, and Diaz, Rafael (2012). The agro-food sector in catching-up countries: A comparative study of four cases. In F. Malerba and R.R. Nelson (Eds.), *Economic Development as a Learning Process: Variation across Sectoral Systems*, Edward Elgar, Cheltenham, UK.

Guillén, Mauro F. (2000). Business groups in emerging economies: A resource-based view. *Academy of Management Journal* 43(3): 362–380.

Guo, B. (2017). The rise to market leadership of Chinese leading automotive firms: A case of Geely Group from the sectoral innovation system perspective. In F. Malerba, S. Mani, and P. Adams (Eds.), *The Rise to Market Leadership*, Edward Elgar, Cheltenham, UK.

Habakkuk, H.J. (1962). *American and British Technology in the Nineteenth Century: The Search for Labour-Saving Inventions*, Cambridge University Press, Cambridge.

Hall, B., Helmers, C., Rogers, M., and Sena, V. (2014). The choice of formal and informal intellectual property: A review. *Journal of Economic Literature* 52(2): 375–423.

Hanusch, H. (Ed.) (1988). *Evolutionary Economics: Applications of Schumpeter's Ideas*, Cambridge University Press, Cambridge.

Hanusch, H., and Pyka, A. (2007). The principles of Neo-Schumpeterian economics. *Cambridge Journal of Economics* 31(2): 275–289.

Harper, D.A. (2014). Intellectual property as a complex adaptive system. In A. Pyka and J. Foster (Eds.), *The Evolution of Economic and Innovation Systems*, Springer, Heidelberg, New York, Dordrecht, London.

Hausmann, Ricardo, Pritchett, Lant, and Rodrik, Dani (2005). Growth accelerations. *Journal of Economic Growth* 10(4): 303–329.

Hausmann, Ricardo, Rodrik, Dani, and Velasco, Andrés (2008). Growth diagnostics. In N. Serra and J.E. Stiglitz (Eds.), *The Washington Consensus Reconsidered: Towards a New Global Governance*, Oxford University Press, New York, pp. 324–355.

Hayami, Yujiro, and Ruttan, Vernon W. (1985). *Agricultural Development: An International Perspective*, Johns Hopkins University Press, Baltimore, MD.

Helfat, C.E. (1994a). Evolutionary trajectories in petroleum firm R&D. *Management Science* 40(12): 1720–1747.

(1994b). Firm-specificity in corporate applied R&D. *Organization Science* 5(2): 173–184.

(1997). Know-how and asset complementarity and dynamic capability accumulation: The case of R&D. *Strategic Management Journal* 18(5): 339–361.

Helfat, C.E., and Campo-Rembado, M.A. (2016). Integrative capabilities, vertical integration, and innovation over successive technology lifecycles. *Organization Science* 27(2): 249–264.

Helfat, C.E., and Martin, J. (2015). Dynamic managerial capabilities: A review and assessment of managerial impact on strategic change. *Journal of Management* 41(5): 1281–1312.

Helfat, C.E., and Peteraf, Margaret A. (2003). The dynamic resource-based view: Capability lifecycles. *Strategic Management Journal* 24(10): 997–1010.

Helfat, C.E., and Winter, S.G. (2011). Untangling dynamic and operational capabilities: Strategy for the (n)ever-changing world. *Strategic Management Journal* 32: 1243–1250.

Helfat, C.E., Finkelstein, S., Mitchell, W., Peteraf, M.A., Singh, H., Teece, D.J., and Winter, S.G. (2007). *Dynamic Capabilities: Understanding Strategic Change in Organizations*, Blackwell Publishing, Malden, MA.

Heller, M., and Eisenberg, R. (1998). Can patents deter innovation? The anticommons in biomedical research. *Science* 280: 698–701.

Henderson, R.M., and Clark, K.B. (1990). Architectural innovation: The reconfiguration of existing product technologies and the failure of established firms. *Administrative Science Quarterly* 35: 9–30.

Henderson, R., and Cockburn, I. (1996). Scale, scope, and spillovers: The determinants of research productivity in drug discovery. *RAND Journal of Economics* 27(1): 32–59.

Hidalgo, C.A., and Hausmann, R. (2009). The building blocks of economic complexity. *PNAS* June 30, 106(26): 10575.

Hidalgo, César A., Klinger, Bailey, Barabási, A.-L., and Hausmann, Ricardo (2007). The product space conditions the development of nations. *Science* 317(5837): 482–487.

Hobday, Michael (1995). *Innovation in East Asia: The Challenge to Japan*, Edward Elgar, London.

Hobsbawm, E. (1968). *Industry and Empire*, Penguin Books, Harmondsworth, UK.

Hodgson, G. (1993). *Economics and Evolution: Bringing Life Back into Economics*, Polity Press, Cambridge.

(2005). The concept of a routine. In M.C. Becker (Ed.), *Handbook of Organizational Routines*, Edward Elgar, Cheltenham, UK.

(2016). On fuzzy frontiers and fragmented foundations: Some reflections on the original and new institutional economics. *Journal of Institutional Economics* 10(4): 591–611.

Holt, R.P.F., Rosser Jr., B., and Colander, D. (2010). The complexity era in economics. *Middlebury College Economics Discussion Paper*, No. 10-01.

Hoopes, David G., and Postrel, Steven. (1999). Shared knowledge, "glitches," and product development performance. *Strategic Management Journal* 20(9): 837–865.

Hoopes, D.G., Madsen, T., and Walker, G. (2003). Why is there a Resource-based View? Toward a theory of competitive heterogeneity. *Strategic Management Journal* 24(10): 889–902.

Hughes, T.P. (1983). *Networks of Power: Electrification in Western Society*, Johns Hopkins University Press, Baltimore, MD.

Hull, D. (2001). *Science and Selection*, Cambridge University Press, Cambridge.

Hume, D. (1762). *History of England*.

Iizuka, Michiko, and Katz, Jorge (2011). Natural resource industries, "tragedy of the commons" and the case of Chilean salmon farming. *International Journal of Institutions and Economies* 3(2): 259–286.

Iizuka, Michiko, and Soete, Luc (2011). Catching-up in the 21st century: Globalization, knowledge & capabilities in Latin America, a case for natural resource based activities. MERIT Working Papers 071, United Nations

University – Maastricht Economic and Social Research Institute on Innovation and Technology (MERIT).

Jacobides, M.G., and Winter, S.G. (2012). Capabilities: Structure, agency, and evolution. *Organization Science* 23(5): 1365–1381.

Johansson, D. (2009). The theory of the experimentally organized economy and competence blocs: An introduction. *Journal of Evolutionary Economics* 20(2): 185–201.

Jones, Benjamin F., and Olken, Benjamin A. (2008). The anatomy of start-stop growth. *The Review of Economics and Statistics* 90(3): 582–587.

Jun, B., Saviotti, P.P., and Pyka, A. (2017). The effect of education on growth and income distribution. Paper submitted to the 23rd Computing in Economics and Finance Conference, New York, June 28–30, 2017.

Kahl, S. (2014). Associations, jurisdictional battles, and the development of dual-purpose capabilities. *Academy of Management Perspectives* 28(4): 381–394.

Katz, Jorge M. (1984). Domestic technological innovations and dynamic comparative advantage: Further reflections on a comparative case-study program. *Journal of Development Economics* 16(1): 13–37.

(2001). Structural reforms and technological behaviour: The sources and nature of technological change in Latin America in the 1990s. *Research Policy* 30(1): 1–19.

(2006). Market-oriented reforms, globalisation and the recent transformation of the production and social structure of developing countries. *International Journal of Technology Management* 36(13).

Kauffman, S.A. (1993). *The Origins of Order: Self Organization and Selection in Evolution*, Oxford University Press, USA.

Khanna, Tarun, and Palepu, Krishna (1997). Why focused strategies may be wrong for emerging markets. *Harvard Business Review* 75: 41–54.

(2000). Is group affiliation profitable in emerging markets? An analysis of diversified Indian business groups. *Journal of Finance* 55(2): 867–891.

Kim, Linsu (1997). *Imitation to Innovation: The Dynamics of Korea's Technological Learning*, Harvard Business School Press, Boston, MA.

Kim, Yoon-Zi, and Lee, Keun (2009). Making a technological catch-up in the capital goods industry: Barriers and opportunities in the Korean case. In Franco Malerba and Sunil Mani (Eds.), *Sectoral Systems of Innovation and Production in Developing Countries*, Edward Elgar, Cheltenham, UK, chapter 9.

Kim, Yee Kyoung, and Lee, Keun (2015). Different impacts of scientific and technological knowledge on economic growth: Contrasting science and technology policy in East Asia and Latin America. *Asian Economic Policy Review* 10(1): 43–66.

Klepper, S. (1997). Industry life cycles. *Industrial and Corporate Change* 6: 145–182.

Klepper, S., and Graddy, E. (1990). The evolution of new industries and the determinants of market structure. *Rand Journal of Economics* 21: 27–44.

Klepper, S., and Simonis, K.L. (1997). The making of an oligopoly: Firm survival and technological change in the evolution of the U.S. tire industry. Paper presented at the Workshop on Economic Evolution, Learning and Complexity. Augsburg, Germany, May 1997.

Klevorick, A.K., Levin, R.C., Nelson, R.R., and Winter, S.G. (1995). On the sources and significance of interindustry differences in technological opportunities. *Research Policy* 24: 185–205.

Knudsen, T., and Levinthal, D. A. (2007). Two faces of search: Alternative generation and alternative evaluation. *Organization Science* 18(1): 39–54.

Kock, Carl J., and Guillén, Mauro F. (2001). Strategy and structure in developing countries: Business groups as an evolutionary response to opportunities for unrelated diversification. *Industrial and Corporate Change* 10(1): 77–113.

Koopmans, T.C. (1957). *Three Essays on the State of Economic Science*, McGraw-Hill, New York.

Kudic, M. (2015). *Innovation Networks in the German Laser Industry*, Springer, Heidelberg, New York, Dordrecht, London.

Kuhn, T. (1962). *The Structure of Scientific Revolutions*, Chicago University Press, Chicago.

Kuznets, S. (1955). Economic growth and income inequality. *The American Economic Review* 45: 1–28.

(1966). *Modern Economic Growth: Rate, Structure and Spread*, Yale University Press, New Haven, CT.

Lall, Sanjaya (1992). Technological capabilities and industrialization. *World Development* 20(2): 165–186.

(2000). The technological structure and performance of developing country manufactured export, 1985–1998. *Oxford Development Studies* 28(3): 337–369.

Lall, Sanjaya, and Teubal, M. (1998). "Market-stimulating" technology policies in developing countries: A framework with examples from East Asia. *World Development* 26(8): 1369–1385.

Landes, D.S. (1969). *The Unbound Prometheus*, Cambridge University Press, Cambridge.

Lazaric, N., and Denis, B. (2005). Routinization and memorization of tasks in a workshop: The case of the introduction of ISO norms. *Industrial and Corporate Change* 14(5): 873–896.

Lazaric, N., and Raybaut, A. (2005). Knowledge, hierarchy and the selection of routines: An interpretative model with group interactions. *Journal of Evolutionary Economics* 15(4): 393–422.

Lazonick, W. (2005). The innovative firm. In J. Fagerberg, D.C. Mowery, and R.R. Nelson (Eds.), *The Oxford Handbook of Innovation*, Oxford University Press, Oxford.

Lee, Keun (2005). Making a technological catch-up: Barriers and opportunities. *Asian Journal of Technology Innovation* 13(2): 97–131.

(2013a). *Schumpeterian Analysis of Economic Catch-up: Knowledge, Path-Creation, and the Middle-Income Trap*, Cambridge University Press, London.

(2013b). Capability failure and industrial policy to move beyond the middle-income trap: From trade-based to technology-based specialization. In J. Lin and J. Stiglitz (Eds.), *Industrial Policy Revolution I*, Palgrave, Basingstoke, UK.

Lee, Keun, and Ki, Jee-hoon (2017). Rise of the latecomers and catch-up cycles in the world steel industry. *Research Policy*, Special Issue on Catch-up Cycles, 46(2): 365–375.

Lee, Keun, and Kim, Byung-Yeon (2009). Both institutions and policies matter but differently for different income groups of countries: Determinants of long-run economic growth revisited. *World Development* 37(3): 533–549.

Lee, Keun, and Lim, Chaisung (2001). Technological regimes, catching-up and leap-frogging: Findings from the Korean industries. *Research Policy* 30(3): 459–483.

Lee, Keun, and Malerba, Franco (2017). Catch-up cycles and changes in industrial leadership: Windows of opportunity and responses by firms and countries in the evolution of sectoral systems. *Research Policy*, Special Issue on Catch-up Cycles, 46(2): 338–351.

Lee, Keun, and Temesgen, Tilahun (2009). What makes firms grow in developing countries? An extension of the resource-based theory of firm growth. *International Journal of Technological Learning, Innovation and Development* 2(3): 139–172.

Lee, Keun, Gao, Xudong, and Li, Xibao (2017). Assessing industrial catch-up in China: A sectoral systems of innovation perspective. *Cambridge Journal of Regions, Economy and Society* 10(1): 59–76.

Lee, Keun, Lim, Chaisung, and Song, Wichin (2005). Emerging digital technology as a window of opportunity and technological leapfrogging: Catch-up in digital TV by the Korean firms. *International Journal of Technology Management* 29(1/2): 40–63.

Lee, Keun, Mani, Sunil, and Mu, Qing (2012). Explaining variations in the telecommunication equipment industry in Brazil, China, India and Korea. In F.

Malerba and R. Nelson (Eds.), *Economic Development as a Learning Process*, Edward Elgar, Cheltenham, UK, pp. 21–71.

Lee, Keun, Song, Jaeyong, and Kwak, Jooyoung (2015). An exploratory study on the transition from OEM to OBM: Case studies of SMEs in Korea. *Industry and Innovation* 22(5): 423–442.

Leff, Nathaniel H. (1978). Industrial organization and entrepreneurship in the developing countries: The economic groups. *Economic Development and Cultural Change* 26(4): 661–675.

Levin, R.C., Cohen, W.M., and Mowery, D.C. (1985). R&D appropriability, opportunity and market structure: New evidence on some Schumpeterian hypotheses. *American Economic Review Proceedings* 75: 20–24.

Levin, R.C., Klevorick, A.K., Nelson, R.R., and Winter, S.G. (1987). Appropriating the returns from industrial research and development. *Brookings Papers on Economic Activity* 3: 783–831.

Levinthal, D.A. (1997). Adaptation on rugged landscapes. *Management Science* 43(7): 934–950.

Lim, C., Kim, Y., and Lee, K. (2017). Changes in industrial leadership and catch-up by latecomers in the shipbuilding industry. *Asian Journal of Technology Innovation*: 1–18.

Lin, Justin Y. (2012a). *New Structural Economics: A Framework for Rethinking Development and Policy*, World Bank, Washington, DC.

(2012b). *The Quest for Prosperity: How Developing Economies Can Take Off*, Princeton University Press, Princeton, NJ.

Lundvall, Bengt-Åke (1988). Innovation as an interactive process: From user-producer interaction to the national system of innovation. In G. Dosi, Ch. Freeman, R. Nelson, G. Siverberg, and L. Soete (Eds.), *Technical Change and Economic Theory*, Pinter, London.

(1992). *National Systems of Innovation: Toward a Theory of Innovation and Interactive Learning*, Pinter, London.

(1993). User-producer relationships, national systems of innovation and internationalisation. In D. Foray and C. Freeman (Eds.), *Technology and the Wealth of Nations: The Dynamics of Constructed Advantage*, Pinter, New York, pp. 277–300.

(2014). Deteriorating quality of work undermines Europe's innovation systems and the welfare of Europe's workers. http://portal.ukwon.eu/guest-essay (last accessed November 7, 2017).

(2016). *The Learning Economy and the Economics of Hope*, Anthem Press, London.

Macher, J.T., and Mowery, D.C. (2009). Measuring dynamic capabilities: Practices and performance in semiconductor manufacturing. *British Journal of Management* 20: 41–62.

Malerba, F. (Ed.) (2004). *Sectoral System of Innovation: Concepts, Issues, and Analyses of Six Major Sectors in Europe,* Cambridge University Press, Cambridge.

Malerba, Franco (2002). Sectoral systems of innovation and production. *Research Policy* 31(2): 247–264.

(2009). Increase learning, break knowledge lock-ins and foster dynamic complementarities: Evolutionary and system perspectives on technology policy in industrial dynamics. In D. Foray (Ed.), *The New Economics of Technology Policy,* Edward Elgar, Cheltenham, UK.

Malerba, Franco, and Mani, Sunil (2009). *Sectoral Systems of Innovation and Production in Developing Countries: Actors, Structure and Evolution,* Edward Elgar, Northampton, MA.

Malerba, Franco, and Nelson, Richard (2011). Learning and catching-up in different sectoral systems: Evidence from six industries. *Industrial and Corporate Change* 20(6): 1645–1675.

(2012). *Economic Development as a Learning Process: Variation Across Sectoral Systems,* Edward Elgar, Northampton, MA.

Malerba, Franco, and Orsenigo, Luigi (1996). Schumpeterian patterns of innovation are technology-specific. *Research Policy* 25(3): 451–478.

Malerba, F., and Orsenigo, L. (1997). Technological regimes and sectoral patterns of innovative activities. *Industrial and Corporate Change* 6: 83–117.

Malerba, Franco, Mani, Sunil, and Adams, Pamela (2017). *The Rise to Market Leadership,* Edward Elgar, Northampton, MA.

Malerba, F., Nelson, R.R., Orsenigo, L., and Winter, S.D. (1999) History-friendly models of industry evolution: The computer industry. *Industrial and Corporate Change* 8(1): 3–4.

Malerba, Franco, Nelson, Richard, Orsenigo, Luigi, and Winter, Sidney (2016). *Innovation and the Evolution of Industries: History-friendly Models,* Cambridge University Press, Cambridge.

Mandeville, B. (1714). *The Fable of the Bees, or, Private Vices, Public Benefits,* Clarendon Press, Oxford. Reprinted in Kaye, F.B. (Ed.) (1924). *Mandeville's The Fable of the Bees, or, Private Vices, Public Benefits,* Clarendon Press, Oxford.

Mani, S. (2017). Market leadership in India's pharmaceutical industry: The case of CIPLA Limited. In F. Malerba, S. Mani, and P. Adams (Eds.), *The Rise to Market Leadership,* Edward Elgar, Cheltenham, UK.

Mansfield, E. (1986). Patents and innovation: An empirical study. *Management Science* 32(2): 173–181.

March, J.G. (1991). Exploration and exploitation in organizational learning. *Organization Science* 2(1): 71–87.

March, J.G., and Simon, H.A. (1958). *Organizations*, John Wiley, New York.

Marengo, L. (1992). Coordination and organizational learning in the firm. *Journal of Evolutionary Economics* 2(4): 313–326.

(1996). Structure, competence and learning in an adaptive model of the firm. In G. Dosi and F. Malerba (Eds.), *Organization and Strategy in the Evolution of the Enterprise*, Palgrave Macmillan, UK, pp. 124–154.

Marengo, L., and Dosi, G. (2005). Division of labor, organizational coordination and market mechanisms in collective problem-solving. *Journal of Economic Behavior & Organization* 58(2): 303–326.

Marshall, A. (1890). *Principles of Economics*, MacMillan, London.

(1892). *Elements of Economics of Industry*, MacMillan, London.

(1919). *Industry and Trade*, MacMillan, London.

Marsili, O. (2001). *The Anatomy and Evolution of Industries: Technological Change and Industrial Dynamics*, Edward Elgar, Cheltenham, UK.

Martin, R., and Sunley, P. (2010). Complexity thinking and economic geography. In R. Boschma and R. Martin (Eds.), *The Handbook of Evolutionary Geography*, Edward Elgar, Cheltenham, UK, pp. 93–119.

Marx, K. (1847). *The Poverty of Philosophy (English version)*, Marx-Engels Institute, Moscow.

Mathews, John A. (1996). High technology industrialisation in East Asia. *Journal of Industry Studies* 3(2): 1–77.

(2002). Competitive advantages of the latecomer firm: A resource-based account of industrial catch-up strategies. *Asia Pacific Journal of Management* 19(4): 467–488.

(2005). Strategy and the crystal cycle. *California Management Review* 47(2): 6–32.

Mazzoleni, R., and Nelson, R.R. (1998). The benefits and costs of strong patent protection: A contribution to the current debate. *Research Policy* 27(3): 273–284.

Mazzoleni, Roberto, and Nelson, Richard R. (2006). The roles of research at universities and public labs in economic catch-up, LEM Working Paper Series, No. 1.

(2007). Public research institutions and economic catch-up. *Research Policy* 36(10): 1512–1528.

Mazzoleni, R., and Nelson, R. (2013). An interpretive history of challenges to neoclassical microeconomics and how they have fared. *Industrial and Corporate Change*: 1–44.

Mazzucato, M. (2013). *The Entrepreneurial State: Debunking the Public vs. Private Myth in Risk and Innovation*, Anthem Press, London.

Meliciani, V. (2002). The impact of technological specialisation on national performance in a balance-of-payments-constrained growth model. *Structural Change and Economic Dynamics* 13(1): 101–118.

Merges, R.P., and Nelson, R.R. (1994). On limiting or encouraging rivalry in technical progress: The effect of patent scope decisions. *Journal of Economic Behavior & Organization* 25(1): 1–24.

Mesoudi, A. (2011). *Cultural Evolution*, University of Chicago Press, Chicago.

Metcalfe, J.S. (1994). Evolutionary economics and technology policy. *Economic Journal* 104(425): 931–944.

(1998). *Evolutionary Economics and Creative Destruction*, Routledge, London.

(2005). Systems failure and the case for innovation policy. In P. Llerena, M. Matt, and A. Avadikyan (Eds.), *Innovation Policy in a Knowledge-based Economy*, Springer, Germany, pp. 47–74.

(2014). Capitalism and evolution. *Journal of Evolutionary Economics* 24(1): 11–34.

Metcalfe, J.S., Foster, J., and Ramlogan, R. (2006). Adaptive economic growth. *Cambridge Journal of Economics* 30(1): 7–32.

Mill, J.S. (1848). *Principles of Political Economy With Some of Their Applications to Social Philosophy*, Longman Green and Co., London.

Mokyr, J. (1990). *The Lever of Riches: Technological Creativity and Economic Progress*, Oxford University Press, Oxford.

(2002). *The Gifts of Athena: Historical Origins of the Knowledge Economy*, Princeton University Press, Princeton, NJ.

(2009). *The Enlightened Economy: An Economic History of Britain 1700–1850*, Yale University Press, New Haven, CT.

(2010). The contribution of economic history to the study of innovation and technical change: 1750–1914. In H.H. Bronwyn and N. Rosenberg (Eds.), *Handbook of the Economics of Innovation, Vol. I*, Academic Press, Burlington, VA, pp. 11–50.

(2017). *Culture of Growth: The Origins of the Modern Economy*, Princeton University Press, Princeton, NJ.

Morrison, Andrea, Pietrobelli, Carlo, and Rabellotti, Roberta (2008). Global value chains and technological capabilities: A framework to study learning and innovation in developing countries. *Oxford Development Studies* 36(1): 39–58.

Mowery, David C., and Nelson, Richard R. (1999). Explaining industrial leadership. In D.C. Mowery and R.R. Nelson (Eds.), *Sources of Industrial Leadership: Studies of Seven Industries*, Cambridge University Press, New York, pp. 359–382.

Mowery, D., and Rosenberg, N. (1979). The influence of market demand upon innovation: A critical review of some recent empirical studies. *Research Policy* 8(2): 102–153.

Mowery, D., Nelson, R., and Martin, B. (2010). Technology policy and global warming: Why new policy models are needed (or why putting new wine in old bottles won't work). *Research Policy* 39: 1011–1023.

Mowery, D., Nelson, R., Sampat, B., and Ziedonis, A. (2004). *Ivory Tower and Industrial Innovation*, Stanford Business Books, Stanford, CA.

Muchie, Mammo, and Baskaran, Angathevar (2013). *Creating Systems of Innovation in Africa: Country Case Studies 2, Asia*, Tut and Aalborg University Publishers, Aalborg.

Muñoz, F.F., Encinar, M.I., and Cañibano, C. (2011). On the role of intentionality in evolutionary economic change. *Structural Change and Economic Dynamics* 22(3): 193–203.

Murmann, J.P. (2003). *Knowledge and Competitive Advantage: The Coevolution of Firms, Technology and National Institutions*, Cambridge University Press, Cambridge.

Murmann, J.P., and Frenken, K. (2006). Toward a systematic framework for research on dominant designs, technological innovations, and industrial change. *Research Policy* 35(7): 925–952.

Narayanan, V.K., Colwell, Ken, and Douglas, Frank L. (2009). Building organizational and scientific platforms in the pharmaceutical industry: A process perspective on the development of dynamic capabilities. *British Journal of Management* 20: S25–S40.

Nelson, Richard R. (1981). Research on productivity growth and productivity differences: Dead ends and new departures. *Journal of Economic Literature* 19(3): 1029–1064.

(1991). Why do firms differ and how does it matter? *Strategic Management Journal* 12: 61–74.

Nelson, Richard R. (Ed.) (1993). *National Innovation Systems: A Comparative Analysis*, Oxford University Press, Oxford.

Nelson, Richard R. (1994). The co-evolution of technology, industrial structure, and supporting institutions. *Industrial and Corporate Change* 3(1): 47–63.

(1995). Recent evolutionary theorizing about economic change. *Journal of Economic Literature* 33(1): 48–90.

(1999). Why do firms differ and how does it matter? *Strategic Management Journal* 12(S2): 61–74.

(2004). The market economy, and the scientific commons. *Research Policy* 33(3): 455–471.

(2006). Reflections on "The Simple Economics of Basic Scientific Research": Looking back and looking forward. *Industrial and Corporate Change* 15: 145–149.

(2008a). What enables rapid economic progress: What are the needed institutions? *Research Policy* 37(1): 1–11.

(2008b). Factors affecting the powers of technological paradigms. *Industrial and Corporate Change* 17: 485–497.

(2008c). Routines as technologies and as organizational capabilities. In M.C. Becker and N. Lazaric (Eds.), *Organizational Routines*, Edward Elgar, Cheltenham, UK, pp. 11–25.

(2008d). Economic development from the perspective of evolutionary economic theory. *Oxford Development Studies* 36(1): 9–21.

(2013). Demand, supply, and their interaction on markets as seen from the perspective of evolutionary economic theory. *Journal of Evolutionary Economics* 23(1): 17–38.

(2016). The behavior and cognition of economic actors in evolutionary economics. *Journal of Evolutionary Economics* 26(4): 737–751.

Nelson, R., and Consoli, D. (2010). An evolutionary theory of household consumption behavior. *Journal of Evolutionary Economics* 20(5): 665–687.

Nelson, Richard R., and Pack, Howard (1999). The Asian miracle and modern growth theory. *The Economic Journal* 109(457): 416–436.

Nelson, R., and Sampat, B. (2001). Making sense of institutions as a factor shaping economic performance. *Journal of Economic Behavior and Organization* 44(1): 31–54.

Nelson, R.R., and Winter, S.G. (1974). Neoclassical vs. evolutionary theories of economic growth: Critique and prospectus. *The Economic Journal* 84(336): 886–905.

(1977). In search of a useful theory of innovation. *Research Policy* 6: 36–76.

Nelson, R. and Winter, S. (1982). *An Evolutionary Theory of Economic Change*, Harvard University Press, Cambridge, MA.

Nelson, R.R., and Wolff, E.N. (1997). Factors behind cross-industry differences in technical progress. *Structural Change and Economic Dynamics* 8(2): 205–220.

Nelson, R.R., Peck, J.M., and Kalachek, E.D. (1967). *Technology, Economic Growth and Public Policy*, The Brookings Institution, Washington, DC.

Niosi, Jorge, Athreye, Suma, and Tschang, Ted (2012). The global computer software sector. In F. Malerba and R.R. Nelson (Eds.), *Economic Development as a Learning Process: Variation Across Sectoral Systems*, Edward Elgar, Northampton, MA, p. 72.

Nordhaus, W.D. (2007). Two centuries of productivity growth in computing. *Journal of Economic History* 67(1): 128–159.

North, D. (1990). *Institutions, Institutional Change, and Economic Performance*, Cambridge University Press, Cambridge.

(2005). *Understanding the Process of Economic Change*, Princeton University Press, Princeton, NJ.

Nuvolari, A. (2004). Collective invention during the British industrial revolution: The case of the Cornish pumping engine. *Cambridge Journal of Economics* 28: 347–363.

Ostrom, E., and Basurto, X. (2011). Crafting analytical tools to study institutional change. *Journal of Institutional Economics* 7(3): 317–343.

Park, Kyoo-Ho, and Lee, Keun (2006). Linking the technological regime to the technological catch-up: Analyzing Korea and Taiwan using the US patent data. *Industrial and Corporate Change* 15(4): 715–753.

Pasinetti, L.L. (1981). *Structural Change and Economic Growth*, Cambridge University Press, Cambridge.

(1993). *Structural Economic Dynamics*, Cambridge University Press, Cambridge.

Pavitt, K. (1984). Sectoral patterns of technical change: Towards a taxonomy and a theory. *Research Policy* 13: 343–373.

(1987). The objectives of technology policy. *Science and Public Policy* 14: 182–188.

Peneder, M. (2016). Competitiveness and industrial policy: From rationalities of failure towards the ability to evolve. *Cambridge Journal of Economics*, bew025. doi: 10.1093/cje/bew025.

Penrose, Edith Tilton (1995 [1st ed. 1959]). *The Theory of the Growth of the Firm*, Oxford University Press, New York.

Perez, C. (1983). Structural change and assimilation of new technologies in the economic and social systems. *Futures*, October, 357–375.

(1985). Microelectronics, long waves and structural change: New perspectives for developing countries. *World Development* 13(3): 441–463.

(2002). *Technological Revolutions and Financial Capital, The Dynamics of Bubbles and Golden Ages*, Edward Elgar, Cheltenham, UK.

(2014). Financial bubbles, crises and the role of government in unleashing golden ages. In H.P. Burghof and A. Pyka (Eds.), *Innovation and Finance*, Routledge, Abingdon, UK, pp. 11–25.

Perez, Carlos, and Soete, Luc (1988). *Catching-up in Technology: Entry Barriers and Windows of Opportunity*, Pinter, New York.

Piketty, T. (2014). *Capital in the Twenty-First Century*, Belknap Press, Cambridge, MA.

Potts, J. (2011). *Creative Industries and Economic Evolution*, Edward Elgar, Cheltenham, UK.

Powell, W.W., Koput, K.W., and Smith-Doerr, L. (1996). Interorganizational collaboration and the locus of innovation: Networks of learning in biotechnology. *Administrative Science Quarterly* 41(1): 116–145.

Pyka, A. (2000). Informal networking and industrial life cycles. *Technovation* 20(1): 25–35.

(2002). Innovation networks in economics: From the incentive-based to the knowledge-based approaches. *European Journal of Innovation Management* 5(3): 152–163.

Ramani, Shyama V., and Guennif, Samira (2012). Catching-up in the pharmaceutical sector: Lessons from case studies of India, Thailand and Brazil. In F. Malerba and R.R. Nelson (Eds.), *Economic Development as a Learning Process*, Edward Elgar, Northampton, MA, pp. 157–193.

Rammel, Ch., Stagl, S., and Wilfing, H. (2007). Managing complex adaptive systems: A co-evolutionary perspective on natural resource management. *Ecological Economics* 63(1): 9–21.

Rasiah, Rajah (2006). Electronics in Malaysia: Export expansion but slow technical change. In V. Chandra (Ed.), *Technology, Adaptation, and Exports: How Some Developing Countries Got it Right*, World Bank, Washington, DC, p. 127.

Rasiah, Rajah, Kong, Xin-Xin, Lin, Yeo, and Song, Jaeyong (2012). Explaining variations in catch-up strategies in Malaysia, China and Taiwan. In F. Malerba and R.R. Nelson (Eds.), *Economic Development as a Learning Process*, Edward Elgar, Northampton, MA, pp. 113–156.

Rhee, Yung W., Westphal, Larry E., Kim, Linsu, and Amsden, Alice H. (1984). Republic of Korea. *World Development* 12(5): 505–533.

Richerson, P.J., and Boyd, R. (2005). *Not by Genes Alone: How Culture Transformed Human Evolution*, University of Chicago Press, Chicago.

Rivkin, J.W., and Siggelkow, N. (2003). Balancing search and stability: Interdependencies among elements of organizational design. *Management Science* 49(3): 290–311.

Robert, V., and Yoguel, G. (2016). Complexity paths in neo-Schumpeterian evolutionary economics, structural change and development policies. *Structural Change and Economic Dynamics* 38: 3–13.

Rodriguez-Clare, Andres (1996). Multinationals, linkages, and economic development. *The American Economic Review* 86(4): 852–873.

Rodrik, Dani (2006). Goodbye Washington consensus, hello Washington confusion? A review of the World Bank's economic growth in the 1990s: Learning from a decade of reform. *Journal of Economic Literature* 44(4): 973–987.

(2015). *Economics Rules: The Rights and Wrongs of the Dismal Science*, Norton, New York.

Rosenberg, N. (1963). Mandeville and laissez-faire. *Journal of the History of Ideas* 24(2): 183–196.

(1976). *Perspectives on Technology*, Cambridge University Press, Cambridge.

(1994). *Exploring the Black Box*, Cambridge University Press, Cambridge.

Rosenberg, N., and Birdzell, L. (1986). *How the West Grew Rich*, Basic Books, New York.

Rosenbloom, R.S., and Cusumano, M.A. (1987). Technological pioneering and competitive advantage: The birth of the VCR industry. *California Management Review* 29(4): 51–76.

Rothaermel, F.T., and Hess, A.M. (2007). Building dynamic capabilities: Innovation driven by individual-, firm-, and network-level effects. *Organization Science* 18(6): 898–921.

Rumelt, R.P. (1984). Towards a strategic theory of the firm. In R. Lamb (Ed.), *Competitive Strategic Management*, Prentice-Hall, Englewood Cliffs, NJ, pp. 556–570.

(1991). How much does industry matter? *Strategic Management Journal* 12(3): 167–185.

Rutherford, M. (1994). *Institutions in Economics: The Old and the New Institutionalism*, Cambridge University Press, Cambridge.

(1996). *Institutions in Economics: The Old and the New Institutionalism*, Cambridge University Press, Cambridge.

Ruttan, V.W. (2006). *Is War Necessary for Economic Growth? Military Procurement and Technology Development*, Oxford University Press, New York.

Sachs, Jeffrey, and Warner, Andrew (1995). Natural resource abundance and economic growth, NBER Working Paper No. 5398.

Safarzyńska, K., Frenken, K., and van den Bergh, J.C.J.M. (2012). Evolutionary theorizing and modeling of sustainability transition. *Research Policy* 41(6): 1011–1024.

Sahal, D. (1981). *Patterns of Technological Innovation*, Addison-Wesley, New York.

(1985). Technological guideposts and innovation avenues. *Research Policy* 14(2): 61–82.

Saviotti, P.P. (1996). *Technological Evolution, Variety and the Economy*, Edward Elgar, Cheltenham, UK.

Saviotti, P., and Pyka, A. (2004). Economic development by the creation of new sectors. *Journal of Evolutionary Economics* 14(1): 1–35.

Saviotti, P.P., and Pyka, A. (2008a). Product variety, competition and economic growth. *Journal of Evolutionary Economics* 18: 167–182.

(2008b). Micro and macro dynamics: Industry life cycles, inter-sector coordination and aggregate growth. *Journal of Evolutionary Economics* 18: 323–348.

(2013a). The co-evolution of innovation, demand and growth. *Economics of Innovation and New Technology* 22: 461–482.

(2013b). From necessities to imaginary worlds: Structural change, product quality and economic development. *Technological Forecasting & Social Change* 80(8): 1499–1512.

(2017). Innovation, structural change and demand evolution: Does demand saturate? *Journal of Evolutionary Economics* 27(2): 337–358.

Saviotti, P.P., Pyka, A., and Jun, B. (2016). TEVECON: Description of model. www.researchgate.net/publication/292130135_TEVECON_Description_of_Model?ev=srch_pub (last accessed November 11, 2017).

Schamp, E.W. (2010). On the notion of co-evolution in economic geography. In R. Boschma and R. Martin (Eds.), *The Handbook of Evolutionary Geography*, Edward Elgar, Cheltenham, UK, pp. 432–449.

Scherer, F.M. (1984). *Innovation and Growth: Schumpeterian Perspectives*, MIT Press, Cambridge, MA.

Scherer, F.M., Herzstein, S., Dreyfoos, A., et al. (1959). *Patents and the Corporation* (2nd ed.), privately published, Boston, MA.

Schmalensee, R., and Willig, R. (Eds.) (1989). *Handbook of Industrial Organization*, Elsevier, Amsterdam.

Schmookler, J. (1966). *Invention and Economic Growth*, Harvard University Press, Cambridge, MA.

Schroeder, H. (2011). Application possibilities of the micro-meso-macro framework in economic geography. *Papers in Evolutionary Economic Geography* 11(15), Utrecht University.

Schumpeter, J.A. (1911). *The Theory of Economic Development*, Harvard University Press, Cambridge, MA. English edition, 1934.

(1934). *The Theory of Economic Development*, Harvard University Press, Cambridge, MA.

(1939). *Business Cycles, A Theoretical, Historical and Statistical Analysis of the Capitalist Process*, McGraw Hill, New York.

(1942). *Capitalism, Socialism and Democracy*, Harper, New York.

(1950). *Capitalism, Socialism and Democracy* (3rd ed.), Harper, New York.

Siggelkow, N., and Levinthal, D.A. (2003). Temporarily divide to conquer: Centralized, decentralized, and reintegrated organizational approaches to exploration and adaptation. *Organization Science* 14(6): 650–669.

Siggelkow, N., and Rivkin, J.W. (2005). Speed and search: Designing organizations for turbulence and complexity. *Organization Science* 16(2): 101–122.

Silverberg, G. (2007). Long waves, conceptual, empirical and modelling issues. In H. Hanusch and A. Pyka (Eds.), *Elgar Companion to Neo-Schumpeterian Economics*, Edward Elgar, Cheltenham, UK.

Silverberg, G., and Lehnert, D. (1993). Long waves and "evolutionary chaos" in a simple Schumpeterian model of embodied technical change. *Structural Change and Economic Dynamics* 4: 9–37.

(1994). Growth fluctuations in an evolutionary model of creative destruction. In G. Silverberg and L. Soete (Eds.), *The Economics of Growth and Technical Change: Technologies, Nations, Agents*, Edward Elgar, Aldershot, UK.

Silverberg, G., and Verspagen, B. (1995). An evolutionary model of long term cyclical variations of catching up and falling behind. *Journal of Evolutionary Economics* 5: 209–227.

(2005). Evolutionary theorizing on economic growth. In K. Dopfer (Ed.), *The Evolutionary Foundations of Economics*, Cambridge University Press, Cambridge.

Simon, H. (1955). A behavioral model of rational choice. *Quarterly Journal of Economics* 69(1): 99–118.

(1957a). *Models of Man*, New York: Wiley.

(1957b). *Administrative Behavior: A Study of Decision-making Processes in Administrative Organization*, Macmillan, New York.

(1976). From substantive to procedural rationality. In S. Latsis (Ed.), *Method and Appraisal in Economics*, Cambridge University Press, Cambridge, pp. 129–148.

(1981). *The Science of the Artificial*, MIT Press, Cambridge, MA.

(2005). Darwinism, altruism and economics. In K. Dopfer (Ed.), *The Evolutionary Foundations of Economics*, Cambridge University Press, Cambridge.

Smith, A. (1776). *An Inquiry into the Nature and Causes of the Wealth of Nations*, Penguin Books, London, 1986.

Soete, L., and Turner, R. (1984). Technological diffusion and the rate of technical change. *The Economic Journal* 94(375): 612–623.

Spender, J.C. (1989). *Industry Recipes: The Nature and Sources of Managerial Judgment*, Oxford University Press, Oxford.

Stadler, C., Helfat, C.E., and Verona, G. (2013). The impact of dynamic capabilities on resource access and development. *Organization Science* 24(6): 1782–1804.

Stigler, G.J. (1951). The division of labor is limited by the extent of the market. *Journal of Political Economy* 59: 185–193.

Stokes, D.E. (1997). *Pasteur's Quadrant: Basic Science and Technological Innovation*, Brookings Institution Press, Washington, DC.

Strohmaier, R. (2014). The evolution of economic structure under pervasive technical change: A methodological and empirical study. *GSC Discussion Paper* No. 07.

Sturgeon, Timothy J., and Gereffi, Gary (2009). Measuring success in the global economy: International trade, industrial upgrading and business function outsourcing in global value chains. *Transnational Corporations* 18(2): 1.

Suarez, F., and Utterback, J.M. (1995). Dominant designs and the survival of firms. *Strategic Management Journal* 16: 415–430.

Syverson, C. (2011). What determines productivity? *Journal of Economic Literature* 49: 326–365.

Szulanski, G. (1996). Exploring internal stickiness: Impediments to the transfer of best practice within the firm. *Strategic Management Journal* 17(S2): 27–43.

Teece, D.J. (1986). Profiting from technological innovation: Implications for integration, collaboration, licensing and public policy. *Research Policy* 15(6): 285–305.

(1987). Capturing value from a technological innovation. In B.R. Guile and H. Brooks (Eds.), *Technology and Global Industry: Companies and Nation in the World Economy*, National Academic Press, Washington, DC.

(2007). Explicating dynamic capabilities: The nature and microfoundations of (sustainable) enterprise performance. *Strategic Management Journal* 28(13): 1319–1350.

(2011). *Dynamic Capabilities and Strategic Management; Organizing for Innovation and Growth*, Oxford University Press, Oxford.

(2012). Dynamic capabilities: Routines versus entrepreneurial action. *Journal of Management Studies* 49(8): 1395–1401.

Teece, D.J, Pisano, G., and Shuen, A. (1997). Dynamic capabilities and strategic management. *Strategic Management Journal* 18(7): 509–533.

Tripsas, M. (1997). Surviving radical technological change through dynamic capability: Evidence from the typesetter industry. *Industrial and Corporate Change* 6(2): 341–377.

Tushman, M.L., and Anderson, P. (1986). Technological discontinuities and organizational environments. *Administrative Science Quarterly* 31: 439–465.

Tybout, James R. (2000). Manufacturing firms in developing countries: How well do they do, and why? *Journal of Economic Literature* 38(1): 11–44.

Utterback, J.M. (1987). Innovation and industrial evolution in manufacturing industries. In B.R. Guile and H. Brooks (Eds.), *Technology and Global Industry: Companies and Nation in the World Economy*, National Academic Press, Washington, DC.

——— (1994). *Mastering the Dynamics of Innovation*, Harvard Business School Press, Boston, MA.

Utterback, J.M., and Abernathy, W. (1975). A dynamic model of process and product innovation. *Omega* 33: 639–656.

Veblen, T. (1898). Why is economics not an evolutionary science? *Quarterly Journal of Economics* 12(4): 373–397.

Verona, G., and Ravasi, D. (2003). Unbundling dynamic capabilities: An exploratory study of continuous product innovation. *Industrial and Corporate Change* 12(3): 577–606.

Verspagen, Bart (1991). A new empirical approach to catching-up or falling behind. *Structural Change and Economic Dynamics* 2(2): 359–380.

Vincenti, W. (1990). *What Engineers Know and How They Know It*, Johns Hopkins University Press, Baltimore, MD.

Viner, J. (1958). Stability and progress: The poorer countries' problem. In D.C. Hague (Ed.), *Stability and Progress in the World Economy: The First Congress of the International Economic Association*, Macmillan, London.

Von Hippel, E. (1988). *The Sources of Innovation*, Oxford University Press, New York.

Weibull, J. (1995). *Evolutionary Game Theory*, MIT Press, Cambridge, MA.

Winter, Sidney G., Jr. (1965). *Economic Natural Selection and the Theory of the Firm*, Ann Arbor, Michigan University Microfilm (Doctoral Dissertation Series). May 31, 1965.

Winter, S.G. (1964). Economic "natural selection" and the theory of the firm. *Yale Economic Essays* 4: 225–272.

——— (1986). The research program of the behavioral theory of the firm: Orthodox critique and evolutionary perspective. In B. Gilad and S. Kaish (Eds.), *Handbook of Behavioral Economics*, JAI Press, Greenwich, CT, pp. 155–188.

(2000). The satisficing principle in capability learning. *Strategic Management Journal* 21(10–11): 981–996.

(2003). Understanding dynamic capabilities. *Strategic Management Journal* 24(10): 991–996.

(2005). Developing evolutionary theory for economics and management. In M. Hitt and K.G. Smith (Eds.), *Great Minds in Management: The Process of Theory Development*, Oxford University Press, Oxford, pp. 510–547.

(2006). Toward a neo-Schumpeterian theory of the firm. *Industrial and Corporate Change* 15(1): 125–141.

(2013). Habit, deliberation and action: Strengthening the microfoundations of routines and capabilities. *Academy of Management Perspectives* 27(2): 120–137.

(2014). The future of evolutionary economics: Can we break out of the beachhead? *Journal of Institutional Economics* 10(4): 613–644.

Winter, Sidney G., and Szulanski, Gabriel (2001). Replication as strategy. *Organization Science* 12(6): 730–743.

Witt, U. (2001). Learning to consume: A theory of wants and the growth of demand. *Journal of Evolutionary Economics* 11(1): 23–36.

World Bank (2005). *Economic Growth in the 1990s: Learning from a Decade of Reform*, World Bank, Washington, DC.

(2010). Exploring the middle-income-trap. *World Bank East Asia Pacific Economic Update: Robust Recovery, Rising Risks, Vol. II*, World Bank, Washington, DC.

(2012). *China 2030: Building a Modern, Harmonious, and Creative High-Income Society*, World Bank, Washington, DC.

Wright, G. (1997). Towards a more historical approach to technological change. *Economic Journal* 107(444): 1560–1566.

Yeon, J., Pyka, A., and Kim, T. (2016). Structural shift and increasing variety in Korea, 1960–2010: Empirical evidence of the economic development model by the creation of new sectors. Hohenheim Discussion Papers, No. 13-2016.

Yonekura, Seiichirō (1994). *The Japanese Iron and Steel Industry, 1850–1990: Continuity and Discontinuity*, St. Martin's Press, New York.

Yu, Jang, Malerba, Franco, Adams, Pamela, and Zhang, Y. (2017). Related yet diverging sectoral systems: Telecommunications equipment and semiconductors in China. *Industry and Innovation* 24(2): 190–212.

Yusuf, Shahid, and Nabeshima, Kaoru (2009). Can Malaysia escape the middle-income trap? A strategy for Penang, Policy Research Working Paper Series, No. 4971. Available at SSRN: http://ssrn.com/abstract=1427631 (last accessed November 7, 2017).

Zbaracki, M.J., and Bergen, M. (2010). When truces collapse: A longitudinal study of price-adjustment routines. *Organization Science* 21(5): 955–972.

Ziman, J.M. (Ed.) (2000). *Technological Innovation as an Evolutionary Process*, Cambridge University Press, Cambridge.

Zollo, M., and Winter, S.G. (2002). Deliberate learning and the evolution of dynamic capabilities. *Organization Science* 13(3): 339–351.

Index

Printed in the United States
By Bookmasters